Pilgrims Until We Die

Pilgrims Until We Die

Unending Pilgrimage in Shikoku

IAN READER AND JOHN SHULTZ

OXFORD
UNIVERSITY PRESS

OXFORD
UNIVERSITY PRESS

Oxford University Press is a department of the University of Oxford. It furthers the University's objective of excellence in research, scholarship, and education by publishing worldwide. Oxford is a registered trade mark of Oxford University Press in the UK and certain other countries.

Published in the United States of America by Oxford University Press
198 Madison Avenue, New York, NY 10016, United States of America.

Library of Congress Cataloging-in-Publication Data
Names: Reader, Ian, 1949- author. | Shultz, John, author.
Title: Pilgrims until we die : unending pilgrimage in Shikoku /
Ian Reader and John Shultz.
Description: New York : Oxford University Press, [2021] |
Includes bibliographical references and index.
Identifiers: LCCN 2020058610 (print) | LCCN 2020058611 (ebook) |
ISBN 9780197573587 (hardback) | ISBN 9780197573594 (paperback) |
ISBN 9780197573617 (epub)
Subjects: LCSH: Buddhist pilgrims and pilgrimages—Japan—Shikoku Region. |
Shikoku Region (Japan)—Religious life and customs. |
Pilgrims and pilgrimages—Psychology. | Religious life.
Classification: LCC BQ6450.J32 S48628 2021 (print) |
LCC BQ6450.J32 (ebook) | DDC 294.3/43509523—dc23
LC record available at https://lccn.loc.gov/2020058610
LC ebook record available at https://lccn.loc.gov/2020058611

DOI: 10.1093/oso/9780197573587.001.0001

1 3 5 7 9 8 6 4 2

Paperback printed by Marquis, Canada
Hardback printed by Bridgeport National Bindery, Inc., United States of America

To Ritsuko

Contents

Acknowledgements

We acknowledge the support of the Japan Society for the Promotion of Science for its research grant No. 17K02237 Perpetual Pilgrims and Religious Authority with the Contemporary Shikoku Henro, which funded the fieldwork and other aspects of the research on which this book is based. The fieldwork and interviews were conducted between February 2018 and November 2019.

We thank two anonymous reviewers for their comments, which helped us develop the final manuscript, and thank Cynthia Read for being supportive from the moment we first contacted Oxford University Press, for answering numerous questions, and for guiding this book through even at a time of great stress during the Covid-19 pandemic.

We would like to thank various personnel from Kansai Gaidai University who facilitated the project. The university staff kindly managed various financial matters with respect to the grant. Likewise, we enjoyed the diligent support of student research assistants, including Sasaki Rie, Kosaka Shion, and Yamashita Asumi, who aided early stages of the work. Kaneko Nachika laboured diligently through the bulk of the project, through to its completion.

We thank all the people we have interviewed for this project: pilgrims, priests, temple officials, and others who are in some way involved in the Shikoku pilgrimage. Besides those met in Shikoku itself, several interviewees kindly came to meet us either at John's office at Kansai Gaidai University or in convenient locations in the Osaka region. We thank all those who responded to our mailed and digital questionnaires as well. Without the cooperation of all these people the research would have been impossible. We thank the staff at the Maeyama Henro Salon for their help and for allowing us to access materials there and thank Ugawa Fumio for his help and for making materials related to Kōgetsu-san (Chapter 3) available to us.

Academic friends have been supportive throughout and offered advice and encouragement. Erica Baffelli has encouraged our research and been a friend and colleague throughout. David Moreton has been a friend to all who are interested in the Shikoku pilgrimage, and he has generously helped our research and kindly shared information and contacts with us. John Eade, a guiding figure in studies of pilgrimage, has helped in engaging in academic discussions with both of us. We have both benefitted from invitations to give papers related to the project at various institutions and workshops. We thank various people and groups for invitations to speak about the project and for their comments and feedback. John thanks the Kyoto Asian Studies group for an invitation to present an overview of the project at a meeting in Kyoto in December 2017 and Benjamin Dorman for the invitation to do so at Nanzan University. Ian thanks Mario Katic for inviting him to speak at a workshop at the University of Zadar, Croatia, and Aura di Febo and Paula Kolata for organising the workshop *Research on Contemporary Japanese Religions* at the University of Manchester in February 2018, where Ian presented an outline of the project before our first period of fieldwork.

Ian also thanks Ritsuko and John for their hospitality whenever he visits Japan, and we both thank Yama-chan for spiritual encouragement as we planned our field trips to Shikoku.

We thank our families for their support and putting up with our absences as we engaged in our own immersion in *Shikokubyō* while doing fieldwork. Ian thanks Dorothy, Rosie, and Phil, as always, for their support, and John thanks Ritsuko. It is to Ritsuko to whom this book is dedicated with gratitude.

Conventions

All Japanese names are given in standard Japanese order (family name followed by given name). We use macrons to indicate long vowels in Japanese words and names except for words and place names that are well known in English (e.g. Shinto, Tokyo, Kyoto). Japanese words are given in italics; we also provide an explanation or translation of them when they are first used. For example, the term used in Japanese to refer to the pilgrimage in Shikoku is *henro*—a term also used to refer to the pilgrims, who may also be referred to as *o-henro* or *o-henro-san*. We will from time to time use these terms, and especially *henro* in place of pilgrimage simply for reasons of style.

We have used pseudonyms when referring to all those we interviewed during our research and whose views and experiences are discussed, so as to preserve their anonymity and protect them. This is so for pilgrims as well as temple priests and officials, and people who provided information about other figures discussed in this book. As will become clear there are times when some of those involved in the pilgrimage are critical of others, and there are some contentious aspects to the issues we discuss—for instance, when pilgrims claim to have done the pilgrimage numerous times and others are sceptical about these claims, or when different figures claim their way to be the 'correct' one and dismiss the views of others. In order to enable interviewees to express their views openly and to ensure that others they might talk about were not maligned by name, we assured everyone we interviewed and everyone who responded to our written questions (see Chapter 4) that we would preserve their anonymity. When referring to historical figures (i.e. those who are dead) we have retained real names; as it happens the contentious issues related in all cases apply to those still living.

The first time we refer to any interviewee or case study by name we use the polite Japanese suffix -san, but thereafter, simply for reasons of convenience and style, do not. Thus in the first line of the book we meet Hara-san, but thereafter he will be referred to simply as Hara.

The eighty-eight Shikoku temples all have names ,but they also are numbered in a standard clockwise order around the island, related to the most common (albeit not obligatory) route followed by pilgrims. Since the temples are most commonly referred to by pilgrims via their numerical designation (*Dai ichiban*, Temple One, and so on) that is how we refer to them in this book.

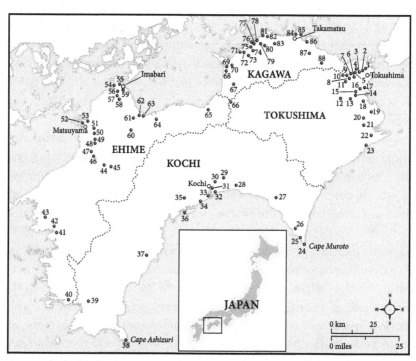

Map of Shikoku, showing prefectures and locations of the eighty-eight temples

Introduction

A pilgrim until I die

In October 2018 the authors of this book interviewed Hara-san,[1] a man in his mid-fifties who was dressed in pilgrimage regalia, outside the gate of one of the eighty-eight temples on Japan's 1400 kilometre-long Shikoku pilgrimage (*Shikoku henro*) route that circles the fourth-largest island in the Japanese archipelago. He was holding a begging bowl and was silently engaged in the Buddhist practice of *takuhatsu* (soliciting alms)—something that many Shikoku pilgrims have done over the centuries. He told us he had been walking the pilgrimage for many years, living and sleeping on the route, and subsisting on the alms (*settai*) he received. He had initially done the pilgrimage aged thirty, and then returned to his home in Yokohama to work. Two decades later, aged fifty, he gave up his work and home (he was unmarried and had no children) to come back to Shikoku where he had been ever since. He spent much of his time walking the pilgrimage and the rest in the mountains doing ascetic practices. In all he estimated he had done around thirty pilgrimage circuits of the island. He viewed his itinerant life as a form of asceticism grounded in faith and told us he would continue doing the pilgrimage 'until I die' (*shinu made*)—a phrase we have heard frequently from other pilgrims, both from those who, like Hara,[2] live on the pilgrimage route and from pilgrims who have made repeated pilgrimages whether by foot, organised bus pilgrimage tours or, most common in recent years, by car. Many of them have been doing the pilgrimage regularly for decades, often doing dozens of circuits a year.

Hara, whom we will encounter again in Chapter 3, is one of a number of people who have spent much of their lives on an unending pilgrimage in Shikoku and who have performed the pilgrimage multiple—even hundreds

---

[1] As we note in the Conventions, we have used pseudonyms to refer to all living informants and interviewees cited in this book.

[2] As stated in the Conventions, when we first refer to a pilgrim or interviewee by name we use the polite Japanese title -san but thereafter do not.

Pilgrims Until We Die. Ian Reader and John Shultz, Oxford University Press. © Oxford University Press 2021. DOI: 10.1093/oso/9780197573587.003.0001

of—times, often over many decades. Historically perhaps the most famous such pilgrim is Nakatsukasa Mōhei who, in 1865 or 1866 (the exact date is unclear) and aged around twenty,[3] left his home on the island of Suo-Ōshima in present-day Yamaguchi prefecture in Japan to walk the *Shikoku henro*. It is unclear exactly why Nakatsukasa initially set out on the pilgrimage. Some accounts claim he was inspired to seek a religious path after hearing stories from an elderly lady about the practice of *settai* (almsgiving to pilgrims) in Shikoku and about the merits of the pilgrimage;[4] others state that he did so in reaction to his family preventing him from marrying the woman he loved, probably because she was seen by his family as beneath his standing.[5] What is known is that Nakatsukasa did not do the pilgrimage just once but kept going around the island on a journey lasting some fifty-six years until his death in 1922. In this time he completed 280 pilgrimage circuits of Shikoku and left the island just twice, the first time to visit some mountain pilgrimage sites on Honshu, the main island of the Japanese archipelago, and the second time to do another of Japan's most famous pilgrimages, the thirty-three-temple Saikoku Kannon pilgrimage, which he walked three times in a row before returning to Shikoku. He became famous throughout Shikoku because of his unending pilgrimage, gaining a reputation for possessing magical healing powers and attracting support from followers along the route, many of who gave him alms and put him up. He also took a Buddhist ordination, published a guide to the pilgrimage in which he set out his views on the correct attitude pilgrims should have, and collected money to erect pilgrimage stones both to guide and encourage other pilgrims, and to commemorate his own pilgrimage activities. Among the occasions on which he erected pilgrimage stones were his eighty-eighth circuit (eighty-eight being significant because of the number of temples on the pilgrimage route), his 100th circuit, and his 137th one. For his 137th circuit he erected fifteen such stones to commemorate having surpassed the 136 pilgrimage circuits by Tada Emon, who died on the pilgrimage in 1862 after having spent much of the latter part of

---

[3] His date of birth is unclear; most accounts think it was in 1845 or 1846 and that he was around 20 at the time when he went to Shikoku. Historical details related to Nakatsukasa here and elsewhere in the book are drawn from Tsurumura 1978; Kiyoyoshi 1984, 1999; Mori 1986; Yoritomi and Shiragi 2001; and Reader 2005.

[4] This claim is in the blog of the Fukujukō pilgrimage group, at http://blog.goo.ne.jp/fukujukai/e/be4dfcb8d3528ae6612968ef352795d5 (accessed June 2018) although we have found no other sources to corroborate this claim.

[5] This is the view expressed in Yoritomi and Shiragi 2001 and Kiyoyoshi 1999.

his life on it and who was considered at the time to have done the most pilgrimage circuits.[6]

While the length of time Nakatsukasa spent—over half a century—on what appeared to be on a never-ending pilgrimage and the number of circuits he made are extraordinary, he is by no means a singular figure in the pilgrimage's history or in its contemporary nature. Rather, he is, like Hara, an example of a phenomenon that has characterised the Shikoku pilgrimage both historically and, perhaps even more, in the contemporary era: some of those who do it are drawn back compulsively time and again to the extent that they end up living on the route as what one of us has elsewhere called 'permanent pilgrims',[7] a term we will discuss in greater depth later, or, like many others who will be encountered in this study, spend significant amounts of their lives making pilgrimages and thinking about being pilgrims in Shikoku.

While we know of no one as yet who has spent as long on an extended unending pilgrimage as Nakatsukasa, we have met several people who have spent many years or decades continuously going around the pilgrimage on foot (see Chapter 3) and others whose history of doing the pilgrimage is longer than Nakatsukasa's fifty-six years. Nor is Nakatsukasa's number of pilgrimages—280—anywhere close to being the most in Shikoku; it has been surpassed by many people in the modern, motorised age. In 2017 Fukuda Shōnosuke died having completed 648 circuits; he had done most of these by car, and in his later years (see Chapter 4) was often doing thirty or forty circuits a year and spending as many as ten or eleven months per year on the pilgrimage. An article in the pilgrimage newsletter *Henro* in July 2008 reports that Fukuda began doing the pilgrimage in 1997 as a memorial (*kuyō*) for fallen war colleagues and to pray that his sick wife could be healed. He said he became captivated by Kōbō Daishi (the central figure of veneration in the pilgrimage) and by *Shikokubyō* (lit. Shikoku illness)—a term widely cited in Shikoku to indicate an all-embracing absorption in and even addiction to the pilgrimage and that we encountered frequently in our research and will discuss later. By 2008, according to the article in *Henro*, Fukuda was spending around 340 days per year on the pilgrimage; his main focus by this point was doing it as a memorial for his wife who had died. The pilgrimage, he said, was his life's meaning (*henro wa ikigai*).[8]

---

[6] Kiyoyoshi 1999: 241; Reader 2005: 70.
[7] Reader 2005: 255–266.
[8] *Henro* 280, July 2008, p. 1.

Pilgrims, confraternities, customised cars, and journeys on foot

Fukuda, like Nakatsukasa before him, had acquired a Buddhist ordination, from Anrakuji, Temple Six (all the temples have both an official temple name and a number designation that is used by pilgrims and in guidebooks and maps).[9] Outside Anrakuji a commemorative stone records Fukuda's 500th pilgrimage and outlines aspects of his life and faith. A priest at the temple told us stories about Fukuda's pilgrimage activities and the reverence other pilgrims were said to have for him, and showed us a collection of Fukuda's pilgrimage commemorative items kept at the temple. Fukuda may not be the person who has done the most circuits of the 1400-kilometre route, however, for we have encountered and interviewed people who claim to have done even more circuits than this—in one case over 700 in a sixty-year period. We also have heard of someone who, as of November 2019, had done 700 circuits and may, at the time of this writing, have gone well beyond the numbers done by any previous pilgrim; although we have not managed to encounter him, and communications sent to his home address have not elicited any response, we have managed to talk to several people who know him. We will discuss him further in Chapter 4.

There are pilgrimage confraternities and societies dedicated to the pilgrimage that are led by people who have done 200 pilgrimages or more, whose members have done dozens or hundreds of circuits and travel together regularly; in Chapter 5 we will outline some of these groups and their leaders. Many of those who have such long histories of pilgrimage and multiple performances have worked most of their lives but on retiring have decided to devote the rest of their lives to the pilgrimage. Frequently they use their retirement and their pensions and life savings to this end.

Often pilgrims adapt their vehicles to facilitate their travels. Some car drivers have done this by removing the passenger seats and inserting a bed in their place so that they can sleep in their vehicles at night, thereby enabling them to cut costs and spend more time on the route. Others drive customised vans with a bed or mattress in the back to sleep on. We first heard of this practice, known as *shachūhaku*, or 'sleeping/overnighting in the car', from

---

[9] In Chapter 1 we discuss the route and numbers more specifically. As we note in the Conventions, throughout the book we normally refer to the temples by their numbers.

Figure I.1 *Shachūhaku*: pilgrim's car adapted for sleeping

a retired lady in her eighties whom we met in Shikoku in March 2018. She told us that since retirement she had done the *henro* some forty times and intended to keep doing it as many times as she could; she said that her way of doing the pilgrimage was *shachūhaku*, a term she explained by opening the back of her car, which was adorned with numerous pilgrimage stickers. She had removed the front and back passenger seats and in their place installed a bed and camping equipment that enabled her to travel cheaply with some comfort and autonomy (see Figure I.1). It was a term and phenomenon we encountered repeatedly thereafter, for *shachūhaku* has become an aspect of the contemporary pilgrimage landscape that enables people to do multiple pilgrimages and spend long periods travelling without the costs of overnight lodgings. Nowadays, too, one can even purchase vans that have been customised for Shikoku pilgrims doing *shachūhaku*, with a tatami floor, futons, cooking space, a place to hang one's pilgrim's hat, and many other facilities for travelling pilgrims.[10] *Shachūhaku* is a term and practice that will be encountered frequently in the pages and stories that appear in this book.

We have also interviewed numerous people who, while not living permanently on the route, have walked the pilgrimage many times, often on a very regular and seasonal basis, and for whom the *henro*[11] forms a key frame of reference for their lives. Since it takes around six weeks or so to walk the whole route, anyone who has walked a number of circuits will have spent significant amounts of time on the route. Many spend a great deal of time before each pilgrimage in preparation as well. For example, Sasaki-san, a man from Sendai in northern Japan whom we met in March 2018 and have subsequently had written correspondence with, told us he comes to Shikoku every year on or around the same date to walk the pilgrimage. When we met him he had done it over a dozen times and planned to continue so doing as long as he was able. Moreover, he said, it took him around two months beforehand to meticulously plan his route, arrange overnight accommodation (he stayed in pilgrim lodges, temple lodgings, and other accommodation), and make sure his family knew where he would be at any day of his planned pilgrimages. Planning was not just an integral part of the actual pilgrimage but a key focus of his life each year. As he said to us, each year as he walks he wonders if this will be his last pilgrimage. Each year, two or so months before his usual visit to Shikoku, he feels the compulsion to go again and starts planning the next pilgrimage.

He is not an isolated case but an example of a phenomenon we found repeatedly: older (usually retired) Japanese men who had walked the pilgrimage several (often ten or more) times and on a regular basis. Some walk the whole route every year at around the same time, and some do it twice a year. Some sleep out all or most of the time while others, like Sasaki, stay in lodges; generally they spend large amounts of their time between pilgrimages thinking of and planning the next one. We discuss such walker pilgrims in detail in Chapter 6. There are others who, having done the pilgrimage, become enamoured of Shikoku to the extent that they decide to move there, as with one interviewee who originally came from Hyogo prefecture on Honshu, but who, after going to Shikoku to do the pilgrimage, decided to move there. He now runs a lodge on the island

---

[10] Website of Mōta Nyusu (car sales magazine) https://autoc-one.jp/suzuki/every/special-5007515/photo/0046.html?fbclid=IwAR3tUPShGoGIRxyF8XLB7b8XCuUAS-tLlocPQ5Uqh66aw UHG6FaJQW0JM1k (accessed 5 June 2020).

[11] As noted in the Conventions, *henro* is the standard term in Japanese for this pilgrimage, and it is a term we will use in the text at times, so as not to keep repeating the word 'pilgrimage'.

and informed us that he has made thirty Shikoku pilgrimage circuits, as well as numerous visits or shorter pilgrimages to some of the temples on the island.

Numbers, scope, and commemorative themes

The numbers of those who either live on the pilgrimage route or who do the pilgrimage dozens or hundreds of times in the course of their lives may not be massive in comparison with the millions who, over the centuries, have done the Shikoku pilgrimage. After all it has long been one of Japan's most historically famous pilgrimages and is nowadays considered to be probably the most commonly performed Buddhist temple pilgrimage in Japan, so that over the centuries the number of pilgrims has amounted to several million.[12] However, as previously outlined, multiple performances of the pilgrimage are a significant element in its make-up; surveys by Japanese scholars indicate that over 40% of those doing the pilgrimage in the early 2000s were doing at least their second circuit of the pilgrimage, while many had done ten or more circuits (and in many cases far more than that).[13] The *Shikoku Reijōkai* (Shikoku Pilgrimage Temples' Association), which serves as the official body coordinating the activities of the eighty-eight pilgrimage temples and regulating aspects of the pilgrimage, runs a system of recognition for those who perform the pilgrimage multiple times and who help in its promotion and practices. Those who do the pilgrimage four or more times can apply for and acquire the title of *sendatsu* (pilgrimage guide). Those who do it more times still can achieve promotion through a system of *sendatsu* rankings that convey status and recognise the contributions that such figures make to the pilgrim community. There are currently over 9000 living *sendatsu*.[14] Not all those who do the pilgrimage multiple times, we should add, seek the status and rank of *sendatsu*; many of those from whom we have interviewed or

---

[12] Exact figures are hard to come by but general estimates are that, since the 1990s, 100 000 people or more a year have done the pilgrimage, while in earlier times, as Maeda (1971) indicates, there were around 15 000 pilgrims a year up to the 1970s. Over the three-and-a-half centuries of the pilgrimage's formal existence this amounts to a significant number of people. Since around the 1980s the Shikoku pilgrimage has become the most popular (and widely reported) pilgrimage associated with Buddhist temples in Japan (Reader 2014: 36–39). Numbers, according to all the informants we talked to in this research, have dropped in the past few years but still run into many tens of thousands.

[13] Satō 2004: 224–226.

[14] This figure was provided to us by an official of the Pilgrimage Temples' Association in an interview at the Association's office at Zentsūji, Temple Seventy-Five (31 Oct 2019).

received questionnaires say that they have not sought this rank even though they are qualified to do so.

There are also numerous signs at the temples that indicate a recurrent tradition of multiple performance and of a wider consciousness about the number of circuits done by others. Nakatsukasa's practice of erecting commemorative stones shows that he was both aware of the performances of other earlier pilgrims such as Tada and was keen to let the world know he had surpassed them. This awareness of the performances of others has been a recurrent feature of our interviews. While few of those we have met have overtly expressed a sense of competitiveness with regard to others, it has sometimes been hinted at, and we consider that such a sense cannot be discounted in examining why some people do the pilgrimage so often. Moreover, many pilgrims commemorate their multiple performance of the pilgrimage, just as Nakatsukasa and Fukuda have done, by erecting stones and other markers announcing particular pilgrimage achievements or the completion of a vow to perform a set number of circuits; the eighty-eighth and 100th are occasions that seem particularly widely commemorated. We will discuss the issues of commemoration and competition further in Chapter 2.

Legends, lifelong practice, and going back again

As we discuss in Chapter 1, the pilgrimage's foundation legends, stories, and related beliefs, along with its structure and symbols, which include the image of a holy Buddhist figure, Kōbō Daishi, incessantly travelling the pilgrimage route and dispensing benefits to those met along the way, themselves manifest a sense of reiteration, recurrence, unending engagement, and permanence. Historically, too, this has been the case, as we also discuss in Chapter 1, where we show how seminal figures in the development of the pilgrimage such as the seventeenth century ascetic Yūben Shinnen (d. 1691) performed the pilgrimage repeatedly and thereby helped develop a tradition of multiple performance. This has endured throughout the known history of the pilgrimage, manifested in such figures as Tada and Nakatsukasa as well as, in more recent times, mendicant itinerants such as Hara and those pilgrims who sleep in their cars, as well as the growing ranks of people who have acquired the position of *sendatsu* after completing four or more pilgrimages.

This sense of continuity and permanent engagement with pilgrimage as an unending lifelong activity was encapsulated in Hara's determination to continue incessantly walking the pilgrimage 'until I die' and was commonly reiterated by those we interviewed. Many interviewees and many whose stories we heard talked in such terms, of wanting to die on the route or of only stopping when too infirm to continue. Fukuda, for example, according to sources who knew him, continued doing the pilgrimage by car well into his nineties, until he was no longer able to drive himself. At this point, for his 648th circuit he was driven by his daughter; it proved to be his final pilgrimage circuit, for thereafter he was hospitalised, was no longer able to travel, and then died.

This sense of wanting to go back and do the pilgrimage again (and again), leading to a compulsive attachment, unending engagement, and per- petual performance, is encapsulated in terms such as the aforementioned *Shikokubyō* (Shikoku illness) and related terms such as *henro boke* (pil- grimage senility) that are commonly used by people connected to the pil- grimage. Often these terms are linked to the notion, expressed by many we talked to, that the pilgrimage is 'addictive';[15] many (although by no means all) of those we interviewed or surveyed used such terms to refer to them- selves. Several of our respondents, for example, recognised that they had *Shikokubyō*, although none saw it as an 'illness' (which is the normative meaning of the term *byō*) in the sense of being something they needed or wanted to be cured of. Rather, they viewed it as something positive. One re- spondent, for example, wrote that, yes, he had *Shikokubyō* and then added that this was a wonderful blessing (*shiawase desu*); this summed up a common attitude to the idea of 'Shikoku illness and addiction'.

Multiple performances, central organising principles, and routines

All these examples—the historical accounts of lifelong pilgrims, the com- memorative signs left by pilgrims, the people who adapt their vehicles so they can sleep in them on pilgrimage, and of people who live permanently as itinerant pilgrims in Shikoku—indicate that repeating pilgrimages so many times that it becomes a core central organising principle in one's life is a sig- nificant aspect of the *Shikoku henro*. This brings us to a key focus of this book, to questions about pilgrimage in general, and to issues that have not been

---

[15] The notion of the pilgrimage as addictive was first discussed by Reader 2005: 255–257.

widely considered thus far in the expanding academic field of pilgrimage studies.

One of the most common and recurring themes in studies of pilgrimage has been to treat it as a '"ritualized break" from routine',[16] a theme that, Hillary Kaell indicates, has been articulated by many prominent scholars of pilgrimage such as Victor and Edith Turner and Alan Morinis.[17] Equally, the depiction of pilgrimage as occurring 'out there' apart from the ordinary and everyday lives of participants—a notion encapsulated in the title of Turner's article 'The Center Out There: Pilgrim's Goal'[18] and standing as a contrast to the idea of 'home'—has been a staple theme in much pilgrimage literature. It was, for example, expressed in Alan Morinis's summary of a conference on pilgrimage in which a recurrent theme was portraying pilgrimage as 'the special going out which contrasts to the habitual staying at home' and in which a contrast between centre and periphery is evident.[19] Similarly, as the subtitle of Turner's article indicates, the idea that pilgrimage is a process or journey towards a specific place or goal, and hence a process with a finite end point, has been widespread in studies of pilgrimage. Such concepts have in many ways shaped how we think of and examine pilgrimage, as something that is transient and a stepping outside of everyday life, routines, and practices. Often as a result pilgrimage is seen as a journey away from home, something set apart from ordinary life, and an escape from or alternative to ideas of the everyday and of routines. Such emphases also project an image of pilgrimage as extraordinary and singular, a one-off rather than a repeated or repetitive activity.

Our study of Shikoku pilgrims offers an alternative perspective to such conceptualisations. For many Shikoku pilgrims, pilgrimage—and specifically the Shikoku pilgrimage[20]—form a core and dominant life motif, while some pilgrims may spend so much of their time on the pilgrimage that they become either distanced from their actual homes or, as is evident in the stories of Nakatsukasa and Hara, abandon any sense of 'home' as a physical

---

[16] Kaell 2016: 2.

[17] Victor Turner and Edith Turner 1978: 34–35; Alan Morinis 1992.

[18] Turner 1973.

[19] Morinis 1981: 282. The theme of pilgrimage as related to movement (in contrast to the stasis of home) is in effect developed also by Coleman and Eade (2004) in an edited volume that argues that movement is the key component of pilgrimage.

[20] Our interviews and questionnaires showed that many people also have done other pilgrimages, mainly in Japan, and some of them several times, but that overall their prime and sometimes sole focus is the Shikoku pilgrimage. We discuss this further in Chapter 4.

entity set apart from the pilgrimage. Moreover, far from being a break from routine, we have found that pilgrimage in Shikoku for many of our subjects is very much a part of their routines. Rather than being extraordinary and 'out there' it is a practice fully embedded in and a normal part of their everyday lives.

We will develop this point by describing a number of case studies in later chapters but will provide two examples here to illustrate the point. The first is Sasaki, the aforementioned man from northern Japan, who walks the pilgrimage at a set time every year, spends two months in advance planning every aspect of the route, has a generally fixed routine of places to stay, and every year at around the same time finds himself meticulously preparing for his next trip. The second concerns Ozaki-san, a businessman whom we interviewed in October 2018 in Osaka where both his family home and business were located. During the working (Monday to Friday) week he lives with his family and ran his business. Every Friday evening, he told us, he closes his business office for the weekend and then sets out by car to Shikoku, carefully planning his trip so that he crosses the toll bridge across the Inland Sea after midnight (thereby getting the cheaper weekend toll rate) before sleeping somewhere in his car until morning. Then he sets out on foot all day Saturday along the pilgrimage route, before making his way back (via public transport) to his car at night, sleeping in it, and then driving to where he finished the night before, after which he walks all Sunday until evening. At that point he makes his way back to his car to drive home during the night to be ready for work on Monday. His home, family, business, and pilgrimages together form a complementary weekly routine. We have interviewed others who have similar routines in which they work during the week and do the pilgrimage each weekend; while one could argue that their weekends thus are a form of ritualised break from their work routines, they are also a routine. Indeed, in the accounts we heard from people who still are working and doing the pilgrimage in the periods when they are not at work, we often felt wondered if their work and home lives were a ritualised break from pilgrimage rather than the other way around. For Ozaki we felt, as we talked to him, that work business and family appeared secondary to pilgrimage. This was a feeling that emerged in interviews with others as well.

Those we encountered who have done the pilgrimage many times or who have spent vast amounts of their lives on the pilgrimage route are not really escaping from routine when they set off on the *henro* so much as engaging in another form of routine. For Hara and the other permanent itinerants whom we will meet in Chapter 3, the pilgrimage is their life and way of living; it is their routine. One such itinerant we interviewed, Shimada-san, whose story is provided in more detail in Chapter 3, was happy to talk at length about his life history and pilgrimage routines; he also indicated that as a permanent itinerant he had a mental schedule by which he travelled. Indeed, he eventually ended the interview by noting that it was now midday and that he needed to start walking again to get to the place where he planned to sleep out overnight. Another walker we met, who was carrying a backpack and pulling a case on wheels behind him, told us he had a house in Matsuyama, one of the main towns on Shikoku, but could not stand living there for more than a day or two at a time because it was noisy, so he was always keen to get away again and go back to his itinerant lifestyle on the pilgrimage. He already knew where he would sleep that night and had a clear idea of what each day would bring. While he had a house in Matsuyama, the pilgrimage route was where he felt at home; it formed the routinised framework of his life.

The pilgrimage is, for multiple performers, more likely to be an integral part of their lives than some sort of rupture or break from it. It is where they feel at home. Many times we heard people say it was 'part of my life'; as one respondent to a questionnaire wrote, he had nothing to do when he retired, and this led him to do the pilgrimage—something he has done many times since, so that pilgrimage had become part of his life (*seikatsu no ichibu*). This and similar phrases surfaced often in interviews. It is not just those who live on the pilgrimage route or who do it hundreds of times who are in an unending attachment to the pilgrimage; repeatedly, pilgrims who had only done it a few times stated that their lives were framed around doing and planning their pilgrimages. At home, in a real sense, they remained mentally 'on the road'; they were always in the process of doing the pilgrimage.

Unexplored issues: pilgrimage studies and multiple performance

While this book therefore challenges many of the themes that have been prevalent in studies of pilgrimage both globally and in Japan,[21] it specifically draws attention to a topic that has received relatively little discussion in

---

[21] For a detailed examination of studies and theories of pilgrimage published in Japanese by Japanese scholars see Reader 2015.

the field, namely people who do pilgrimages (and in the cases we are examining, one specific pilgrimage) again and again. There have been a very few studies that have touched on this issue. One of the authors of this study devoted a section of a previous book about the Shikoku pilgrimage to a brief examination of what he termed 'permanent pilgrims', a category that included Nakatsukasa and a number of pilgrims met during earlier Shikoku fieldwork.[22] Studies on other pilgrimages too have briefly touched on the issue. Nancy Frey, for example, refers briefly to the ways in which some pilgrims doing the Santiago de Compostela pilgrimage told her it was 'addictive' and she speaks of a 'pilgrimage bug' and of 'serial' pilgrims 'hooked' on the Camino'.[23] Other examples include Simon Coleman's comment that the English pilgrimage site of Walsingham was a 'second home' for some people and Philip Taylor's study of pilgrimage in Vietnam, which shows how multiple performances are common there, with some people having a recurrent itinerary of pilgrimages—something especially so for traders who combine pilgrimage with mercantile activities.[24]

Historically cases of repeat and recurrent pilgrims can be found in studies of medieval Christianity. Diane Webb, for example, states that there were people in medieval England who 'who made a life's work' of pilgrimage.[25] Examples include the Norfolk female mystic Margery Kempe, who made numerous pilgrimages in the fifteenth century, visiting the Christian Holy Land, Santiago de Compostela, and several other pilgrimage sites on the continent such as Rome and Assisi, as well as many sites within England. Kempe collected indulgences from the sites she visited, relied on alms and begging to sustain her, and frequently annoyed her fellow pilgrims by excessive demonstrations of piety and recurrent weeping. Each pilgrimage she did seemed to increase her desire to go on another, as her life became a cycle of pilgrimage activities. Examples of similarly extended pilgrimage lifestyles can be found in the Tibetan Buddhist tradition too, such as the female lama Jetsun Lochen who was born in 1865 and spent her first thirty-nine years travelling as a pilgrim until she took up residence in a hermitage. Initially she travelled with her parents and then for some thirteen years with her spiritual teacher Pema Gyatso; after his death she then spent the next fourteen years on pilgrimage either on her own or with devotees. Her focus was on pilgrimage

[22] Reader 2005: 255–266.
[23] Frey 1998: 211.
[24] Coleman 2000; Taylor 2004.
[25] Webb 2000: 216.

places associated with famous lamas and figures in the Tibetan tradition such as Padmasambhava and Milarepa.[26] Examples of pilgrims who become so involved in specific sites that they take up residence there—static pilgrims, as it were, continually on pilgrimage to the places of their new residence—can be found in the academic literature, such as the Hindu pilgrims cited by Diane Eck, who travel to the sacred pilgrimage city of Varanasi and then stay there until they die, and devotees of the Catholic priest Padre Pio, who journey to San Giovanni Rotondo, stay in the town, attend the shrine all the time, and become resident devotees.[27]

Michael Agnew has added to this literature by outlining cases of people who go back time and again on pilgrimage to Lourdes. Agnew describes them as 'serial pilgrims' and shows that not only do they go back there repeatedly but that they also constantly think about the site so that they are 'spiritually always in Lourdes'. Yet Agnew also states that such themes of repetition have been little discussed or analysed in the field of pilgrimage studies. According to Agnew the only examples of such discussions or analysis have been Reader's aforementioned discussion of 'permanent pilgrims' and Frey's references to addiction and serial pilgrims to Santiago.[28]

However, as Reader has pointed out, Frey shies away from any further analysis of this idea of repetition and addiction, instead treating it as a disturbing disjuncture from the 'stimulant for self-exploration' that, in her view, pilgrimage should be.[29] Nor is Reader's study primarily focused on 'permanent pilgrims'; rather they form a relatively small part of a study aimed at developing an understanding of what he portrays as the encompassing dimensions and narrative of pilgrimage. While he raises the issue of permanent or perpetual pilgrims, they remain an element in the broader framework and context of his study rather than a specific analytical case study.

In other words, this is a topic that has as yet been barely focused on in studies of pilgrimage. The only one study that is—at least in terms of its title—directly focused on the topic is C. Bawa Yamba's book *Permanent Pilgrims: Role of Pilgrimage in the Lives of West African Pilgrims*[30]—a study interestingly not cited by Agnew or in Reader's discussion of 'permanent pilgrims'. Yamba examines Muslims from West Africa (predominantly

[26] Havnevik 1998: 92–97.
[27] Eck 1983: 28; McKevitt 1991: 93.
[28] Agnew 2015: 526–529; see also Agnew 2014.
[29] Reader 2005: 264–265; Frey 1998: 211–212.
[30] Yamba 1995.

northern Nigeria) now living in Sudan who had travelled (usually by foot) across Africa to perform the pilgrimage to Mecca. They had, as a rule, never arrived at their intended goal of Mecca, instead running out of resources on the way. Needing to stop and find work in order to glean the wherewithal to move on again they had ended up living in enclaves in the Sudan, raising children, and becoming, in effect, permanent residents there. However they did not see themselves in this light; even the fourth and fifth generations of those who initially arrived in Sudan continued to view themselves as West African pilgrims on the way to Mecca. Their villages were temporary way stations, and they were transients. In analysing their views Yamba suggests that although they appear to be resident in Sudan, they were sustained by the idea that they are still on pilgrimage and thus not locked into what appears to be a marginalised and impecunious situation. Yamba refers to them as 'permanent pilgrims' because the idea of being on pilgrimage to Mecca and of being pilgrims is the core motif of their lives.

While Yamba thus draws attention to the potential of pilgrimage to be a life-framing and permanent state of mind, his case study differs from ours in that he focuses on people who, although they conceptualise themselves as being on the way somewhere as pilgrims, are actually static, living in makeshift villages from one generation to the next and raising children there. Yamba's conceptual framework thus relates to a state of mind that helps people feel they are not tied to their present place and state of being. His study is not about people who have performed (and completed) pilgrimages and yet do them again and again. While we also focus on states of mind (for example, in considering such things as *Shikokubyō* and in noting how the pilgrims we focus on think of themselves as pilgrims even while in between pilgrimages), we are looking at people who are actually performing pilgrimages, often incessantly and always repeatedly, and are in regular or constant states of motion and repetition, rather than people who, while static, conceptualise themselves as transient.

In other words, our discussion of Shikoku pilgrims is addressing a topic as yet under-discussed and barely theorised in the literature. By looking at issues of multiple performance and repetition, and of the idea that pilgrimage is an unending, perpetual, and temporally unbounded practice,[31] we present a new perspective on pilgrimage. We focus on Shikoku

---

[31] The notion of pilgrimage being temporally unbounded has been specifically developed and discussed by Shultz 2020.

because of our mutual interests in studies of pilgrimage in Japan and because Shikoku provides plentiful examples of the types of figures we are interested in, both historically and in the present day. We seek to broaden our discussion to the wider field based in the understanding that—as has been widely mooted—pilgrimage is a phenomenon that is universal in nature, found across different traditions and cultures. As such, there have been continuing attempts to construct broader theories of pilgrimage via the use of specific examples, grounded in the view that since pilgrimage is universal, examples from any given cultural or religious context could offer analytical insights into and theoretical perspectives on the topic in general. At the same time, however, such attempts at analytical and theoretical framing have generally been located within a Western- and Christian-centric context, as has been evident in the meta-theories proposed by scholars, for example, Victor and Edith Turner, and John Eade and Michael Sallnow.[32] On such grounds, of course, as one of us has argued elsewhere, if pilgrimage is indeed universal in nature to the extent that one can make broader comments about it based in specific religious or cultural examples, then it is equally valid to use non-Western and non-Christian cases such as Japan, as any other.[33] As such here we use the issue of repetition and multiple performance in Shikoku to explore wider issues related to pilgrimage.

In so doing we also recognise an inherent tension at the heart of pilgrimage studies in which the field's embrace of the subject's universality has introduced such a wide array of experiences and examples from across the globe and across the socio-religious spectrum that meaningful theoretical assertions about pilgrimage, derived from localised data, are often seen to be lacking in other cultural contexts or time periods. One can see this in the widespread counter-arguments made, based on specific case studies, to meta-narrative theoretical arguments such as Turner's notion of communitas, initially critiqued by Sallnow on the grounds that it did not work among the Andean Indian pilgrims he studied.[34] Eade and Sallnow's subsequent counter-theory to the Turnerian argument on communitas posited contest as a key analytical element in pilgrimage. This, too, has been critiqued by case studies, to the extent that, as Eade has later recognised, meta-narratives do not really work, or at least cannot remain viable across all pilgrimage

[32] Turner and Turner 1978; Eade and Sallnow 1991.
[33] Reader 2014: 22–24.
[34] Sallnow 1981, 1987.

contexts.[35] We concur with this, aware that as the field develops further and more studies become available, it becomes increasingly problematic to make grand and over-arching theoretical claims. It may be, indeed, that methodologies and theories have reached something of an impasse that requires a deep critical re-assessment. The basic question becomes: how can pilgrimage studies flourish given the difficulty of making even the most basic generalisations about the phenomena?

Our response to this is not to propose another grand meta-theory but to draw attention to the value of developing analyses of pilgrimage with a methodological focus on how key variables create diversities of interpretation. Indeed, the narratives and data covered in this book demonstrate obvious and significant variability with respect to key areas of theoretical debate in pilgrimage studies, including the social character of the experience, the role of place, appeal to austerity and the degree of free choice among individuals. While resisting the call to make a universal proclamation about pilgrimage (or about all pilgrimages) derived from specific localised data, we wish to use our findings from Shikoku to raise questions about the general nature of pilgrimage, challenging assumptions that have commonly portrayed it as an exceptional practice done predominantly by people taking breaks from normal routines, and making suggestions about how the example we focus on can spur new thoughts and research about, and understandings of, pilgrimage in general. While our case studies are focused on a minority, albeit a sizeable one, within the wider number of Shikoku pilgrims, we argue not only that the notion of unending pilgrimage is *the* dominant trope for the *henro*, but that this phenomenon is an under-appreciated dynamic evident in global pilgrimage more broadly. Further, this diverse minority can be seen to have an outsized influence on the social system of the pilgrimage, culturally and authoritatively speaking. As we discuss in subsequent chapters, during our research we not only met and interviewed pilgrims who have done the Shikoku pilgrimage hundreds of times, but also others who aspire to follow in their footsteps and who have goals to attain similar numerical levels of performance. The examples of existing and previous multiple performers of pilgrimage thus may serve as an inspiration for others; they have created a culture of continuing unending performance in the pilgrimage. Moreover, people who have done multiple, and at times many hundreds of, pilgrimages in Shikoku spent much of their time thinking about Shikoku. They were, to

---

[35] Eade 2000.

borrow and adapt Agnew's phrase 'spiritually always in Shikoku'. Pilgrimage was a significant part of their identity and it was something to which they were constantly drawn.

While we are not saying that pilgrimage inherently leads to addiction and to permanent performances, we do suggest that it has that potential. Perhaps this is more evident in some cultural contexts than others but it can become an all-embracing practice and life framework—a pilgrimage identity that remains so whether on or off the trail. This is certainly the case for those who are drawn into a permanent relationship with the Shikoku pilgrimage. It gives them a sense of identity in their everyday lives and is not just an addiction but a central organising force in their lives.

The spectrum of practice and engagement

This is a theme that is common across what is, as our subsequent chapters indicate, a broad spectrum of practice, attitudes, and approaches to the pilgrimage, among those who do the *henro* multiple times. We have found an immense amount of variation among such people: from permanent itinerants who live on the route; to those who embed it as a routine within their working lives; to those who travel repeatedly as members of social confraternities led by an inspirational pilgrimage leader; to those who adapt their cars to facilitate their pilgrimages; to those who are just starting their pilgrimage careers but who envision doing it repeatedly in future. There are immense variations of actual performance: from walking regularly; to speedy circuits by car; from doing the whole circuit in one go; to breaking it up into numerous shorter sections and visits. Within such broad frameworks, too, there are numerous variations. There are relatively few people who now live as permanent itinerants on the route even if they serve as an important category, associated with the historical roots of the pilgrimage and its enduring elements. Yet even among this very small minority one finds multiple variations of attitude and practice, a point we illustrate via the case studies in Chapter 3 where we show, for example, how two such itinerants, who know and respect each other, have significantly different orientations. One sees his pilgrimage as an austerity and primarily identifies himself as an ascetic who came to Shikoku as a pilgrim in order to follow this path; the other first did the pilgrimage as a reaction to losing a job and home, and after finding it suited him to remain free and unencumbered by walls continued to walk the pilgrimage. For one, faith and asceticism were dominant elements, while for the other they appeared to play little part compared to the sense of freedom the pilgrimage gave him along with the ability to subsist in an era in which he had been thrown out of work. This is just one example of the many differences of attitude, practices, and motivations we have encountered among those who have done the pilgrimage multiple times. As such we recognise that variability is a significant theme in this pilgrimage—as we suggest it is for pilgrimages in general. The Shikoku pilgrims we discuss are all following their own paths and doing the pilgrimage in the ways they think fit. What unites them and remains constant are in essence three themes: that all these people, with their many differing ways of travel and attitudes, are engaging in the same practice, namely the Shikoku pilgrimage, visiting the same temples, and sharing the same route; that they are drawn back again and again to it; and that it serves as a central organising principle that gives meaning and motivation to their lives and provides them with a sense of identity as pilgrims whether at home or circuiting the route.

Methods, fieldwork, and our engagement with the pilgrimage

We will shortly outline the framework of this book, but first will add a short note about our methods of study. Both authors have studied pilgrimages in general, and most notably in Japan and especially in Shikoku, for many years, using a mixture of field-based, textual, and historical research. One of us (IR) first went to Shikoku in 1984 and has since then visited the island dozens of times and conducted numerous interviews with pilgrims, temple priests, and others involved in pilgrimage support activities in Shikoku, as well as doing archival research on the pilgrimage's history. The other author (JS) also has been doing field research in Shikoku for over a decade and a half and has done extensive studies of pilgrims' diaries and writings about their pilgrimages. Both have travelled extensively in Shikoku, have walked the pilgrimage route on at least one occasion, and have travelled with groups of pilgrims at different times. We have thus built this current research on the foundations of our earlier work and have used various contacts in Shikoku to facilitate the current research.

Our fieldwork for this study was primarily done in three intensive visits to Shikoku between February 2018 and November 2019, in which we went round most of the pilgrimage route on each occasion, stopping to talk to and interview pilgrims at the temples or whenever we saw them along the route itself. Whenever we encountered someone who had done the pilgrimage more than once we explained the project and asked if we could interview them. We also arranged formal interviews (and at times follow-up interviews) when possible, and conducted several such with pilgrims at various locations suitable to them, usually when they were not on the pilgrimage route. We also used many published resources, reading pilgrim accounts and examining back issues of *Henro*, the aforementioned monthly newsletter that is sent to all registered Shikoku *sendatsu*. We also published a short article in *Henro* that outlined our project and asked people to contact us if they were willing to be interviewed. That produced numerous responses and subsequent interviews at mutually convenient locations. The internet provided a further source of information and contacts; some interviews with our field subjects came about after reading the blogs and online writings of pilgrims. We also met some interviewees on a number of occasions. In addition there were other shorter visits by one of the authors to Shikoku plus extensive interactions with a pilgrimage confraternity whose leader and members have done many pilgrimages; this group is discussed in Chapter 5.

Besides such interviews we collected data and views via a lengthy written questionnaire that we sent to people who had done the pilgrimage many times, and we outline their responses in Chapter 4. In addition we made use of things that pilgrims have left behind during their travels and that contained data and information about their multiple journeys. These included commemorative stones and inscriptions that pilgrims have erected to celebrate their own performances or to honour famed pilgrims and the pilgrim name slips (*osamefuda*, also known simply as *fuda*) that pilgrims commonly carry with them. Such *fuda* normally are inscribed with an image of Kōbō Daishi and various invocations, along with the name of the pilgrim and often, too, his or her address, and prayers or wishes for the pilgrimage. Pilgrims commonly leave them at offertory boxes at the temples. They also hand them out to people they meet on the route, especially if such people give them alms (*settai*), a practice that has contributed significantly to the culture of multiple pilgrimage performance in Shikoku (see Chapter 1). *Fuda* come in various colours to signify the number of times a person has done the pilgrimage (see Chapter 2 for further details), and we met many pilgrims who were keen to qualify for the highest ranked of them all, the brocade type (*nishiki fuda*) that signifies one has done over one hundred circuits. We were also able to examine numerous brocade *fuda* through various channels, including the kindness of temple priests and officials who allowed us to inspect collections of such items that had been left at their temples, and through encounters with pilgrims who carried such items. These brocade *fuda* proved a valuable source of data to chart the schedules of some of the most active multiple performers (see Chapter 4) and to gather addresses of such people so that we could contact them to request further information and to whom we could send the questionnaires we referred to earlier.

The structure of this book

In Chapter 1 we present a general outline of the pilgrimage, in historical and legendary terms, showing how these themes are closely woven together. The chapter outlines how traditions of asceticism and legends of eternal mendicancy helped shape the culture of pilgrimage, while local customs of almsgiving provided needed support for earlier pilgrims. This chapter shows how the physical structure of the pilgrimage contributes to the sense that it is an unending journey, introduces some well-known pilgrims of earlier ages, and shows how feelings of competition and commemoration developed in the pilgrimage.

Chapter 2 looks at how modern developments have enhanced the culture of repetition in Shikoku, through the rise of modern transport systems and economic advances (including a modern pension system) that enable people to finance multiple pilgrimages. In particular a new category of 'pensioner pilgrims' has arisen who, as one informant remarked, have the three things needed for doing the pilgrimage many times: free time, money, and health (the last being the one element that eventually causes pilgrims to cease their travels). We examine the phenomenon of *shachūhaku* (sleeping in the car) as a new factor in this context and look also at how a variety of elements in the modern pilgrimage—such as the *sendatsu* ranking system and *osamefuda* (pilgrim name slips)—have spurred a culture of multiple performance, competition, and status acquisition. We discuss also how the idea of *Shikokubyō* (Shikoku illness) and hence of pilgrimage as an addictive and alluring practice has become prominent in explanations of why people do the pilgrimage and how it has been readily embraced by practitioners.

In Chapter 3 we look at a very small but enduring aspect of the pilgrim community in Shikoku, but one that continues the pilgrimage's original patterns of asceticism, mendicancy and continual performance, namely those pilgrims who live permanently on the route, subsisting mainly by begging for alms. We show that such people are often the focus of criticism, accused of freeloading, and that some have problems with alcohol. However this is not so for all. Some permanent itinerants are devout ascetics who have found meaning in the pilgrimage that they lacked in everyday life. They may be rigorous in their practices, live by clear guidelines, and never touch alcohol. We present depth case histories of eight such figures, including one itinerant who became (in)famous in Japan as a criminal and fugitive from the law while also being revered by many who knew him in Shikoku. Recurrently, too, such pilgrims indicated that the only thing that would stop their pilgrimages was death itself.

In Chapter 4 we present results of an extensive 'interview by mail' with twenty pilgrims who had done the pilgrimage large numbers of times. This supplements our direct interviews and helps flesh out the profiles of those who do repeated pilgrimages, indicating aspects of their background, age profiles, number of times they have done the pilgrimage, how they finance it, their attitudes to other pilgrims, and much else. The questionnaire also examined issues of addiction and Shikokubyō—something that most readily admitted to and embraced. We also found that many of those surveyed did not only do the Shikoku pilgrimage but also several other pilgrimages in Japan as well—something that indicated that pilgrimage in general, and not just Shikoku, was often a significant factor in their lives. These figures also responded in a similar way to the 'permanent itinerants' of Chapter 3, when asked if or when they would stop doing the pilgrimage: when I die or when I am no longer able to do it. We also in Chapter 4 look closely at schedules, at the time those who do the most pilgrimages take for their journeys, and the intensity of their performance. Here we focus in particular on the case studies of two pilgrims from recent times who both have done over 600 circuits, often averaging around forty pilgrimage circuits a year, along with reasons why they became so immersed in the pilgrimage.

While many of the pilgrims cited in Chapters 3 and 4 travel alone, pilgrimage is not necessarily a solitary activity. In Chapter 5 we focus on those who travel by motorised transport and also draw attention to the social dimensions of such pilgrimages. We look first at pilgrimage confraternities, led usually by a prominent pilgrim with an extended history of performance, and at how such groups encourage multiple performances while creating a sense of social bonding and conviviality among members. These themes emerge also when looking at pilgrims who travel in their own vehicles, for example, by providing examples of one of the most common patterns of multiple performance in this context, namely retired husband and wife couples who make multiple pilgrimages together, often in converted vehicles. We also show that although female pilgrims constitute a minority among those who do large numbers of pilgrimages, they are prominent in the *shachūhaku* community, and we include interviews and accounts of some such women to this end. The chapter also draws attention to a point that is further developed in Chapter 6: that while many of those interviewed are not continually on the pilgrimage in a physical sense, they are always thinking about the 'next time' in Shikoku. As we discuss here and in Chapter 6, even those who have only done the pilgrimage once or twice are often already thinking in such terms—something we illustrate both via examples of such pilgrims and through statistical data. Our case studies here and in the next chapter thus not only focus on people with very high numbers of pilgrimages but those, while only just starting out, already see themselves as having a long-term engagement with the pilgrimage.

Chapter 6 picks up on these themes through an examination of those who walk the pilgrimage multiple times. Most commonly these are older male Japanese, although we also show this category includes some women and a growing number of non-Japanese (mainly Western) people. We examine their motives and attitudes, noting that while some talk about how through doing the pilgrimage they have gradually developed a sense of faith, they more commonly place less emphasis on faith than do those who travel by car, talking more about motives related to health, fitness, and self-exploration. Repeatedly, too, they speak of being permanently drawn to the pilgrimage and embrace the idea of *Shikokubyō* to explain what they are doing. They often have regular schedules and say that even when at home they may be mentally on pilgrimage. We also introduce a husband and wife couple who had done five circuits by foot but who were rare among interviewees in saying this was really their last time—because of age, since he was 90 and she, a cancer survivor, was 83. Finally we turn to foreign (mostly Western) pilgrims, a very small minority but one that has grown in the past decade or so, with some of these pilgrims now returning again and again to Shikoku.

Our Conclusion draws together the key themes and theoretical questions posed at the outset, arguing that the Shikoku case should not be seen as unique but as a representation of a wider dynamic in which pilgrimage becomes a core life action and process. We set out some challenges to the wider field that emerge from our study and argue that more attention needs to be paid in studies of pilgrimage, not simply to the point that some people do the same pilgrimage repeatedly, making it a central facet of their lives, but that pilgrims who visit one site or route may well (as is the case with many Shikoku pilgrims) visit numerous other pilgrimage sites as well. Finally, we discuss the extent to which the idea expressed by some in Shikoku that pilgrimage is a metaphor for a journey through life and that 'life is pilgrimage' might resonate more widely in studies of pilgrimage, returning to the point made earlier that the Shikoku pilgrimage is not a transient activity set apart from home or routines, but an unending journey that permeates the lives of its participants.

1

The Shikoku pilgrimage

History, legends, ascetics, and the structure of repetition

The Shikoku *henro*: a brief description

Henro is one of many Japanese words that are commonly translated in English as 'pilgrimage'.[1] It is a term that developed specifically for the pilgrimage in Shikoku and refers to a route that goes around the island; *henro* in essence means a route (*ro*) that goes everywhere (*hen*) and that encompasses and encircles the island. Pilgrims in Shikoku are also referred to as *henro* (or, more formally, *o-henro-san*). The pilgrimage route is about 1400 kilometres in length and takes pilgrims on a circuit of the island in which they visit eighty-eight Buddhist temples along the way. Most (eighty in all) of the temples belong to the Shingon sect, an esoteric branch of Buddhism established in Japan in the ninth century by the monk Kūkai; the other eight belong to other sects such as Tendai, Jōdo, Zen, and Jishū. Although Shingon is thus dominant in sectarian terms, the pilgrimage is non-denominational, and those who do it come from a wide spectrum of institutional backgrounds and none.[2]

Each temple contains a main temple hall (*hondō*) enshrining the temple's main image of worship and a *Daishidō*, a hall of worship to Kōbō Daishi, the legendary Buddhist figure who features prominently in the Japanese tradition as a miracle worker and spiritual guide central to the pilgrimage. Pilgrims are expected to visit and perform acts of veneration at each of these halls of worship at every temple. All the temples have names, but each is also known to

---

[1] For a comprehensive discussion of Japanese terms translated by the English 'pilgrimage' and their meanings, see Reader and Swanson 1997. See also Reader 2005: 33 for why it is appropriate to use the term 'pilgrimage' in non-Western contexts.

[2] Osada, Sakata, and Seki 2003: 234–236 provide a breakdown of the sectarian affiliation and religious backgrounds of pilgrims they surveyed in the early 2000s. Respondents to our questionnaire and in interviews indicated a variety of sectarian backgrounds along with numerous responses, saying that they no sectarian affiliation or that they were not interested in 'religion' (*shūkyō*), even as they were doing the pilgrimage.

Pilgrims Until We Die. Ian Reader and John Shultz, Oxford University Press. © Oxford University Press 2021.
DOI: 10.1093/oso/9780197573587.003.0002

pilgrims and identified in guidebooks and accounts of the pilgrimage also by numbers in a circuit that goes round the island clockwise. Ryōzenji, for example, is the name of a temple in Tokushima prefecture close to ports such as Naruto at which, in earlier eras, many pilgrims coming from major population centres such as Osaka arrived. Because it was the first temple that these pilgrims came to, it became known as Temple One (*Daiichiban*). Gokurakuji, the next temple to it on the circuit, just over a kilometre away, is known as Temple Two (*Dainiban*) and so on. Although the pilgrimage has—in numerical terms—an order (from one to eighty-eight), this is simply a matter of convenience. In reality pilgrims can visit the temples in any order they wish and start from wherever is most convenient for them. They need not go clockwise, although this is regarded as the most convenient and normal way, and some pilgrims do it counter-clockwise (*gyaku uchi*). Some of those we have interviewed say they sometimes do it counter-clockwise just for a change.

Nor is there any injunction to say how one should do it; until the latter part of the nineteenth century and the advent of trains and other forms of motorised transport, pilgrims had little choice but to walk, and many continue to do so to this day. However, as new means of travel have developed, pilgrims have made use of them, from ferries across inlets that saved time in the seventeenth and eighteenth centuries, to trains, buses, and cars in more recent times.[3] Nor does one have to do it in one single journey. It is common for people, whether by bus, by car, or on foot, to do the pilgrimage in a number of sections (a practice known as *kugiri*); this is something that, for example, people in work often do because they cannot get enough time off to do the whole route in one go. Walkers, too, often do it in sections—something especially common among older walkers, many of who say they like to go home and rest up for a while after walking arduous sections of the route, which involves numerous ascents to mountain temples.

In essence, the way one does the pilgrimage is a matter for personal choice. Some always walk, others do it in a variety of ways, sometimes with a group of fellow pilgrims by bus and sometimes on foot or by car. In more recent times, and aided by Japan's excellent transport system, some do it in a series of overnight or even, for those living in or near Shikoku, in day trips.

---

[3] Reader 2005: 107–186 provides a detailed account in English of the pilgrimage's development, including the development of various modes of transport and their impact, while Hoshino 2001: 311–334 and Mori 2005, 2014 provide comprehensive accounts in Japanese of its development, especially in relation to modern contexts.

Basically it is the prerogative of the pilgrim to do it in the way and time frame she or he sees fit, and in our studies of Shikoku we have encountered all sorts of ways of doing the pilgrimage; one of its attractions is that each person can determine how he or she will do it, and decide their own schedules and practices as they do so. As we will see (especially in Chapter 2) modern developments that have opened up multiple new modes of doing the pilgrimage and have enabled people to do it more quickly have influenced the development of multiple performances significantly.

There is no clear explanation as to why there are eighty-eight sites in all[4] or why they are situated where they are. There is, for example, no pattern to the distances between the temples. There are areas where temples are close together. Temples One and Two, for example, are barely one kilometre apart, others are even closer, and in one place two temples (Sixty-Eight and Sixty-Nine) stand next to each other in the same precinct. In other areas there may be long distances between them; there are stretches of eighty or more kilometres between temples on occasion, with the longest being the 100 kilometres between Temples Thirty-Seven and Thirty-Eight.

The temples are spread across the four prefectures of Shikoku: Tokushima, Kōchi, Ehime, and Kagawa. These are the modern names of the four fiefdoms that in feudal times covered Shikoku (Awa, Tosa, Iyo, and Sanuki respectively) and to this day it is common for pilgrims, priests, and guidebooks alike to use these old feudal era names. Temples 1–23 are in Awa (Tokushima), 24–39 in Tosa (Kōchi), 40–65 in Iyo (Ehime) and 66–88 in Sanuki (Kagawa). These four sections have given rise to the image and structure of the pilgrimage as a symbolic journey to enlightenment based in Buddhist thought as follows:

Temples 1–23 (Awa): *hosshin* (awakening of the Buddha mind; setting out on the path)

Temples 24–39 (Tosa): *shugyō* (practice—the ascetic practice needed to achieve awakening)

Temples 40–65 (Iyo) *bodai* (opening of the Buddha mind/enlightenment)

Temples 66–88 (Sanuki) *nehan* (Nirvana; release from the cycle of existence, ultimate liberation)

---

[4] See Reader 2005: 277–278 for some general and popular theories—all of which rely on speculation and surmise, and none of which is conclusive or with much historical evidence to substantiate them.

While this symbolic structure appears to be a rather modern invention of the Buddhist authorities and temples associated with the route,[5] this structure has its roots also in the ascetic travels that were important in the pilgrimage's development and signifies a theme that has been important to some pilgrims, namely the idea of the *henro* as a journey of spiritual self-development. This is not something that all pilgrims may view as significant, as there are multiple motivations for doing the pilgrimage, including seeking worldly benefits, performing memorial services for their deceased kin, seeking to eradicate bad karma for themselves and acquire merit to ensure post-death salvation, and many other reasons including, increasingly in modern times, finding oneself, keeping fit, and the wish to travel.[6]

The pilgrimage route, in circling the island, takes pilgrims through mountains, along the often-rugged coast and through areas of dramatic scenery. It also passes through towns, cities, and industrialised areas, and in modern times along highways as well as (for walkers) quiet paths through forests. Several temples are situated in the mountains—the highest at an altitude of around 1000 metres—while others are in flat areas and in river valleys. Many areas, especially in southern Shikoku, are sparsely populated (and suffering from depopulation). As such the pilgrimage encompasses all aspects of Shikoku's terrain and scenery, from urban sprawl to mountains, sea shores and forests; one is rarely too far from either dramatic natural scenery or elements of the built environment such as shops and places to eat and stay overnight. This in itself often serves as a spur to pilgrims who readily talk about how they find travelling in Shikoku enables them to enjoy good scenery and nature, yet rarely be far from the conveniences of modern life.

A central concept in the pilgrimage is that of *dōgyō ninin*, a term that translates as 'two people, one practice'. This refers to the idea that Kōbō Daishi travels with and guards over each and every pilgrim, so that the pilgrimage is thus not an individual journey but one performed in the company of the spiritual figure who also is venerated at every site. Pilgrims commonly wear clothing that reflects this association with Kōbō Daishi, such as a white pilgrim's shroud (*hakui*) that bears an image of him or her and the ideograms for the phrase *dōgyō ninin*, and a pilgrim's staff (*tsue*) that symbolically represents her or him. The clothing and accoutrements pilgrims wear and carry also are symbolically associated with death, indicating that

---

[5] Hoshino 2001: 329–331.
[6] See Reader 2005: 75–106; Osada, Sakata, and Seki 2003: 327–361; and Satō 2004: 220–224 for broad overviews of common motives and reasons for doing the pilgrimage.

pilgrims are set apart from the everyday world and are 'dead to the world' while on pilgrimage.[7] In addition pilgrims also commonly carry items such as a *nōkyōchō* (lit. pilgrim's stamp book) and *osamefuda* (pilgrim name cards/ name slips), that have special significance for pilgrims, especially those who do the *henro* multiple times.

The *nōkyōchō* is a fold-out book in which each page relates to one of the pilgrimage temples. When pilgrims visit the temple concerned, a temple official will, for a small fee, affix a red temple seal (*shuin*) and paint an ink-brush calligraphy relating to the temple in the appropriate page of the book. A completed book is indicative of having done the whole pilgrimage, and in the eyes of many pilgrims is seen as a sign of merit and as a passport to the Pure Land (Jōdo) at death. Those who do the pilgrimage multiple times often get their books stamped again with the red seals on every visit so that their books end up appearing wholly red. Pilgrims also generally carry pilgrim name slips—*osamefuda*—that usually bear an image of and invocation to Kōbō Daishi on them, as well as a space in which pilgrims can write their names, address, wishes and other details, such as their age and the number of times they have done the pilgrimage. These *osamefuda* may be left in offering boxes at the temples as a form of prayer calling card, but they are also given to other pilgrims met along the way and to anyone who gives the pilgrim alms—a practice found widely in Shikoku that is central to the pilgrimage's dynamic (discussed in the next section). It is not obligatory to carry either a *nōkyōchō* or *osamefuda*; quite a number of the multiple performers, notably those who live permanently on the route, have informed us that they ceased getting stamps or never carried a book to start with, and some no longer carry *osamefuda*. However both these are widely used among the pilgrimage community, and for those who do the pilgrimage many times they can serve as a marker of status and also as a stimulus and motivation to do the *henro* more times— issues we discuss in Chapter 2.

Pilgrimage origins: Kōbō Daishi and the intertwining of history and legend

The historical roots of the pilgrimage are imprecisely documented. Although there are references to some form of ascetic route around Shikoku from

---

[7] See Reader 1993a for a discussion of this image of Shikoku pilgrims being 'dead to the world'.

around the late twelfth century, the first historically verifiable mention of a pilgrimage with eighty-eight sites to be visited is from the seventeenth century. It is in this era—the mid-seventeenth century—that the route is considered to have coalesced in its later structural (i.e. eighty-eight site) form.[8] Its roots, however, date back some centuries earlier to ascetic travels around Shikoku by priests and mendicants mainly from the mountain temple complex of Kōyasan in the hills south of Osaka and associated with the Shingon Buddhist tradition in Japan. Its history is also intricately associated with legends that have given meaning to the pilgrimage and have been central to its appeal historically.

The cult of Kōbō Daishi is a central element in the pilgrimage. Kōbō Daishi is the posthumous name of Kūkai (774–835), the Buddhist monk and founder of the Shingon tradition in Japan and of its holiest centre, Kōyasan. Kūkai was originally from Shikoku and practised austerities there in his early life as a Buddhist seeker before going to the Japanese mainland to further his Buddhist training. He established a reputation for erudition and ritual skills before travelling to China to study Buddhism there. He returned to Japan bearing the teachings, ritual practices, and implements of the esoteric Shingon Buddhist tradition he had encountered in China and which he then established in Japan, starting Buddhist temples in the then-capital Heiankyō (present-day Kyoto) and at Kōyasan. Regarded as one of the greatest figures in Japanese cultural and religious history, Kūkai died in 835 at Kōyasan.[9]

However, legends promoted by the Shingon sect averred that he had not died but entered eternal meditation in his mausoleum at Kōyasan. As such he could still be visited there—and to this day pilgrims visit Kōyasan for such reasons.[10] The bestowal of the posthumous honorific title Kōbō Daishi (the great teacher who spread the law [of Buddhism]) by the Imperial household on Kūkai in 921 enhanced the legends developing around him and helped promote a cult of reverence in the founder that has been central to Shingon's popular development. In these legends Kōbō Daishi not only sat in eternal meditation at Kōyasan, but also travelled around Japan as a wandering ascetic dressed in pilgrim's robes, dispensing miracles, rewarding the worthy, assisting the sick, punishing wrongdoers, carving Buddhist statues, and

---

[8] For histories of the pilgrimage and its formation from early textual references to an ascetic path in Shikoku, to the formation of a clear eighty-eight stage pilgrimage route—the *henro*—see Reader 2005: 107–122. In Japanese we have drawn especially on the following sources: Maeda 1971: 28–44; Shinjō 1982: 479–491; Kondō 1982: 18–281; and Yoritomi and Shiragi 2001.

[9] For details of Kūkai's life see Hakeda 1972 and Abe 1999.

[10] Nicoloff 2008 provides a good accessible account of Kōyasan in the present day.

opening temples; numerous temples and statues have foundation legends attributing their origins to Kōbō Daishi.[11]

One such foundation legend involves the pilgrimage in Shikoku, the island of Kūkai's birth. In this legendary construction the pilgrimage is depicted as a route created by his ascetic travels around Shikoku. The eighty-eight temples themselves are either founded (according to legend) by him or in some way associated with him (e.g. as sites where he performed austerities). While few of the sites can historically be verified as places where the historical Kūkai was active, the legendary tales around his posthumous incarnation as Kōbō Daishi have created a form of hyper-reality that permeates and shapes the pilgrimage.[12] Kōbō Daishi is not only depicted as the initiator of the pilgrimage; he is also a permanent pilgrim on it, constantly travelling around Shikoku as a Buddhist mendicant pilgrim carrying a begging bowl, soliciting alms, bestowing benefits and miraculous cures on those who help him and punishing those who do not (see Figure 1.1). As such the pilgrim who travels around the Shikoku pilgrimage is following the path of and walking in the footsteps of Kōbō Daishi. Likewise, at its spiritual core, the journey is unequivocally represented as unending.

These images are significant elements in the practice of almsgiving to pilgrims (settai), a custom that (as we discuss further later in this chapter) has historically supported pilgrims and facilitated the custom of recurrent pilgrimages. Not only is Kōbō Daishi the archetype of the mendicant ascetic pilgrim, but he is also the guardian, protector, and companion of all pilgrims, as is illustrated by the phrase dōgyō ninin (two people one practice) written on pilgrim shirts. This in itself creates a link between pilgrims and the idea of unending pilgrimage, while numerous pilgrimage stories and legends attribute all manner of pilgrim experiences and miraculous benefits to his protection and intercession.[13]

The figure of Kōbō Daishi thus imbues the pilgrimage with a theme of itinerancy and incessant travel, while faith in Kōbō Daishi (Daishi shinkō) is

---

[11] On the legends and development of a cult around Kōbō Daishi see in particular Abe 1999; Hinonishi 1988; and Saitō 1984, 1988.

[12] For a discussion of how the legendary founding transcends historical realities see Reader 2005: 45–46.

[13] There are a number of historical texts and volumes that contain stories of miracle intercessions by Kōbō Daishi along with tracts written by ardent proponents of the pilgrimage asserting that his interventions can aid pilgrims. See, for example, Reader 1999 for a translation and commentary on the earliest such pilgrimage tract, and Shikoku Hachijūhakkasho Reijōkai 1984 for a compendium produced by the pilgrimage temples narrating stories about Kōbō Daishi's miraculous assistance to pilgrims.

Figure 1.1 Kōbō Daishi statue: Daishi the ascetic pilgrim

highly important for many pilgrims as well as for many of those associated with its temples. *Daishi shinkō* is a popular mode of faith in Japan, promoted by the Shingon sect and deeply embedded in the Japanese popular religious and folk traditions. Kōbō Daishi is a figure of worship to whom numerous generations have prayed for help and benefits, while Daishi faith has been central to the development of the pilgrimage and a significant motivating factor for many pilgrims historically and in the present. Many of the pilgrims we have interviewed have expressed deep devotion to Daishi. One man, for example, who claimed to have done the pilgrimage hundreds of times, drives a van emblazoned with numerous pilgrimage badges and stickers and always, even in his daily life when doing his shopping, dresses in pilgrim clothes that, as he told us, affirm his association with, devotion to, and constant engagement with Daishi.[14] Indeed, he saw Daishi's hand in enabling us to get in contact with and interview him—something that was reiterated by other informants who considered it was due to Daishi's grace that they were able to be interviewed by international researchers and thereby teach them about the merits of the pilgrimage and of Daishi, and, as a result, hopefully spread word about Daishi and the pilgrimage abroad.[15]

While faith and devotion to Daishi are predominantly associated with Japanese folk religious culture, there are also non-Japanese pilgrims for whom it is significant. One female Canadian resident of Japan, for example, who had done the *henro* some fourteen times and who continues to walk sections of it whenever she can find time away from her day job in Japan, spoke of faith in Daishi as a factor in her continuing pilgrimages during an interview in March 2018. She first did the pilgrimage (like many foreign pilgrims) due to her interest in Buddhism and Japanese culture. Her awareness of Kōbō Daishi as a significant figure in Japanese Buddhist history grew as she became immersed in the pilgrimage, and as she did it more and more times a sense of faith in Daishi developed in her.

For some pilgrims the idea of the pilgrimage as an ascetic practice and path to enlightenment enables them to feel akin to Kōbō Daishi.[16] While this is a view sometimes expressed by Japanese pilgrims both historically and in the present, it has been especially embraced by the recent influx of international pilgrims in Shikoku, some of whom view the journey predominantly in terms of Buddhist self-actualisation.[17] While the actual pursuit of an enlightened status like that of Kōbō Daishi is comparatively rare compared to *Daishi shinkō*, it represents a potentially influential minority, some of whom have written lengthy accounts of the journey in this context.[18]

We should add that not every pilgrim emphasises *Daishi shinkō* (faith in Daishi) as will become clear in subsequent chapters. Informants we

[14] Pilgrims commonly refer to him simply as Daishi, thus displaying a sense of close familiarity with him.

[15] See also Reader 2005: 253–255 for a similar account of a pilgrim who believed Daishi had brought about his meeting with the fieldworker for the same reasons.

[16] See Shultz 2016 for a discussion of this issue.

[17] Shultz 2018.

[18] See, for example, the account of her pilgrimage by *Japan Times* writer Amy Chavez (2013) that follows this line.

interviewed or received questionnaires responses from indicated that their main focus was on doing the Shikoku *henro* repeatedly, but many also said they had performed various other Japanese pilgrimages as well, including the Saikoku, Chichibu, and Bandō pilgrimages, all of which focus on the bodhisattva Kannon. As such, while they might be motivated in part by *Daishi shinkō*, they were also focused on performing pilgrimages in general. Among those who live as permanent itinerants, too, we found less emphasis on *Daishi shinkō* when talking about their motives or reasons for being pilgrims. Some pilgrims—notably, we found, older Japanese men who had walked the pilgrimage multiple times—appeared to pay less or little attention to the idea of faith in Daishi, stating that their interests in walking and seeing the natural environment of Shikoku were what motivated them, rather than faith. Several respondents, too, spoke more in terms of respect and admiration, viewing Daishi more as a special and inspirational person who serves as an example for others to follow, than as a deity-like miracle-working holy figure. Some used modern terms to describe him, as was the case with a male pilgrim who said he was a 'Daishi fan' (using the foreign loan word: fan) rather than an adherent of *Daishi shinkō*; he also said that the problem with faith (*shinkō*) was that it meant accepting all manner of clearly fictitious things. Others described Daishi in personal ways as a 'friend' (a comment made initially to us—and reiterated by others—by a female pilgrim who will be met again in Chapter 5 and who was interviewed twice on successive days in November 2018) and as a supremely talented human being.

The path of salvation: the legend of the rich man who became a pilgrim

There is another pilgrimage foundation legend that is aligned to the cult of Daishi and the image of the permanent mendicant: that of Emon Saburō, said to have been the richest (and most miserly) man in Shikoku. According to this legend, Emon drove away and insulted a pilgrim who came to his door begging for alms. Shortly after, Emon's eight children died one after another, at which point he realised the pilgrim he had insulted was Kōbō Daishi himself, and that he was being punished for his meanness and for insulting the holy figure. Repenting, he set out on foot around the island on a penitential pilgrimage to find Kōbō Daishi and seek forgiveness. He did twenty circuits without success but on the twenty-first, as he fell dying, Kōbō Daishi appeared before him, forgave him his sins and enabled him to have a good rebirth. This legend, which first appeared in 1567 according to extant historical records,[19] affirms a belief found among pilgrims in Shikoku that they can, if they persevere, meet Kōbō Daishi, attain salvation and be forgiven for past misdeeds. Emon's multiple circuits and incessant pilgrimage are the keys to his legendary salvation and rebirth, showing that even a rich miser who insults a holy figure can gain forgiveness and that repeated pilgrimages can wipe away all transgressions. The legend of Emon Saburō articulates the belief that pilgrims will meet Kōbō Daishi—something that is emphasised in the earliest collection of miracle tales relating to the pilgrimage, the *Shikoku Kudokuki* of 1690, by the ascetic Shinnen. The *Shikoku Kudokuki* repeats the Emon Saburō legend, affirms that Kōbō Daishi is ever-present on the route and thus can be encountered by any pilgrim, and emphasises the importance of giving alms to pilgrims and of treating all pilgrims as if they were Kōbō Daishi.[20] The Emon Saburō legend was clearly created by pilgrims with this in mind, but it also helps underline the view that doing it many times is beneficial. Along with the image of the wandering holy figure of Kōbō Daishi as a permanent pilgrim, the Emon Saburō legend helped develop a culture of repetition and constant pilgrimage in Shikoku.

Asceticism and *hijiri*

By the end of the sixteenth century—the century in which the Emon legend appeared and when the first vestiges of the pilgrimage as a coordinated route around the island were manifest—we also have evidence that priests and ascetics were doing multiple circuits of the island. Data compiled by Ehime prefecture's research centre about the historical development of the pilgrimage shows that quite early on there were ascetics and priests doing multiple journeys around the route. Thus an inscription at one temple from 1572 records that a priest named Jikaku had done twenty-one circuits of Shikoku (the same number, one might add, as Emon in his legendary journey),[21] while an inscription dating from 1591 at Kure, in Kōchi prefecture, cites an ascetic named Kanshin who had done the pilgrimage seven times.[22] References to

[19] Kondō 1982: 26–28.
[20] See Reader 1999 for a translation and commentary of the *Shikoku Kudokuki* and Reader 2005: 118–119 for further discussion of this text and its significance in the pilgrimage.
[21] Ehime ken Shōgaigakushū Sentā 2001: 270–271; Shirai 1982.
[22] Kiyoyoshi 1999: 33.

priests and ascetics such as these show that the pilgrimage was from early on associated with Japanese traditions of asceticism exemplified by figures such as the *hijiri*, wandering ascetics who generally had connections to (and usually an ordination at) one or more major Buddhist temples or religious sites, and who travelled around preaching a popular Buddhist creed and offering religious services. Such figures also engaged in alms gathering on behalf of the temple(s) they were associated with and performing ritual and religious services on their behalf, while acting as popular proselytisers of Buddhism and of the cults of Buddhist figures of worship. As such they fulfilled a historically significant role in expanding the popular remit of Buddhist institutions and temples in Japan.[23]

Historical studies of the pilgrimage indicate that its roots are particularly grounded in the travels of *hijiri* and other mendicants from Kōyasan who, in the centuries after Kūkai's death, and as the cult and image of his posthumous incarnation as Kōbō Daishi developed, began travelling in Shikoku to follow in the footsteps of their founder. Through these ascetic travels a formal pilgrimage route (one that also incorporated a number of local pilgrimage routes around the island) began to develop. In historical terms, it first appears to start taking shape in the sixteenth century, although as was noted earlier, it was not until the mid-seventeenth century that historically verifiable references to and evidence of the pilgrimage as an eighty-eight site route around the island can be found.

The circuit that developed thus owed much to the Japanese ascetic tradition, which, especially in Buddhist contexts, involved being permanently or semi-permanently itinerant. Such notions of itinerancy—evident also in Zen Buddhist concepts of the monk as an *unsui* (lit. wandering cloud) or unfettered figure on a journey of self-realisation—were integral to the development of the Japanese Buddhist tradition and also to the culture of pilgrimage associated with it, and of which the Shikoku *henro* is perhaps the most striking example. Buddhist notions of transience and the image of the pilgrimage purveyed in Buddhist contexts, as a journey in the realms of transience and to enlightenment, also contributed to this framework.

[23] On the roles of *hijiri* and similar figures in Japanese history, and notably in connection with proselytising popular Buddhist ideas and practices while fund raising for temples, see Goodwin 1994; Gorai 1975, 1989; and Shinno 1978, 1980, 1986, 1991.

Multiple performance as a Japanese ascetic and religious characteristic

Another aspect of Japanese asceticism and Buddhist practice that is important in this context is an emphasis on repetition based in the idea that by performing practices multiple times (and, especially, incessantly) one can accumulate merit, eradicate any karmic hindrances, purify the spirit, and attain spiritual transcendence. In various branches of Buddhism that have developed in Japan one finds examples of such incessant practice, for instance, in the Zen tradition of intense meditation periods and in the Nichiren Buddhist practice of *hyakumanben* (one million recitations), reciting the *daimoku* (the seven-syllable mantra that introduces each section of the Lotus Sutra that is central to the Nichiren tradition) over and over again. In the Pure Land Buddhist tradition repeatedly chanting the *nembutsu* (the invocation to Amida Buddha) is a venerated practice that was performed by figures such as Hōnen, the founder of the Jōdo tradition in Japan. In the Tendai sect, monks have performed repeated pilgrimage circuits around Mount Hiei, the sect's headquarters, as part of their ascetic training in the Tendai tradition. The most famous such practice at Hiei is the *sennichi kaihōgyō*—the 1000-day mountain circumambulation practice—in which monks perform extended pilgrimage-style circumambulations of the Hiei mountain area; besides this practice involving 1000 separate pilgrimages around the mountain, shorter (for example 100-day/100-circuit) practices also are undertaken by Tendai practitioners at Hiei.[24] In the *yamabushi* (mountain ascetic) tradition, which has associations with the Tendai and Shingon traditions and also with the Shikoku pilgrimage, too, practices that emphasise multiple repetition also are significant.[25]

The concept of constant repetition as a means of achieving higher levels of spiritual awareness and as a mark of devotion is thus embedded in the Japanese religious tradition and contributes to the practice of multiple pilgrimage performances in Shikoku. Some interviewees, for example, have expressed the view that multiple performances of the pilgrimage are a way of attaining salvation and enlightenment. Others also identify themselves,

[24] For a discussion of such practices and the longer *sennichi kaihōgyō* see Rhodes 1987 and Stevens 1988.
[25] Several mountains in Shikoku where pilgrimage temples are located have close links to the *yamabushi* tradition, and various studies have pointed to the influences of this tradition in the development of the pilgrimage; see, for example, Tanaka 1979, Hoshino 1979, and Shinno 1991.

due to their multiple performances, with the *hijiri* tradition. Thus, for example, Tabuchi Yoshio, now deceased, who was interviewed by one of the authors in 1991 at a time when Tabuchi had done the pilgrimage 110 times, stated that doing it multiple times enabled the spirit to be purified and the practitioner to attain enlightenment.[26] Similarly, a charismatic leader of an active *sendatsukai*, a confraternity of official pilgrim guides, explained that he envisions himself as a modern *hijiri*, despite the fact that his more than 230 circuits of the journey were accomplished almost entirely by motorised transport. This point is reinforced in printed advertisements for his monthly pilgrimage tours, which directly speak of the opportunity for participation in the leader's ascetic practice (*dōgyō*), the term so closely associated with shared practice with Kōbō Daishi (see earlier discussion).[27]

There is, in other words, from its very earliest days a tradition of repetition embedded within the Shikoku pilgrimage. We should add here that this does not make it unique in Japanese pilgrimage terms. The Saikoku Kannon pilgrimage (*Saikoku junrei*[28]), another prominent Japanese Buddhist pilgrimage route that has thirty-three temple sites, also in earlier times had a tradition of itinerant ascetics known as *sanjūsan gyōja* (thirty-three-stage ascetics) who went round the route repeatedly. These ascetics, who carried portable shrines containing small figurines representing the pilgrimage temples on their backs, had permanent homes but spent much of their lives travelling around the Saikoku route preaching and promoting the pilgrimage. However, this is a custom that gradually disappeared in the modern era, with the last *sanjūsan gyōja* dying in 1967.[29] We have encountered pilgrims who have done other pilgrimages in Japan many times too, and in Chapter 4 will draw attention to the tendency of many serial pilgrims in Shikoku to do other pilgrimages several times as well—albeit rarely as often as they do Shikoku. As we note there, and affirm here, when people repeat pilgrimages in Japan multiple times, it is most commonly the Shikoku pilgrimage that they do. There are historical reasons for this, as we have noted earlier, with the notion of endless pilgrimage ingrained into the pilgrimage's legendary and

[26] Reader 2005: 88–89.
[27] See Chapter 5 for further discussion of this figure and the pilgrimage confraternity he leads.
[28] *junrei* is the term most commonly used for Buddhist temple pilgrimages in Japan. *Henro* is normally used just for Shikoku and other eighty–eight-stage Kōbō Daishi routes, while *junrei* is more generic and can be applied to circuits such as the Saikoku Kannon pilgrimage as well as to the Shikoku pilgrimage (Reader and Swanson 1997).
[29] Speidel 1977; see also Hayami 1983 for more on this pilgrimage.

historical foundations, but there are also geographical and structural factors at play too, and this is what we turn to next.

Geography and structure

The physical structure of the Shikoku *henro* plays an important part in facilitating multiple and unending pilgrimages. Shikoku is an island, and the eighty-eight pilgrimage temples are ranged around it to form a circuit that encompasses the entire island. Pilgrims who visit all the temples circumnavigate virtually the whole island. The common practice of *orei-mairi* (thanks pilgrimage visit) of returning to the temple where one started to give thanks for successful completion means that they return to their starting point and complete a circle of the island. Some pilgrims on returning to where they began their pilgrimage are as a result tempted or drawn into just carrying on and doing it again rather than returning home; several interviewees indicated that this was a factor in their continuing engagement with the pilgrimage. As such the Shikoku *henro* is not a pilgrimage with a single goal or end point from which the pilgrim then returns home. This contrasts with a common structure of pilgrimage exemplified by pilgrimages such as that to Santiago de Compostela in Spain. Nancy Frey, in her account of the Santiago de Compostela pilgrimage, comments that some pilgrims who walk to Santiago experience a feeling of disconnection and unease, when, after reaching their goal, they have to make their journey homewards, usually by boarding a train, plane or some other form of modern transport. Although she mentions one pilgrim who was so unsettled by this that he instead turned round and started walking home, the standard pattern is for them—even if disturbed by a sense of abrupt return to the everyday world—to make their way home from the end point, the pilgrimage goal.[30] There is thus a rupture between pilgrimage and return—a theme that has run through many studies of pilgrimage, which have talked of the outward journey to the goal as an occasion for austere behaviour and the return a playful break from the rigours of pilgrimage.[31] While this type of pattern is not uncommon in Shikoku,[32] pilgrims also may also be conscious that they are, even as

---

[30] Frey 1998: 179–181.
[31] See, for example, Turner and Turner 1978.
[32] See Reader 2005: 247 for a description of playful activity by a party of pilgrims on completion of their journey around Shikoku.

they finish their pilgrimage, also at its start. Some just carry on, as was the case with Nakatsukasa and other historical figures we will mention in this chapter, and with some of the contemporary pilgrims who live their lives on the *henro*. As one such pilgrim indicated in an interview in November 2018, he initially walked the pilgrimage some ten years earlier after losing his job, felt at ease on the pilgrimage, and when he completed his circuit and got back to the temple where he started, he just kept going—and had been walking it ever since.

This sense of the pilgrimage as unending came through also when one of us went to Kōyasan with the pilgrimage confraternity mentioned earlier whose leader had done over 230 Shikoku pilgrimages, many of whose members had done large numbers of circuits. The confraternity met every month to do sections of the pilgrimage and always visited Kōyasan as a thanksgiving pilgrimage visit after completing a circuit; as well as returning to the temple from which one started the pilgrimage, many pilgrims also visit Kōyasan in this way to give thanks after completing their pilgrimages in Shikoku. Although this group were conscious as they visited Kōyasan that they were finishing that particular circuit of the pilgrimage, there were no words of congratulations or statements of completion. There was, instead, a feeling of continuity and consistency; the confraternity members knew that, rather than reaching an endpoint in their pilgrimage, they were also at a beginning and would start another circuit in their next monthly gathering, thus continuing on what was for them an unending pilgrimage.

Settai, takuhatsu and subsistence

Local customs allied to ascetic practices also have created a context in which multiple pilgrimage performances flourish. In the Introduction we mentioned the practices of *takuhatsu* (begging for alms) and *settai*, (giving alms to pilgrims), both of which have been important aspects of the pilgrimage historically. The Buddhist monastic practice of begging for alms, traditionally as a support mechanism for mendicants, was widely used by the ascetics who first helped develop the route around Shikoku. Begging and receiving alms are portrayed in Buddhist contexts as a means not just for mendicants to support themselves and live a life of austerity and practice, but of enabling donors to acquire merit and enhance themselves spiritually by giving alms. The Emon Saburō legend has at its heart the practice of *takuhatsu* and the virtues of giving *settai*; Kōbō Daishi came to Emon's door to do *takuhatsu* and Emon, on rejecting him, was punished for not giving alms. The moral of the story is that every pilgrim could be Kōbō Daishi and that hence one should give alms to pilgrims. The *Shikoku Kudokuki* of 1690 that promotes the Emon legend also contains numerous miracle stories that encourage almsgiving and emphasise its benefits; those who give alms to a mendicant (who always turns out to be Kōbō Daishi) are rewarded with various blessings. The text also shows what happens to those who do not give alms, via stories of retribution and strife that come to those who do not help pilgrims.

Pilgrims in Shikoku, especially in pre-modern times, often relied on alms to support themselves, while the custom of *settai*, giving alms, has been a major element in the shaping of the pilgrimage from early times and one widely supported by local people in Shikoku.[33] Shikoku residents have over the centuries given alms to pilgrims for many reasons. These include the belief that doing so enables the donor to share in the benefits and merits of the pilgrimage and that giving to pilgrims is in essence an offering to Kōbō Daishi. A further factor is that many pilgrims in Shikoku are residents of the island. Historically they used to constitute the single largest group among pilgrims by region of residence, while in the present day they remain a significant part of the pilgrim community.[34] Having done the pilgrimage and been given *settai* thus serves as an encouragement to thereafter give to pilgrims whom they encounter in their daily lives. Moreover, for many in Shikoku *settai* is a local custom, viewed as integral to their identity and to the culture of their island, and hence something to maintain.[35] The practice has also been maintained by almsgiving groups (*settaikō*) and pilgrimage confraternities, some of which were formed by people who, having done the pilgrimage and received alms from people in Shikoku, have decided, in their turn, to contribute to the continuing support of the pilgrimage, with some almsgiving groups having histories of close to two centuries old in this respect.[36]

---

[33] See Asakawa 2008, which is the most extensive recent examination of almsgiving in Shikoku.

[34] Maeda 1971: 160–161; Satō 1990: 442; and Hoshino 2001: 264 all show that Shikoku residents were the single largest group of pilgrims historically and right up to the 1980s, while even at the end of the twentieth century they constituted 20% of all pilgrims (Reader 2005: 26).

[35] We base these comments on discussions with local people in Shikoku over the past three decades. For detailed discussions of the local dimensions of almsgiving in Shikoku see Kouamé 1998, 2001 and Asakawa 2008.

[36] Maeda 1971: 234–249 outlines some prominent *settai* groups from around half a century ago, at least one of which is still active today (information provided by officials at one temple). Reader (2005: 95–96) also describes one such group active in Shikoku in the 1990s and still is in existence.

Settai can be a means of support for those with little or money, and many pilgrims we have interviewed have indicated that it has helped them significantly, notably the homeless itinerant pilgrims whom we will discuss in Chapter 3. Moreover as people perform more circuits they get to know more people, learn where *settai* might be available and become known because of their continual circuiting—and hence receive more *settai* and support.[37] The permanent pilgrim Unkai whom we will encounter in Chapter 3, informed one of the authors that he knew places around the route to stay and to get *settai*, and this considerably aided his permanent life of itinerant pilgrimage. Another pilgrim whose story we tell in Chapter 3, known as Kōgetsu, who lived on the pilgrimage route for six years in the early part of this century and who became both famous and infamous as a result, also had a circle of friends and acquaintances around the island who helped and supported him during his circuits of the island. Similar examples can be found elsewhere in the historical records and in pilgrim diaries from pre-modern times. In a written account from 1836, for example, a pilgrim from the Musashi fiefdom (present day Saitama prefecture) gives details of the alms he received, including over fifty places where, the writer indicated, *settai* was regularly handed out.[38] Yoritomi and Shiragi also cite a pilgrim from 1819 who wrote a diary that included multiple references to receiving *settai* and who seems to have enjoyed a rather relaxed pilgrimage in which he imbibed saké and enjoyed bouts of sightseeing along the way, all aided by the alms he received.[39] Nakatsukasa Mōhei, during his fifty-six years of circling Shikoku, certainly found that this helped his continuing pilgrimage; in his journal he recorded the *settai* he received, and he had numerous places where he was known and where people would put him up.[40]

[37] It should be noted that for all of its importance in providing practical and psychological support to continuing Shikoku pilgrims through the years, the concept of *settai* has begun to fall out of use in contemporary pilgrimage narratives. In connection with both the solicitation of and in preparation for the 2020 Tokyo Olympics (subsequently postponed due to COVID-19), the term *omotenashi* was ushered in by the TV announcer and Japanese ambassador to the Olympic committee Takigawa Christel. *Omotenashi* is a term that comes from the Japanese service industry, especially those in connection with traditional style inns, and it conveys a sense of unobtrusive hospitality. Japanese have been encouraged to cultivate this spirit to welcome international Olympic fans. The term *omotenashi* has developed also in Shikoku related to the pilgrimage, as a sort of secular substitute for the traditional notion of *settai*. For example, places once called designated as *settai-jo* (or *settai* places), sheltered spots for rest and refreshment, have been re-named 'omotenashi stations'. It remains to be seen what the long-term trends and changes might be as a result of this significant re-branding.
[38] Shinjō 1982: 1080–1082.
[39] Yoritomi and Shiragi 2001: 169, 176; see also Reader 2005: 124, 131.
[40] Kiyoyoshi 1999: 237–288; Reader 2005: 121–123.

Settai and alms solicitation thus have helped sustain recurrent and ascetic practitioners historically and enabled them to continue on their travels; they also enable local sedentary people to feel part of the pilgrimage. That in turn encourages those who remain on the road to continue their journeys. The very fact that the pilgrimage is a circuit helps here as it means pilgrims can come back again—but not too often—to call again on supporters and to show that they are a continuing element in the pilgrimage structure. This, again, is a factor aiding the permanent itinerants whom we discuss in Chapter 3.

It is clear, too, that the custom of *settai* and the kindness shown to pilgrims by local people led some people to go to Shikoku as pilgrims in the Edo (1603–1868) period (the historical era in which the period developed a clientele beyond that of ascetics) for reasons not connected to asceticism and faith in Kōbō Daishi. Although historical records of such people are comparatively rare, stories of people fleeing their homes after committing crimes and then seeking sanctuary by dressing as and hiding out amongst the pilgrims, or of surreptitiously leaving home or being chased out by their families or neighbours because they suffered from contagious diseases, were not uncommon in Edo-period Shikoku. Notable among these were sufferers of Hansen's disease (leprosy), many of whom turned in desperation to becoming pilgrims because they were exiled from their homes and found that the only way to maintain themselves was by taking on the guise of pilgrims, continually moving on while begging for alms.[41]

As such, while the custom of *settai* has been a central and valued element in the pilgrimage, it has also given rise to hostility and negative attitudes towards pilgrims at times. Shikoku's feudal authorities in earlier times saw pilgrims as a potential drain on the economy, as causing disruption via their begging, and possibly also as health risks.[42] As such the authorities periodically imposed restrictions on pilgrims and on the extent to which they could solicit alms, with draconian punishments for those who breached such rules.[43] Suggestions that some people were doing the pilgrimage not for religious or ascetic reasons but primarily to 'get things' (*monomorai*) while avoiding work or because they were ill or fugitive miscreants were common in pre-modern Shikoku.[44] In the early years of the Meiji (1868–1912) era,

---

[41] Hoshino and Asakawa 2011: 57–64; Maeda 1971: 258–259; Reader 2005: 132–135; Mori 2014: 131–134.

[42] Mori 2014: 118–135.

[43] Asakawa 2008: 247–254.

[44] Kojima 1989.

when Japan was being transformed into a modern nation state, there were attempts to ban the pilgrimage and suppress *settai* for such reasons.[45] Negative attitudes towards such pilgrims were common in earlier times in Shikoku and were reflected in the use of terms such as *hendo*, a derogatory term in Shikoku that plays on the word *henro* but implies someone who is really just a beggar who uses the pilgrimage to avoid working,[46] and *shokugyō henro*, 'professional pilgrims', a term with dualistic undertones that initially referred to people who used the pilgrimage as their means of subsistence.[47] We will discuss these terms further in Chapter 3, where we show that such dualistic issues and images are to a degree still found in the pilgrimage, and that the idea of the homeless pilgrim as a potential fugitive from justice has also come to the fore in recent times.

Historical examples: in the footsteps of others

As we mentioned earlier, from the late sixteenth century onwards we find references to ascetics doing multiple pilgrimage circuits around Shikoku. Such references increase thereafter and point to the presence of an influential set of pilgrims: multiple performers who inspire others and help create and develop a tradition of repetition in the pilgrimage. One of the most famous and significant of such figures was Yūben Shinnen, an ascetic Kōbō Daishi devotee from the Osaka region and with ties to Kōyasan. His date of birth is unclear but it is known that he died in Shikoku (where his grave can be found in Kagawa prefecture) in 1691. Shinnen played an important role in developing and publicising the pilgrimage as a practice associated with veneration of Kōbō Daishi. He made around twenty pilgrimage circuits himself, devoted energy to erecting *henro ishi*, pilgrimage stone markers that helped guide pilgrims, and established a hall of worship (Shinnen-an) where pilgrims could stay. He also produced the first Shikoku pilgrimage guidebooks and the first collection of miracle stories, which not only helped pilgrims understand the structure of the route but encouraged them by assuring them that they would encounter Kōbō Daishi on their pilgrimages and receive his grace. He also drew attention to the practice of multiple performance; in his 1687 guidebook *Shikoku Michishirube* Shinnen refers to an ascetic named Dōkyū Zenji

[45] Reader 2005: 140–141.
[46] Asakawa 2008: 192; Mori 2014: 135.
[47] Asakawa 2008: 190–192; Mori 2014: 131.

who worshipped Kōbō Daishi and died in 1684, having done the pilgrimage twenty-seven times, twelve of them barefoot.[48] Other figures from a similar era include Takabayashi Genshū from Hanta in Kōchi prefecture, who, according to a commemorative stone inscription at Enkōji (Temple Thirty-Nine) dated 1680, did the pilgrimage thirty-six times, although no further information has surfaced about him.[49] Others who are known to have done the pilgrimage many times in the Edo period include Bukkai (1710–1769), Takeda Tokuemon (dates unknown but late eighteenth century), and Tada Emon (d. 1862). Bukkai was from Shikoku. He began religious training when very young and from the age of fifteen travelled around the country on an ascetic journey that took him to Kōyasan, Mount Fuji and other sites. Aged forty, he returned to Shikoku and then did the pilgrimage twenty-one times, mostly during a three-year period between 1752 and 1754.[50] Takeda came from the Imabari region of Shikoku; little is known of his early life, though records indicate that he had a family, but that between 1781 and 1792 his eldest son and four of his daughters perished, causing him to set out on the pilgrimage to cure his grief. Between 1792 and 1807 he made around three circuits per year as well as erecting some seventy pilgrimage guide marker stones.[51] Little is known about Tada save that he was from the Hiroshima region and that he died in 1862 having done 136 pilgrimage circuits; his grave is located in Nagao, Shikoku, near Temple Eighty-Seven, suggesting that he died while on the pilgrimage.[52]

We have already referred to Nakatsukasa Mōhei's extended pilgrimage in which he spent all his life (apart from his two excursions in 1878 and 1885 to the mainland to do other pilgrimages) from the age of around twenty until his death over half a century later on the pilgrimage. He was motivated by faith in Kōbō Daishi and published a pilgrimage guidebook in which he emphasised that the pilgrim was following the path set out by Kōbō Daishi and should venerate Daishi and chant sutras in praise of the gods and buddhas.[53] Nakatsukasa also kept records of where and when he received *settai*, and raised funds via donations and alms solicitation to put up over 230 pilgrimage stones to help others. Nakatsukasa separated himself physically from his birth home and family, never returning while alive, although he

[48] Kiyoyoshi 1999: 35–36; Asai 2004: 79; Yoritomi and Shiragi 2001: 81.
[49] Kiyoyoshi 1999: 34.
[50] Ehime ken Shōgaigakushū Sentā 2001: 234–237.
[51] Ehime-ken Shōgaigakushū Sentā 2001: 244–245; Reader 2005: 121.
[52] Kiyoyoshi 1999: 36–38.
[53] Mori 2014: 80–81.

apparently performed memorial rituals for deceased kin while on pilgrimage, kept in touch with some family members by letter, and expressed the wish to be buried in his family grave; he lived and died on the pilgrimage, returning to his home village only after death. He usually averaged around six circuits a year and made occasional diversions off the pilgrimage path to visit other temples around the island. From around the age of seventy his pace slowed, initially to three or four circuits a year and then more slowly; his last few circuits took as many as six months with frequent longer halts. He also, particularly in later years, occasionally used ferries and steam trains as well.[54]

Other well-known pilgrims who did multiple circuits in the period after the Meiji Restoration of 1868 (which is regarded as heralding the advent of Japan as a modern nation-state and the beginning of its rapid modernisation and embracing of modern technologies including transport systems) include Yamamoto Genpō (1866–1961), who went blind aged nineteen and, seeking a cure, did the pilgrimage in 1888. In all Yamamoto walked the *henro* seventeen times, seven of them barefoot. He became an ordained Zen Buddhist priest at Sekkeiji (Temple Thirty-Three), which belongs to the Rinzai Zen sect, during one of his pilgrimages. He went on to become a prominent Buddhist teacher and head of the Myōshinji Rinzai Zen sect in Japan, but never lost his connection to the pilgrimage, walking it for a final time near the end of his life when he was ninety-five.[55]

Nakatsukasa is generally considered to have done the most circuits of any pilgrim until very recent times, and it is likely that he has walked it more than anyone else. However, there are others who, while less well known, clearly made multiple circuits and must have spent many years on the pilgrimage, such as Miyashita Eshun (dates unknown) who is recorded as having done it 210 times.[56] Kiyoyoshi Eitoku gives the names of twenty-two people who made more than fifty circuits in the period from the seventeenth century to the end of Nakatsukasa's life—an era in which doing the *henro* meant walking it and when a circuit by foot would take forty or more days.[57] As Kiyoyoshi notes, in 1895—the year that Nakatsukasa did his 137th circuit, thereby surpassing Tada Emon, and erected fifteen pilgrimage stones to commemorate this feat (see Introduction)—another pilgrim named Gokyū

[54] Ehime ken Shōgaigakushū Sentā 2001: 253–267.
[55] Ehime ken Shōgaigakushū Sentā 2001: 260–270; Obigane 2002. There is also a stone inscription at Temple Thirty-Three that details Yamamoto's life and which contains similar information.
[56] Shirai 1982: 219; Ehime ken Shōgaigakushū Sentā 2001: 271.
[57] Kiyoyoshi 1999: 40–43.

Kichigorō published a *banzuke* (ranking list[58]) of pilgrims who had done the *henro* multiple times.[59] Gokyū, about whom little is known, indicates that he himself had done it 162 times, but he was not on top; prime place was held by someone named Mitsuharu, whom Gokyū referred to as a *gyōja* (ascetic) and who, it was said, had done it 199 times.[60] The *banzuke* lists fourteen others who had done it between fifty and 100 times, forty-five who had done it over twenty but under fifty times, and 211 who had done it between seven and twenty times.[61]

Gokyū's ranking chart and Nakatsukasa's commemoration of overtaking Tada Emon's number of pilgrimages also point to further factors that encourage multiple performances of the pilgrimage—a sense of competition with others and the idea that one can achieve status and authority through such multiple performance. These are issues we discuss in more detail in the next chapter, as modern developments have not only expanded the potential for doing the pilgrimage many times but have also offered new inducements to people to do so.

Besides the pilgrims named earlier, there were others who remained constantly on the pilgrimage, existing mainly on *settai*, whether as fugitives from justice or because of illnesses such as leprosy that caused them to be exiled from their homes. We do not know, and have no real record of, the extent to which this was the case, although oral testimonies indicate that some such people were still doing the pilgrimage recurrently in the 1930s.[62] In the immediate post-war period, too, there were instances of soldiers returning home after Japan's war defeat, to find their homes destroyed and families lost, and then setting out for Shikoku to become pilgrims as a result; Tezuka Myōken, a nun who has written about people she met on the Shikoku pilgrimage, recalls a former soldier who told her that after returning home from war and finding he had lost his home and family he had thereafter spent the next thirty years as an itinerant homeless pilgrim in Shikoku.[63]

---

[58] *Banzuke* are published before each Sumo wrestling tournament to indicate the current ranking of every wrestler, and sometimes this format is used elsewhere in Japan to rank different people and things.

[59] This *banzuke* was apparently found in the Daishi hall of worship at Temple Twenty-Two but has since been lost; however, the details of it were noted down at the time, according to Kiyoyoshi (1999) and Hoshino and Asakawa (2011: 89).

[60] Kiyoyoshi 1999: 40–43; Satō 2004: 225.

[61] Hoshino and Asakawa 2011: 88–89.

[62] Reader 2005: 134.

[63] Tezuka 1988: 48.

In other words, there is a historical legacy of multiple and incessant pilgrimage performance in Shikoku, and this has certainly been an influential factor in the continuing practice of repeated and unending pilgrimage in the present day. As we will see in Chapter 3, although there may be few people now continually walking the pilgrimage, the tradition of permanent or almost incessant itinerancy continues to this day, and there remain a small number of pilgrims in this mode. This historical legacy continues in other ways too; some of those who began doing the pilgrimage on foot in the first part of the twentieth century continued to do so in the post-war era, as well as making use of Japan's expanding transport system, especially as they grew older. Many also did multiple pilgrimages by motorised transport while serving as a leader of pilgrimage groups and promoting the pilgrimage to new generations. Tabuchi Yoshio, whom we have mentioned already, was one such; he first did the pilgrimage on foot in 1929 with his father, walked it many times, and then began leading pilgrimage groups on organised pilgrimages by bus and acting as a pilgrimage proselytiser and evangelist in the post-war period.[64]

This tradition of recurrent performance has been enhanced also by modern developments such as transport systems and notably the advent of widespread car ownership and greater economic well-being that have characterised Japan in recent times. Other factors, too, including what we term 'technological enabling'—such things as satellite navigation systems and social media services that help people find their way around quickly and easily and provide, via social media, pilgrims with ways of sharing and receiving encouragement in real time—have also facilitated pilgrimage in the modern day. Such things have increased the possibilities for multiple performance, offering pilgrims a greater choice in how they do this and opening up scope for more, quicker, pilgrimages, while structural developments in the pilgrimage also have encouraged people to do the pilgrimage many times. They have also increased the scope and types of multiple performing pilgrim, and it is to these issues that we turn to next in Chapter 2.

[64] Reader 2005: 88–90.

2

Modern stimulations

Money, health, time, and commemoration

The impact of the modern age

The historical patterns of repeated pilgrimage and of life absorption as pilgrims in Shikoku have been given new impetus in the contemporary era. Especially since the 1950s the pilgrimage's clientele has expanded due to the rise of modern transport systems, initially through organised bus tours and in recent decades by the growth in car ownership and travel in what people term 'my car' pilgrimages.[1] Japan's highly integrated transport system has made doing pilgrimages easier and enabled people from outside Shikoku to get to and from the island quickly. Those who live in more distant parts of Japan—for example the northern prefectures of Japan and the northern island of Hokkaidō—would have taken weeks to just get to Shikoku in earlier times when the only viable means of travel was by foot, making pilgrimages there either a once in a lifetime experience or simply impossible. They can now get to and from there easily by plane or high-speed trains. Studies of the pilgrimage in the Tokugawa period indicate few pilgrims at all from Japan's northern regions and relatively few from many of the areas around the Tokyo (Edo) region.[2] Even in the 1930s pilgrims from such regions were a small minority.[3] By contrast, during our research we have met and received communications from numerous people from such areas who perform repeated Shikoku pilgrimages. The depth survey of pilgrims in the late twentieth century by Osada, Sakata, and Seki shows that pilgrims from the Tokyo region and from northern Japan together accounted for around one-sixth of all Shikoku pilgrims.[4]

---

[1] Reader 2005: 154; Satō 2004: 228–229.
[2] Maeda 1971: 158–161.
[3] Hoshino 2001: 264–284 shows from his study of pilgrim lodge records of the 1930s that only around 2% of pilgrims came from the region around Tokyo.
[4] Osada, Sakata, and Seki 2003: 228–231; Reader 2005: 155.

Pilgrims Until We Die. Ian Reader and John Shultz, Oxford University Press. © Oxford University Press 2021.
DOI: 10.1093/oso/9780197573587.003.0003

Travelling around Shikoku, too, has been made easier by bus and train services there. These developments mean that people can do the pilgrimage more quickly—something that facilitates multiple performances—and can go back and forth between their homes and the pilgrimage route easily and often, as we saw in the Introduction with the example of the businessman Ozaki who is able to go back and forth between the pilgrimage route and his workplace in Osaka on a weekly basis. Such developments have also opened the pilgrimage up to a wider number of people—notably older pilgrims, especially female, who in earlier eras were less likely to make what was an arduous journey but for whom organised pilgrimage bus tours, and later the ability to travel by their own cars, made it accessible.[5]

Along with the growth in motorised transport has come the development of better roads and other facilities such as GPS systems and enhanced road signs that have enabled pilgrims to be faster and more 'efficient' in their pilgrimages. Internet access and mobile and smart phones enable pilgrims to find lodgings easily, arranging and planning their trips well in advance, while for those who sleep in their cars the development of convenience stores and roadside service areas (*michi no eki*) that have shops, food stalls, toilets, and sometimes also shower facilities enable them to stay overnight and deal with their travel and food needs. We have spoken to many current pilgrims who say they can visit all the temples in under a week by car while performing rituals and getting their pilgrim books stamped during temple opening hours; this contrasts with the fourteen or more days the first bus tours took in 1953.

Economic factors, pensions, and healthcare

Economic growth and pension systems have also played a significant role in enabling more people to do pilgrimages more frequently. Whereas pilgrims of earlier eras who made multiple circuits were often dependent on alms, those who do it repeatedly in the present day are generally able to finance their pilgrimages from their pensions and savings. Many are 'pensioner pilgrims' who have made the pilgrimage the focus of their post-retirement life and who use their pensions—often enhanced by their savings from a lifetime

---

[5] This outline of transport changes and their impact is drawn from Reader 2005: 155–167; Hoshino and Asakawa 2011: 23–26; Mori 2005; Osada, Sakata, and Seki 2003; and Satō 2004. Satō 2004: 228–229 indicates the majority of pilgrims (61%) by the early 2000s went by car, although it is likely that the figure is higher now.

of work—to support their pilgrimage habits. In our questionnaire for multiple performers (see Chapter 4) the majority of respondents said they were retired and that they used their pensions, often supplemented by savings, to this end, while those who embed the pilgrimage within their working lives said they used their salaries and savings. We have also interviewed unemployed people walking the pilgrimage who told us that they did not need to rely on alms but were able to live for very little on the *henro* because they slept out and ate cheap food. Improved healthcare, too, has played its part as life expectancy has risen and people have been able to remain active longer. Sociological studies of Shikoku pilgrims have shown that those in their sixties and above have in recent decades become the single largest pilgrimage cohort, something rather different from the pre-modern era when older pilgrims were comparatively rare.[6] We have met people in their eighties with twenty or more years' experience of doing the pilgrimage after retirement and who are active enough to spend long periods travelling and sleeping in their cars; as cases such as that of Fukuda Shōnosuke indicate, some manage to carry on into their nineties.

A pilgrim from Kurashiki in Okayama prefecture whom we met at Maegamiji, Temple Sixty-Four, in March 2018, summed up the conditions that aided multiple performance. Aged seventy-two, he had done eighty-eight circuits in all, always sleeping in his car, and he said he planned to continue doing the pilgrimage as long as he could. It took him six or seven days each time, and his reasons for doing it, he said, were to eradicate his bad karma, to remain fit, and because he revered Kōbō Daishi. There were, he said, three elements necessary for continued performance: *genki, hima, okane* (health, free time, money)—all of which he, as a retired person with a pension, currently had. One of those, health, would be the determining factor in how long he could continue and hence how many more circuits he might be able to make—something we heard repeatedly during our interviews.

Pilgrimage structures, work schedules, and multiple options

Another factor that has increased the potential for multiple performance is that, as we stated in Chapter 1, there is no obligation to do the whole

[6] Osada, Sakata, and Seki 2003: 226–227; Satō 2004: 219.

pilgrimage in one go. This is not something specific to the Shikoku pilgrimage but a common feature of Japanese multi-sited pilgrimages; the thirty-three temple Saikoku Kannon pilgrimage is, alongside Shikoku, the best-known of such routes, and similarly to Shikoku many people do it in a series of journeys. Pilgrims can thus 'step in and out' of the pilgrimage depending on circumstances.

While this has always been the case, modern transport and facilities have made doing it in this way increasingly convenient, especially for those who work, to break up the journey into a series of short visits or even day or weekend trips. Many of those who walk do it this way, using Japan's efficient transport system to get to and home from the places they started and finished each stage. This has enabled many people to do multiple circuits while still employed and to fit their pilgrimage activities into their modern work structures and family life; many of our interviewees said they were doing it this way, taking short holidays from their work or doing it over weekends before returning to their day jobs. Older walkers have told us that even though they might be retired, and thus had plenty of time available, they preferred doing it in sections, walking for a week or so at a time then going home to rest up before tackling the next part of the route. Some interviewees have indicated that they are happy to continue in this mode throughout their lives. For others retirement offers the opportunity to expand their pilgrimage activities beyond short breaks from work, when they do sections of the route at a time, into doing the whole pilgrimage repeated times a year.

Related to this is that, as we noted in Chapter 1, there is no obligatory way to do the pilgrimage. Pilgrims have a multiplicity of choices how they do their pilgrimages; they can go on foot, use trains and buses, travel on organised tours, go by car, and so on. They can combine different modes as well; some walkers said that they used trains or buses on some of the long sections between temples where the pilgrimage route followed the main highway and that they found less pleasant to walk. One can do it in one go, either the normative clockwise way around the island (*tōshiuchi*) visiting the temples in their numerical order, or counter-clockwise, reverse numerical order (*gyaku uchi*), or in sections as one wishes, and so on. This spectrum of choice itself encourages multiple performance—something we found repeatedly during interviews even with pilgrims who had only done a very small number of pilgrimages. It was not uncommon, for example, to meet pilgrims on their second circuit who said that they had, for example, initially done the *henro* by car and were now going on foot to see how different it was that way, or who, having done it the first time the normal clockwise way were now doing it counter-clockwise. A man from Shiga prefecture met at Temple Eighty-Seven at the end of October 2018, for example, had done the pilgrimage once on his motorbike and now was doing it again counter-clockwise as a new experience. A couple from Osaka met two days later at Temple Thirty-Three were also on their second circuit—this time by foot, doing it in sections and in reverse order, after having previously done it clockwise by car. Asked why they were doing it again they ventured that they liked walking, that they were captivated by 'Shikoku's charms' (*Shikoku no miryoku*), and that praying and chanting sutras (*okyō*) made them feel peaceful. The man added that if one does it once, one will want to do it again (and again). On their pilgrimages they had met people who had done it repeatedly, and they felt that they were on their way to this as well, even hinting at incipient addiction. A couple from Tottori, aged in their sixties, was travelling by car and said they had done it once carrying a pilgrim's book (*nōkyōchō*). While doing it they saw other pilgrims who carried pilgrimage scrolls, and this made them think it would be good to get such a scroll for themselves. As a result they were doing it again, this time carrying a scroll. We have met people who have tried it a multiplicity of ways one after another—going by car, then walking to see what it is like that way, then by car again but this time with a scroll and so on; in trying out these different variations, some may settle on a particular mode they find most suitable to them, while others continue to experiment with new ways. What seems common is that through doing it various ways they get drawn in and start to embrace the pilgrimage as an unending factor and element in their lives, and that every pilgrimage is in itself a new experience. As pilgrims repeatedly said to us, they were not doing the same pilgrimage over and over so much as experiencing it anew and seeing it in a new light on every occasion.

Professional themes, promotion, and performance

The increase in pilgrim numbers, along with the growth of organised pilgrimage tours and of groups travelling together, has also given rise to a form of professionalisation in the pilgrimage. This is not new, as historically there have been examples of pilgrimage groups being led by an experienced guide

(*sendatsu*) or *hijiri*.[7] Those who, in the Edo period, performed repeated pilgrimages, or who in effect like Shinnen, spent their lives largely focused on
the pilgrimage and soliciting alms for its benefit, were also, in a sense, professionals. Nakatsukasa Mōhei also could be seen in this light; famed because of
his constant circumambulations of the island, he attracted crowds and supporters who gave him alms and enabled him to finance his pilgrimage stones
and guidebook. An article in the *Osaka Mainichi Shinbun* (newspaper) of 17
May 1907, for example, described him as 'a kind of professional' (*hitokusa no
shōbaijin*).[8]

In the contemporary era, the increased popularity of the pilgrimage has
increased the potential for professionalisation and for ardent pilgrims to
support their pilgrimage activities by serving as guides or by engaging in
other ways with the pilgrimage, for example, by writing about it. The development of bus tour pilgrimages from the 1960s onwards helped expand the
pilgrimage clientele and led to an increased demand for people who were
experienced in and knowledgeable about the pilgrimage and its customs and
practices, and who could act as guides for such tours. Many bus companies
have made use of well-known pilgrims to lead pilgrim groups on organised
tours. Such people were thus able to do multiple pilgrimages in a professional
capacity, as is shown by the example of Mori Masamitsu, a devout pilgrim
whose services as a pilgrimage guide were frequently sought by the Iyo Tetsu
transport company (historically the largest provider of organised pilgrimage
bus tours in Shikoku) in the early 1990s. Mori, as an official of the bus company informed one of the authors, was representative of the pilgrimage
leaders they used, in that he was devout, deeply versed in pilgrimage legends
that he could narrate to those he led, and in modes of practice so that he
could lead parties in prayer and show them the correct ways to worship at the
temples. Mori was retired and, because of his status as a venerated guide, he
was able to do multiple pilgrimage circuits in the service of Iyo Tetsu, so that
the pilgrimage became both a focus of faith and professional engagement for
him.[9] There are others, too, as we discuss in more detail in Chapter 5, who
combine devotion to the pilgrimage with leading pilgrimage parties and/or

---

[7] By the mid-seventeenth century there is evidence that *sendatsu* were leading pilgrim groups in
Shikoku, as shown by the account of the priest Chōzen who did the *henro* in 1653 and who records
meeting groups of pilgrims led by guides on two occasions (Reader 2005: 115).
[8] Mori 2014: 79.
[9] Reader 1993b: 45. See also Reader 2005: 220–221.

running pilgrimage confraternities, and who thus have a professional relationship with the pilgrimage alongside their devotional engagement with it.

There are many others who could be considered to have a professional relationship with the pilgrimage, including multiple performing pilgrims who have written about the *henro* and whose knowledge of it has helped them acquire a form of celebrity status in the pilgrimage community.[10] One such figure is a Buddhist priest well known for her studies of the pilgrimage, who stated to us in an interview that she received fees for leading pilgrimage tours and that such activities were in a sense a 'business' (*shigoto*). However, such 'business' is in her view a means of enabling her to do other pilgrimage activities, notably allowing her to do her own personal pilgrimages of faith in Shikoku and to carry out volunteer work guiding pilgrims as well. Such things, she considers, are expressions of her faith in Daishi, things that are enabled and supported by what she calls her 'business' pilgrimages. Widely respected among fellow pilgrims[11] her professional activities thus are integrated into a wider framework of academic studies, personal faith, performance and promotion of the pilgrimage.

Another well-known figure who has developed a powerful pilgrimage persona in Shikoku is the Buddhist priest and writer Ieda Shōko. Ieda is a Shingon Buddhist priest who is also well known as an often controversial writer of fiction and non-fiction, especially about sexual themes. Previously married and with a child, she became interested in Shingon Buddhism and Kōbō Daishi, studied at Kōya University, and entered the Buddhist priesthood in 2007. Subsequently she has continued to write extensively on numerous subjects, with an increasing focus on religious, and notably Buddhist, issues, including the Shikoku pilgrimage;[12] she had done the pilgrimage (at the time she was interviewed in November 2018) some thirteen times by foot[13] and twice also by car. Her website carries a blog of her pilgrimage visits to Shikoku along with publicity about her numerous books and writings.

[10] See Shultz 2009 and 2011 for a comprehensive discussion of celebrity pilgrims who have acquired status through their writings and online publications.

[11] We say this from observing her interactions at conferences and meetings with academics researching the pilgrimage and with other pilgrims, and from interviews with pilgrims, leaders of confraternities and priests, as well as academics, in Shikoku.

[12] Ieda 2009 (2014).

[13] Although Ieda talks of going by foot (*aruite*), she has a flexible interpretation of this practice. Her website indicates she uses buses and trains at times (notably when there are long distances between temples), suggests that her book provides the best way to do the *henro* on foot while using transport, and tells readers that it helps them cut out problematic sections of the route. See http://www.gokutsuma.com/henro2/index.htm (accessed 3 January 2020).

Ieda does the *henro* as a series of short visits, and she has been an active proponent of such forms of pilgrimage, seeing them as a way to enable ordinary people to fit the pilgrimage into their work and other schedules. Her pattern is to visit Shikoku each month for a short period—usually, her website indicates, two nights and three days—to traverse sections of the route. She does this throughout the year, thus completing one circuit per year and always ending up with a visit to Kōyasan, where she states she is often greeted by well-wishers and friends celebrating the completion of her circuit. She also notes that although she likes to walk alone,[14] sometimes women who have read the blog she writes while on pilgrimages try to meet up and walk with her for part of the route.

Ieda commented in our interview that she had become so attuned to the route through recurrent performances that her body knew where to go almost automatically, without her having to think about it. She is devoted to Kōbō Daishi, seeing him as a powerful figure whose path should be followed; although she had not personally experienced any Daishi-related miracles, she felt that the benefits (*riyaku*) he bestowed on her have allowed her to continue doing the pilgrimage. Although she is a Buddhist priest, she currently does not run a temple, although she said that in the future she intended to do so; she had received a message from Daishi at the end of one of her pilgrimages, in which he told her to do this after she had completed eighteen circuits of the *henro*. At that point, she felt, running the temple would take up much of her time and thus limit her ability to do the pilgrimage at the same rate as at present. Nonetheless she intended to remain involved with and doing the pilgrimage as long as her health allowed.

Ieda, when we talked to her, was critical of people she saw as seeking to live off the pilgrimage, whether serving as pilgrimage guides or living as pilgrims reliant on begging. Nor, she said, does she make money from leading pilgrimage groups. At the same time, her writings about the pilgrimage, promoted on her website, serve to enhance her status as a celebrity pilgrim; various publicity items on display around the route also draw attention to her.[15] As an advocate of the pilgrimage who encourages ordinary people to do it whichever way they can, she is both a promoter and beneficiary of the

---

[14] However, she also counsels about the potential problems women might have walking alone in the mountainous and less inhabited parts of the island.

[15] For example, copies of magazine articles about Ieda and her writings were displayed on the wall of a restaurant frequented by pilgrims outside Temple Twenty-Five in Kōchi prefecture, along with a note from Ieda, who had eaten there.

pilgrimage, as well as someone who is a regular performer whose life patterns are framed around her regular monthly pilgrimage visits to Shikoku. As such, while she is not a professional pilgrim per se, she is certainly someone whose pilgrimage activities benefit from her celebrity status and for whom the pilgrimage enhances her celebrity and provides a source of remuneration that helps sustain her activities while encouraging others to be pilgrims.

Sendatsu and public manifestations of numbers

In the post-war era, as the number of people performing the pilgrimage multiple times grew and as organised tour parties led by experienced pilgrims increased in number, the Shikoku Pilgrimage Temples' Association, which had itself only become formally instituted in the 1950s, established a formal *sendatsu* system.[16] The term *sendatsu*, which literally means 'someone who stands in front' (i.e. a guide or leader), appears regularly in historical accounts of pilgrimage in Japan to refer to people—usually in earlier times to ascetic practitioners such as *hijiri*—who act as guides to and leaders of pilgrim groups, whether in Shikoku or elsewhere.[17] The Pilgrimage Temples' Association's establishment of a *sendatsu* system represented a modern institutionalisation of this rank; it also encouraged multiple performances of the pilgrimage. People who have done the pilgrimage four times can apply for *sendatsu* status; they have to pay a fee for acquiring this and in return receive a number of items identifying them as *sendatsu* (including a badge with their names and their *sendatsu* number and rank, and a *wagesa* or Buddhist stole to wear around their necks). *Sendatsu* are expected to promote the pilgrimage. faith in Kōbō Daishi, and to take part in meetings and training sessions for *sendatsu* held each year in Shikoku. The system has a number of ranks, and one can rise through them through performing the pilgrimage more times; for example, one can ascend from the basic rank of *sendatsu* to the next—*gonchū sendatsu*—by doing the pilgrimage twice more and paying an additional fee. It does not matter how one does the pilgrimage, although,

---

[16] See Reader 2005: 167–169, which shows that the establishment of this association was closely linked to the development of organised tours, while the establishment of the *sendatsu* system is connected to both.

[17] For historical accounts of the role of *sendatsu* (which became prominent especially in the Kumano pilgrimage but later in Shikoku as well) see Shinjō 1982: 200–220 and Shinno 1991: 17–18.

at least in theory, those who act as professional guides cannot go beyond the basic rank.[18]

The *sendatsu* system has encouraged continuing performance of the pilgrimage, both by bestowing ranks and status on people for so doing and by helping foster a culture—enhanced by regular *sendatsu* meetings and by regional *sendatsu* associations that organise pilgrimage-related activities—in which doing the pilgrimage again and again becomes a norm. We have even met people who said that the wish to become a *sendatsu* was a prime reason for doing the pilgrimage multiple times.[19] Not everyone who does the pilgrimage many times seeks this formal status; none of the itinerants we discuss in Chapter 3, for example, had done so, perhaps partly because of the costs involved but also because they had little interest in issues of status. Quite often interviewees, especially those on foot (see Chapter 6), indicated that, although they had done many pilgrimages, they had no interest in acquiring the status and title of *sendatsu*. However, many do so, and while a number of our questionnaire respondents said they were not *sendatsu*, the majority were (see Chapter 4). Often, too, people are keen to ascend the ranks; having a higher *sendatsu* rank serves a mark of pride and status for many pilgrims. It also means doing more pilgrimages.

Related also to this formal system are other ways in which people are encouraged to do multiple pilgrimages and in which multiple performance may be portrayed in ways that confer status on the pilgrim. The newsletter *Henro*, for example, is sent on a monthly basis to all registered *sendatsu*. It regularly features articles about those who have done multiple pilgrimages, always in ways that bestow praise on them and portray them in a reverential light. In issue number 335, in 2013, for example, *Henro* featured a pilgrim named Takahashi from Fukuoka prefecture, who had vowed to do the pilgrimage 321 times and had thus far done it 236 times—eighty-six times on his own and 150 times with a group. Takahashi, who had walked it once, aged sixty-nine for his 114th circuit, said he had been inspired to make this vow after being given the *osamefuda*, in 2011, of a ninety-year-old pilgrim named Yoneda who had done 333 circuits and whom Takahashi viewed as his inspirational pilgrimage teacher. At that moment, Takahashi said, he decided he

---

[18] For a detailed outline of the system see Reader 2005: 171–177.

[19] This was the case with a striking encounter with a male pilgrim from Matsuyama, at Temple Eighteen in November 2019, who said he was on his fourth circuit, with just six more temples to go, and that his reason for doing it was to become a *sendatsu*, something he wanted to do because he was a resident of Shikoku.

should do 321 circuits himself—the number coming from the date of Kobo Daishi's entry into nirvana (the twenty-first day of the third month of the year, according to Shingon belief).[20] The article emphasised the number of Takahashi's pilgrimages while adding that he worshipped extensively at the temples and did the pilgrimage without rush. Another article, in *Henro* 329 in August 2012, reported the death of Hayashi Sanae, a female pilgrim from Imabari in Ehime prefecture. Hayashi, it reported, had done the *henro* 188 times with her husband before he passed away; his last wish was that she should continue and fulfil his vow to do it 200 times. She did this, eventually completing 223 circuits and spending the rest of her time helping run a free lodging place for pilgrims. The article, which concludes by reporting that Hayashi died (or, as it put it, 'passed to the other world' [*takai sareta*]) clutching Buddhist prayer beads before the family Buddhist altar, thus lauds Hayashi as a devout person whose life of pilgrimage has culminated in a worthy death.[21] The January 2007 newsletter highlighted on its front page the achievement of a *daisendatsu* (great *sendatsu*, the fifth-highest rank) from Matsuyama named Ōmoto, who had done 209 Shikoku pilgrimages and whose commemorative stone celebrating his 200th circuit could be seen at Temple Sixty-Three. The article stated that he had done all his pilgrimages by car and tabulated that this meant he had driven some 290 220 kilometres, the equivalent of seven times around the world.[22] This was reported in a manner that implied admiration for the achievement with no comment about what impact such amounts of driving might have on a fragile environment. Since 2007 when this article was published, our awareness of environmental problems and the damage being done by the burning of carbon gases and by driving have increased exponentially, although we have as yet found little consciousness of this issue among those who drive repeatedly.

Material signs: the pilgrim's name slip

There are also a number of material items that encourage multiple performances of the pilgrimage. These are, in particular, the *osamefuda*, the pilgrim's calling card or name slip mentioned in Chapter 1 that by custom pilgrims

---

[20] *Henro* 335, February 2013, p. 8.
[21] *Henro* 329, August 2012, p. 2.
[22] *Henro* 262, p 1.

leave at the temples and hand out to people they meet and to those who give them *settai*, and the *nōkyōchō*—the book that pilgrims may carry and get stamped at each temple visited. Of these the *osamefuda* (often referred to simply as *ofuda* or just *fuda*) is especially prominent. A system of coloured *osamefuda* has developed in Shikoku, with different colours indicating how many times one has done the *henro*. The system is informal. No one regulates it, and it is up to each pilgrim to determine what colour she or he should use. Those who are doing it for the first up to their fourth time use plain white *osamefuda*; five to seven times use green; eight to twenty-four use red; silver is used for twenty-five to forty-nine; and gold is used for fifty and above.[23] Those who have done it 100 times or more usually get special brocade (*nishiki fuda*) ones made. Pilgrims often write on their *fuda* which number pilgrimage circuit they are on, along with their names, prayers and other information. It is unclear when this practice of using coloured *fuda* originated. Brocade ones appear to be relatively recent; the pilgrim met at Maegamiji (see the earlier section 'Economic factors, pensions, and healthcare') said he had only encountered them in recent years; one of the current authors, who first did research on the pilgrimage in 1984, cannot recall seeing any at that time and first encountered them in Shikoku in 1991.

Both gold and more particularly brocade *fuda* have become desired objects for many pilgrims in recent years and have encouraged their repeated pilgrimages. This was brought home to us in an interview with a retired couple from Kurashiki in Okayama prefecture who were travelling in a small truck and whom we met at Temple Thirty-Four, Tanemaji, in March 2018. Both were *sendatsu* who carried impressive red pilgrim staffs (*kongōtsue*) and were, they told us, on their ninety-third pilgrimage. They said they felt 'called' (*sasoete*) by Kōbō Daishi to do the pilgrimage, which was a matter of faith for them and something that kept them healthy and brought them good fortune. They also had a specific aim: to do 100 circuits and get brocade *fuda*. Indeed they talked excitedly of the possibility of reaching their goal in 2018. They planned each pilgrimage carefully, taking six days each time, and averaged around ten circuits per year, normally intensively in the March–May and September–November periods, when the weather was best. Hence they

---

[23] This colour/number system is what is followed at present, although it has not always been so. As Satō (2014: 232–234) indicates, at different eras, and according to different sources, guidebooks, and historical accounts, the relationship of coloured *fuda* to numbers of circuits has varied. In a guide to the pilgrimage dating from 1934, for example, white *fuda* were to be used for the first seven times, red up to twenty-one times, silver from thirty onwards, and gold from fifty upwards.

thought they could reach their goal in autumn. They also made it clear that this would not be the end of their pilgrimages, given their faith in Daishi, their sense of being called by him to do the pilgrimage, and their feeling that it kept them healthy and brought them benefits. They would continue to do the pilgrimage, carrying their brocade *fuda* with them to hand out to others they met. We have heard similar thoughts from other pilgrims throughout our research.

The *fuda* of those who have done the pilgrimage multiple times have become akin to holy relics, protective amulets and good luck charms in the eyes of many pilgrims. Nakatsukasa's *fuda* were viewed as protective amulets; miracle stories associated with the *fuda* of prominent pilgrims are passed around orally in Shikoku.[24] One of our respondents, a recurrent and experienced pilgrim who had performed seven Shikoku pilgrimages, wrote to tell us that she had received brocade *fuda* from someone who had done it 337 times and also from other pilgrims who had done it over one hundred times, and that she valued these items highly. One author of this book was given a pair of these name slips from a married couple at the Temple Eleven, Fujiidera, and was told that they would serve as protection on the arduous mountain climb to the next temple. There are scattered reports of the theft of gold and brocade *fuda* from temple offering boxes, suggesting that their perceived value sometimes trumps decorum.[25] At Temple Thirty-Seven, Iwamotoji, a Buddhist nun was so impressed to hear that one author had slept outdoors the previous night in freezing conditions that she rewarded him with a *nishiki fuda*, but before placing it in his hands, she made him swear that he would not resell it on the internet. Likewise, while temple priests eventually ritually burn the *fuda* offered onsite, these colourful ones are often considered special and are stored at the temple instead.

Avid pilgrims sometimes have proud collections of brocade *fuda*, making them something like prize baseball cards of the journey. A pilgrim who had done fifty-five circuits in his minivan and who was encountered at a small wayside temple between two of the pilgrimage temples in Ehime prefecture not only gave one of the authors his gold *fuda* but then proudly showed him a collection of the brocade *fuda* he had received over the years. He said he liked doing the pilgrimage so as to meet other pilgrims, give alms to them,

---

[24] Reader 2005: 176.
[25] See Reader 2005: 62 for an example. We have heard reports at various temples that people sometimes do this.

and collect their names and *fuda* in return. He was especially proud of a collection of brocade *fuda* from Fukuda Shōnosuke, which he had mounted in an album and with which he posed so the author could take a photograph. At a meeting of a *sendatsu* association in Niihama in Ehime prefecture several pilgrims produced their collections of brocade *fuda*, which were carefully placed in photo albums. Their knowledge of various multiple performing pilgrims and their respective calling cards led to an interesting dialogue, with comments such as 'oh, that is a good one and hard to find . . '. With one such collection, the pilgrim was careful to note which ones she had received directly from the pilgrim and which were obtained via a secondary source. Those who make the pilgrimage many times and carry brocade *fuda* may also give them to the temple officials who stamp their books and to those who run pilgrim lodges. This has provided a good source of research materials for us and a means of contacting some of those who have done the highest number of pilgrimages in Shikoku, as temple officials and those running temple pilgrim lodges have allowed us to examine the collections of brocade *fuda* they hold and to gather the information written on them.

For example, the temple lodge and pilgrimage centre at Temple Twenty-Four has a scrapbook in which they have pasted in the brocade *fuda* left by pilgrims who have stayed there between 2003 (when the scrapbook started) to November 2019; we examined it both in November 2018 and a year later in 2019. Some pilgrims visited regularly and had numerous *fuda* in the book. In all there were thirty-eight pilgrims represented, ranging from a couple who, in June 2018 were completing their 100th circuit, to one pilgrim (Fukuda Shōnosuke) whose *fuda* appear multiple times from his 334th circuit up to two *fuda* left in December 2013 from his 641st and 643rd pilgrimages. Many of those leaving *fuda* had done over 200 and some over 300 pilgrimages. Thus the female pilgrim Hayashi Sanae from Ehime prefecture whose death was reported in *Henro* (see above) had left two *fuda*, one from her 201st pilgrimage in May 2005 and the other from her 210th circuit in November 2006, indicating a total of nine pilgrimages around Shikoku in some eighteen months. She was at the time aged seventy-nine. In May 2005, too, the pilgrim named Ōmoto whose multiple circuits by car were cited in *Henro* (above) left a *fuda* from his 200th circuit while in 2006 a couple named Takezawa left a *fuda* inscribed with praise for the Buddha Amida and indicating this was their 325th pilgrimage. Another who had done close to 300 circuits left a succession of *fuda* between 2011 and 2018, the first of which in 2011 was from his 228th circuit and last on display in 2019 (with no month indicated) citing 293 pilgrimages—a total of sixty-five pilgrimages around Shikoku in seven years. Sometimes, too, such *fuda* indicate how particular events and issues might be central to individual pilgrims and their pilgrimages. A man from Osaka named Uchida for example, left a number of *fuda* from different pilgrimages between 2011 and 2015, from his 210th to 215th pilgrimages, citing in succession a pilgrimage to commemorate his promotion to a higher *sendatsu* rank, prayers for the spirits of those killed in the March 2011 tsunami and earthquake disaster, and (in 2015) when he was aged seventy-seven, commemoration of the 1200th founding of the pilgrimage.[26]

Collections such as these are tangible evidence of a dedicated core of people who perform hundreds of pilgrimages and who commemorate and celebrate this through their *fuda*. It should be mentioned also that brocade *fuda* have to be specially made,[27] are expensive and drive up the cost of the pilgrimage for those who carry them. They generally cost at least 100 yen apiece, meaning their standard ritual use (i.e. leaving one each at the main hall of worship and Daishidō at each of the eighty-eight temples) would add something like an additional 17 600 yen to the cost of a circuit. If they are given out freely to people along the way, costs would rise even more. As a result some pilgrims make their own; one pilgrim, Shimamura-san, who claims to have done the journey more than 700 times, laser prints his own version on paper, rather than using cloth, a technique met with some scorn by traditionalists. He also makes a special amulet version of his own *fuda* that can be placed in a wallet or on a keychain, and sees the distribution of these and his laser printed version as something of a community service, bringing good fortune and health to those who receive them. Nonetheless most pilgrims we have met who carry brocade *fuda* appear to have had them specially made and also have been ready to pass out their *fuda* when asked (see Figure 2.1).

Such brocade *fuda* also can give rise to criticisms and even to questions about their validity. As we noted above, there is no authority or official body that regulates such things; as one temple priest commented to us, pilgrims are the sole arbiters of how many times they have done it. Temples do not keep records of how many times a pilgrim visits (although officials are often aware of those who come regularly) and generally accept what pilgrims say.

---

[26] This actually represents the celebration of one of the pilgrimage's legendary foundation dates—815, the year Kūkai passed away. In reality the pilgrimage did not develop until centuries after.

[27] The *fuda* for lower numbers are paper, come in standard formats, and can be bought at the temples; pilgrims fill in their names and details by themselves. By contrast the brocade *fuda* need to be done individually since pilgrim names and other information are imprinted directly into the brocade (which is itself a more costly medium than paper).

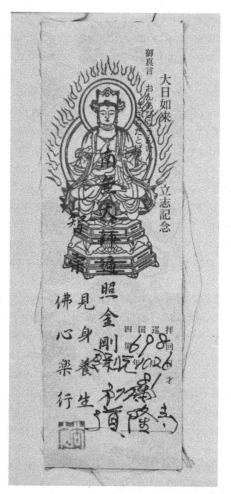

Figure 2.1 *Osamefuda*: brocade pilgrim's name slip indicating 698 circuits

In other words, it is each pilgrim's prerogative to determine or assert how many pilgrimages they have made, and to make or have made their own brocade *fuda* and tell other pilgrims about such things. This in turn can cause questions to be raised and even to accusations that (some) pilgrims might use the symbolism of the brocade *fuda* to impress others and enhance their personal status. We have at various times in our research heard doubts raised about particular pilgrims and their claimed number of circuits; whether such doubts are the result of jealousy because someone has done it more times, or whether they are the product of genuine knowledge of fraud or overstatements is often hard to discern. [28] Sometimes concerns have been raised about whether some pilgrims use brocade *fuda* to enhance their personal status, to impress other pilgrims, or even just as a means of boasting about their own achievements. During interviews, some pilgrims have referred to brocade *fuda* as *misemono* (display items, something associated with showing off).

Hoshino and Asakawa comment on this by citing a scene from the 2009 Japanese television drama series 'Walkers' (*Uōkāzu*), which was set against the backdrop of the Shikoku pilgrimage. In one episode a *sendatsu* named Sakata hands out a brocade *fuda* to another character, thereby indicating he had done it over one hundred times. He did so, Hoshino and Asakawa note, somewhat boastfully, as if to draw attention to his performance and impress others.[29]

There is, in other words, a degree of scepticism among some pilgrims about the implications of coloured *fuda* and their implicit meanings of publicly proclaiming how many times one has done the pilgrimage. Moreover, not all pilgrims carry *osamefuda*; none of the itinerants who live on the road whom we have interviewed proffered them to us, perhaps because they could not afford to spend their limited money on such things but also because, as we indicate further in Chapter 3, they appeared unconcerned about matters of status.

However, while there are therefore some questions surrounding *fuda*, it is clear that they form a significant element in the contemporary dynamic of the pilgrimage and play an important role in encouraging multiple performance and offering rewards—in terms of potential admiration from others along with a sense of achievement and satisfaction—for so doing. While we have not heard any pilgrim say that being able to carry a brocade *fuda* is their sole motivation for doing multiple pilgrimages, we have repeatedly been told—as with the couple from Kurashiki cited above—that it is a motivation, alongside others, to keep going. At the same time, it is also important to reiterate that brocade *fuda* are widely viewed as meritorious items that can bring benefits to those who receive them, and this can serve as a gratifying

---

[28] For example, we have heard one group of pilgrims from a confraternity assert that a man who claims to have done over 700 circuits is overstating the case. We have interviewed that person and are aware of his dedication to visiting the pilgrimage temples; we have not seen any compelling evidence to determine which (that he has done over 700 circuits or that he is exaggerating) of these claims is correct. See also Reader 2005: 241–243 for a case in which a pilgrimage party leader suggested another pilgrim who claimed to have done the *henro* 109 times was not being truthful.

[29] Hoshino and Asakawa 2011: 85.

motivation for those who have done 100 circuits. A priest at one temple commented that people are often overjoyed to be given brocade *fuda*, and this gives the donor a reciprocal sense of good feeling and elation, something that reinforces their sense of self-worth and encourages them to keep doing the pilgrimage.

Material signs: the pilgrim's book

The pilgrim's book (*nōkyōchō*) also serves as a similar motivation. As we noted in Chapter 1, pilgrims can get their books stamped each time they visit a temple, and as such the pages of their books—initially white—can get saturated in red ink. Nakatsukasa Mōhei went through two *nōkyōchō* during his lifelong pilgrimage career, both of which became saturated and bright red.[30] The aforementioned couple met at Tanemaji carried a *nōkyōchō* whose pages were bright red because of the number of stamps they had received, which they showed us proudly. We have frequently been shown heavily stamped *nōkyōchō* by pilgrims keen to tell us how many times they had done the pilgrimage. We also have been shown *nōkyōchō* whose pages were only partially covered in red stamps, whose owners have told us that in time they hoped to do enough circuits to get them wholly red (see Figure 2.2). Interestingly, it was suggested to us from several sources that the complete reddening of a *nōkyōchō* might speed up pilgrimage performance. Since after a certain number of stamps[31] the book is completely red and new stamps will not change the colour further, some pilgrims may abandon their use, allowing them to become unbound by the temples' regular office hours as well as not having to sometimes queue at the office to get the book stamped. One priest suggested that this could significantly reduce the time necessary to do a circuit by car.

A good example of how *fuda* and *nōkyōchō* can serve as motivations for pilgrims came in an encounter with a *sendatsu* at Temple Seventy, Iyadaniji, in Kagawa prefecture, in November 2018. Aged seventy-three, he was from Hiroshima and said he had done the pilgrimage around forty times, the first

---

[30] Ehime ken Shōgaigakushū Sentā 2001: 263.

[31] It is hard to estimate how quickly a book will become completely red, but as a general rule we would suggest this occurs at some time around 100 or more circuits; Tabuchi Yoshio's book, for example, was wholly red, for example, when he had done 110 circuits (Reader 2005: 92) and we have seen other books that are similarly totally red from pilgrims who have done around 120 circuits.

Figure 2.2 Pilgrim's book showing multiple stamps

of them approximately thirty to forty years ago. (We have often found that pilgrims can be a little vague when talking about dates, such as when they first started doing the pilgrimage.) After that first pilgrimage he was not able to do it for a long time due to work, but having retired at the age of sixty (and after his children had grown up and left home) he began doing the pilgrimage regularly in earnest. He had done it sixteen times by group bus tours and the other times by himself (and sometimes also with his wife) by car. His motives included doing memorial services for deceased people he knew, including his brother and sister with whom he had done his first pilgrimage but who had since died. His subsequent pilgrimages have been as *kuyō*—memorials—for them but also on his own behalf. He said he wanted to do one hundred pilgrimages so as to be able to get the brocade *fuda*, although he also felt it was now unlikely, given his age. As such he thought a goal of fifty pilgrimages (and a gold *fuda*) was more likely, since he tended only to do the pilgrimage at weekends. Nonetheless the possibility of a brocade *fuda* continued to motivate him. He added that another ambition was to have a 'completely red' (*maaka*) *nōkyōchō*; as he said this, he pulled out his book, opened it and said, gesturing at it as he did so, that while it had lots of stamps and red ink there were also lots of white spaces between the stamps, so that he needed to do more circuits in order to make it wholly red.

At the *Maeyama O-Henro Kōryū Saron* (hereafter referred to as the Maeyama Henro Salon), a publicly run pilgrimage information centre and museum located between Temples Eighty-Seven and Eighty-Eight, there are various display cases containing displays and historical items associated with famed pilgrims, including Nakatsukasa, Shinnen, and others. One such case contains the bright red *nōkyōchō* of Kishigami Kōkichi who did the *henro* 308 times from 1965 until the early 1990s. Alongside his *nōkyōchō* were displayed items such as his photograph, a commemorative silver brocade pilgrim's shirt that he wore for his 200th pilgrimage, and a pilgrimage towel Kishigami had made to commemorate his 300th pilgrimage. The museum also has collections of the *fuda* of various pilgrims who had done it over 100-plus times, including one from Fukuda Shōnosuke on his 646th pilgrimage, and several left by people commemorating their 100th circuit and who had stopped by specifically to donate their *fuda* on this occasion. In this way the Maeyama Henro Salon not only serves as a reference point and place for pilgrims to celebrate and memorialise their achievements; it also helps spur multiple performance by validating and valorising such people through displaying their *fuda* and making them part of the continuing public history of the pilgrimage.

One can at times also see pilgrim books saturated with red ink on display; at the temple office at Temple Sixty-Four one such book is in a display case with a sign indicating that the pilgrim in question (a local man) had donated the book to the temple when he had done 129 pilgrimages—and that (at the time we saw the sign in March 2018) he had now done it 265 times. On a subsequent visit the temple official informed us that this pilgrim was now on his third *nōkyōchō*. Sometimes, too, pilgrims not only wear a *hakui* (white pilgrim's shirt) but also carry one as well, that they get stamped at each temple. It is more common to get such *hakui* stamped once by each temple, with the shirt being using as a burial shroud, following a common Shikoku practice of pilgrims being placed in their burial caskets dressed in pilgrimage attire.[32] However, some pilgrims will carry one that they get stamped multiple times. We have on occasion been shown such shirts that are totally red for this reason.

Getting pilgrim books and shirts stamped at the temples not only identifies the pilgrim as a repeater but provides scope for officials at the temples to offer special encouragement to them. This is something one of the authors, who had previously walked the whole pilgrimage with a friend, experienced in 2019 when he walked part of the pilgrimage for the second time. At each temple as he presented his pilgrim book, he received words of encouragement and praise from those working at the temple—something that he noted happened to other pilgrims as well. In other words, there is a culture of encouragement and reinforcement evident at the temples—something of course shown also by the *sendatsu* system that the temples have established— that gives credit to repeaters and helps them feel they are doing the right thing by returning again (and again) as pilgrims.

One further point to note about *nōkyōchō* is that they (along with other pilgrimage items such as the pilgrim's shirt) are often used in funerary practices. In popular pilgrimage lore a completed *nōkyōchō* is viewed as a passport to the Pure Land after death. As such it is not uncommon for those who have done the pilgrimage and who have died, to be placed in their funeral casket for cremation with their completed *nōkyōchō* and sometimes also dressed in pilgrimage clothing, [33] thereby reflecting the notion that death is just another part of a continuing life journey. In such ways pilgrimage is unending and unbounded by the physical ends of life.

Material commemorations: stones and inscriptions

Some pilgrims also draw attention to the numbers of times they have done the *henro* by erecting commemorative stones at the temples or along the route. Such stones not only commemorate an individual's (or a pilgrimage confraternity's) performance of pilgrimage but can also enhance the standing

---

[32] Imai 1981: 171. See also Chapter 5 for further examples of this practice.
[33] Reader 2005: 63–64 and 292, n.81.

of the people concerned while encouraging others to follow in their footsteps. Sometimes such stones are associated with or the result of vows made by pilgrims, before departure, to complete the pilgrimage or to do a specific number of circuits. They then erect stones or markers to commemorate the completion of their vow. From the commemorative stones and markers we have examined at Shikoku pilgrimage temples, some numbers (notably eighty-eight and 100 circuits) appear especially significant in this context (see Figure 2.3).

Figure 2.3 Commemorative stone celebrating the eighty-eighth circuit of the pilgrimage

Outside Temple Six there is a large stone erected on 13 December 2010, according to its inscription, to commemorate the 500th circuit of Fukuda Shōnosuke (and also noting his Buddhist ordination name Yuhō, which had been bestowed on him by Temple Six). Fukuda was eighty-four years old at the time, and the stone inscription recorded a brief history of his life and pilgrimage engagement. It states that he was born in the Itano district, Shikoku, not far from Temple Six, although he lived most of his life in the Osaka area, where he ran his business and from whence he later did his pilgrimages. It indicates that from 1998 onwards he devoted himself to doing the *henro* and that for the next eleven years (up to the time when the stone was erected) he had done so incessantly, come rain or shine. Fukuda's stone thus stands to remind future generations about his decades of almost unending pilgrimage.

At Temple Fourteen, a stone put up by a *sendatsu* named Sugiura from Kamakura celebrates his completion of a vow to do one hundred pilgrimages (*hyakkai ketsugan jōju*) in December 2000. Several such commemorative stones at Temple Seventy-Three similarly record significant numerical feats. These included a stone commemorating the eighty-eighth pilgrimage by Hori Kenichi in 2004, one for the 100th circuit by a *sendatsu* named Shikishima (whose brocade *fuda* the authors have seen on display at other temples), and two commemorating the completion of 150 circuits, one by Okamoto Shōkū in 2003 and the other dated March 2007 by Suzuki Hiroshi, a *tokunin daisendatsu* (a high ranking *sendatsu*) from Gifu prefecture. Suzuki's stone bore the phrase *jinsei wa henro nari* (life is a pilgrimage), a phrase that clearly encapsulates the attitudes of many of those who devote themselves to doing it multiple times.

Some stones have been erected by social groups and confraternities. At Temple Thirty-Eight, for example, a stone marker celebrates the sixty-fifth circuit by six *sendatsu* from the Maruyama Daishikō (Maruyama Daishi confraternity) in Okayama prefecture in July 2002. Another stone erected at this temple in 2000 by a Daishi confraternity from Nerima ward in Tokyo commemorates the group's twenty-one years of pilgrimaging in Shikoku. At Saba Daishi, a temple halfway between Temples Twenty-Three and Twenty-Four, which is not one of the official pilgrimage temples but is popular with pilgrims and is known as a *bangai* (temple outside the official numbers),[34]

---

[34] *Bangai* are temples that, although not included in the eighty-eight temples, have some connection with the route and that some pilgrims may visit during their travels; see Reader 2005: 16–17 for further discussion.

numerous pilgrims and groups have erected stone markers. These include a stone celebrating ten continuous years of pilgrimage by one pilgrim, one commemorating twenty-one years of pilgrimages in Shikoku by a person from Sapporo in Hokkaidō, and another recording fifty years of *henro* activity—this time erected by a priest from Sapporo who was a Shikoku *genro daisendatsu* (venerated elder *sendatsu*—the highest rank of *sendatsu*).

These are but a few examples of the large number of commemorative stones that can be seen on the route, especially clustered around the temples. Of course erecting such stones not only commemorates the performance and the pilgrim but also makes their achievement into something permanent (or at least as near permanent as a large stone marker can be). It inscribes the pilgrim on the route, making him/her forever part of it, encapsulated in a physical presence that can be seen by subsequent pilgrims and, of course, by the person him/herself on later pilgrimages.

Competition and multiplicity

All these material signs generate an awareness of multiple performance and encourage others to follow suit, just as was the case with the man who was spurred to make a vow to complete 321 circuits after meeting and receiving a *fuda* from an elderly pilgrim who had done 333 circuits. They can also stimulate a sense of competition that urges some pilgrims on. This is a point we think needs to be given more consideration in studies of pilgrimage. Issues of contest and competition have been discussed in the field, notably through the work of Michael Sallnow and John Eade. However, although such studies provided a theoretical paradigm that has influenced later studies, the themes that have arisen relating to contest have largely been projected through the prism of social relations between different interest groups. As Eade and Sallnow noted, for example, shrine priests trying to keep commerce out of their sanctuaries and stall holders wanting to sell pilgrimage memorabilia and souvenirs might come into conflict around shrines. Sallnow's examinations of Andean pilgrimages drew attention to how different groups of pilgrims competed for positions and status at Andean shrines, while Glenn Bowman's account of how different religious groups contest each other over authority and space in Jerusalem shows how they—not just Christians, Jews, and Muslims but different denominations within these traditions—compete for control of the same city and of sacred places within it.[35]

There is another dimension to contest and competition that has not been given as much attention, however, and that relates to contest and competition between individual pilgrims not just over status and experience but—especially evident in our studies of pilgrims in Shikoku—the numbers of times they have performed pilgrimages. It is especially pronounced when pilgrims make a show of telling others how many times they have done it—as with the aforementioned example of the 'boasting' pilgrim handing over his brocade *fuda* in the television drama 'Walkers'—or when they emblazon their *fuda* with the number of circuits they have done.

This emphasis on numbers can spur not just contest and competition but also, we suggest, jealousy. The ideal of pilgrims doing the pilgrimage together and feeling a sense of bonding and community with other fellow pilgrims is present in Shikoku in the idea of *dōgyō*, 'doing the pilgrimage together'. As we noted in Chapter 1, *dōgyō ninin*—doing the pilgrimage with Daishi—is a common image of the pilgrimage; pilgrims also often refer to fellow pilgrims as *dōgyō*, suggesting a bond and community among pilgrims. Yet alongside this sense of shared community, they may also be deeply conscious of differences indicated by such things as numbers and status; *sendatsu* badges and other items announcing a *sendatsu* ranking and their *fuda* indicating what category (first-time; fifth, tenth, fiftieth, or 100th or more) they fall into, speak volumes about status and difference.

Consciousness of numbers can as such generate a sense of competition among pilgrims. This is not something new, as the 1895 *banzuke* with its ranking list of multiple performers mentioned in Chapter 1 indicates. Nakatsukasa's evident knowledge of other multiple performers, and his sense of competition with them, came through as well in his stone markers commemorating significant pilgrimages, such as when he surpassed Tada Emon's 136 circuits. Contemporary pilgrims, too, may be similarly focused. While they may feel a sense of awe at hearing about Fukuda Shōnosuke and his 648 circuits, some are also be spurred on in a competitive sense, seeing such high numbers as a challenge: 'If Fukuda has done it 648 times, I too can do it many times and may perhaps surpass him'. We have heard this mooted on occasion, notably from a temple priest in late October 2018, who drew our attention to such themes of competition. The priest knew two pilgrims who have made

---

[35] Sallnow 1981, 1987; Eade and Sallnow 1991; and Bowman 1991.

statements about their multiple performances. One of them, Nakano-san, had done—according to a *fuda* dated 8 October 2018 that he had left at the temple—625 circuits. The priest told us that he knew Nakano quite well, as he stopped by to chat to him every so often, and that he was aware that Nakano was conscious of homing in on what was thought to be the highest number of pilgrimages—Fukuda's 648 times. However, around that time a short article appeared in *Henro*, by the aforementioned Shimamura, the man who prints his own *fuda*. He hails from northern Shikoku and in the article he said he had been doing the pilgrimage for over sixty years and had done 703 circuits. We have interviewed Shimamura and are aware that he spends much of his time visiting the temples, dresses all the time in pilgrim clothes, and travels in a van covered in pilgrimage stickers and with a mattress in the back for him to sleep on. We are also aware that there are a number of people involved in the pilgrimage who have expressed doubts about his claim of over 700 circuits,[36] and we will discuss his case in more detail later in this chapter. The priest who was talking to us about Nakano and his interest in the number of times people had done the pilgrimage also knew Shimamura because he lived locally. The priest told us that Shimamura was a sincere devotee of the pilgrimage but that he (the priest) also was not convinced that he had done that many circuits and that he had assured Nakano of this. However, Nakano was deeply concerned about the article and, rather than being reassured by the priest's comment that Shimamura might have overstated his number of circuits, instead said that he had to strive harder to do more circuits still, in order to surpass the number that had been claimed by this other person. We heard later from another priest that Nakano, whom everyone we have talked to has portrayed as a devout pilgrim and whom we will meet again in Chapter 4, was very concerned about numbers of circuits, to the extent that the priest thought he clearly wanted to be the person who had done the most of all.

In the questionnaire we sent out to people whose names and addresses we had collected and who had done multiple circuits, we asked about attitudes to issues related to competition, numbers, and records. Our respondents invariably rejected any idea of competition and said they were put off by anyone boasting about their numbers. However, they also displayed a keen awareness of how many circuits they had done, and often remarked on the numbers done by others. Competition may be understated, but it is also part

---

[36] See note 28.

of the dynamic for pilgrims who see the pilgrimage as a way of affirming their identity and marking them out as special. The man who had written the article speaking of his 700-plus circuits emphasised that he did not have a competitive spirit, but he also cited his 700-plus circuits as well as telling us, in an interview in March 2018, about how else he was special. He had, for example, done a special ascetic practice at Cape Muroto (where Kūkai was said to have performed austerities) that, he claimed, no one else apart from Kōbō Daishi (i.e. Kūkai) had done. Similarly, he leads a pilgrimage tour every spring to Xian in China to the temple where Kūkai trained, Seiryūji, which he refers to as pilgrimage site 'zero' as he considers this to be where, in his view, Kūkai began his life journey of association with Shingon Buddhism; as such, he contends, it is the true starting place for the *henro*. In making these claims he was doing something we have encountered several times in our studies: pilgrims telling us about their practices that (in their eyes) mark them out as special and different from all others. The leader of one pilgrimage confraternity we conducted interviews with, for example, told us that his group was different from other confraternities in that it focused on hard practices (unlike, the implication was, other groups that simply went around the pilgrimage in comfort). We have heard many similar comments and will discuss these more in the later section 'Status, authority, reverence, and ambivalence', when we look at wider issues of status and authority.

Deepening faith, understanding the pilgrimage, and wholehearted commitment

A factor in encouraging continual pilgrimages is the notion that by doing it more times one deepens faith, accrues more merit and understands the pilgrimage and oneself better. We touched on this in Chapter 1 where we cited Tabuchi Yoshio's view that doing the pilgrimage many times could purify the spirit and bring enlightenment, and the Canadian pilgrim who said that as she did it more times the more she became aware of the nature of Kōbō Daishi. This is something that in various ways emerged repeatedly in interviews and questionnaires about the value of doing the pilgrimage again and again, and making it a central facet of one's life. Thus, for example, members of the pilgrimage confraternity we mentioned above stated that one did not really understand the meaning of the *henro* if one did it just once. In an interview in late October 2018 at Enmyōji (Temple Fifty-Three) with a male pilgrim in his fifties who was wearing a blue pilgrimage shirt, similar themes emerged. Illustrating how pilgrims can be pragmatic and determine their own rules, he told us why he wore a blue shirt; by mistake he had washed his *hakui* (i.e. white pilgrimage shirt) with blue items of clothing whose colour ran. He found the result amusing and decided to carry on wearing his now blue 'white shirt'; it marked him out as distinctive. He also told us about his history of pilgrimages. Brought up in a Shingon Buddhist household in Okayama prefecture, at a young age he was taken by his mother to local pilgrimage sites and temples associated with Kōbō Daishi. Later she took him to Shikoku to do the pilgrimage. That first time, he said, was just *asobi* (fun, entertainment, tourism) and not serious in nature. He then, some years later, took his son to do the pilgrimage, again as a form of entertainment and relaxation, and not, he stressed, related to faith. However, then his parents died one after another, and he did the *henro* again as a memorial service (*kuyō*) for them; later other people close to him died, so he did the pilgrimage as a memorial for them too. As he did so, he said, his attitude changed. The pilgrimage was no longer something related primarily to enjoyment and tourism; it had developed deeper meanings for him. He had, by the time we talked to him, done it ten times by car (he said he was limited to once a year for economic reasons) and through those journeys his thoughts had changed. The pilgrimage was now, he said, a way of finding meaning in life, of helping him deal with the loss of family and friends, and of thinking about how to live in future.

Such experiences and ways of thinking recurred regularly in our interviews. Pilgrims we talked to often said that they did not really know much about the pilgrimage the first time they did it. This lack of knowledge is often a reason why many pilgrims choose to travel with someone else more experienced, for instance, as part of a pilgrimage group under the guidance of an experienced *sendatsu*. After this initial experience they felt motivated to do it again, perhaps to spend more time at each temple or to check up on aspects of the pilgrimage and temples they might have missed or overlooked in their first visit. As they did this they became more aware of the contours and nature of the pilgrimage and learned more about themselves, perhaps also feeling that their sense of faith was deepening and that they could become authorities able to guide others. This in turn was something that further inspired them to do the *henro* again, and again. Doing the pilgrimage, in other words, opens up a path to repetition and to deepening one's experience and awareness of the pilgrimage—and of oneself as well. Sometimes, too, we heard pilgrims say that it is important in whatever one does to do it whole-heartedly; as members of the aforementioned pilgrimage confraternity said, if one is going to do something one should do it *isshokenmei* (wholeheart-edly)—something that frequently with Shikoku pilgrims means making it the main focus of their lives.

Status, authority, reverence, and ambivalence

As we have indicated already, there is a flexibility to the Shikoku pilgrimage; pilgrims can determine how they travel, whether to do it in one go or in short stages, and so on. Although there is a formal organisation, the *Shikoku Reijōkai*, that coordinates temple activities, it has little authority over how pilgrims operate and how they engage with the pilgrimage. The image of Kōbō Daishi being with each pilgrim gives pilgrims an autonomy that is an important element in its appeal. This lack of overarching authority, some-thing not uncommon in pilgrimage in general, opens up space for pilgrims to develop a sense of individualised authority and to enhance their standing within the wider pilgrim community.

Performing pilgrimages multiple times is one avenue towards acquiring such authority. Shinnen is an early such example. The knowledge he built up, enabling him to know where best to place pilgrimage guideposts and what to include in his guidebook, could only have been gleaned from multiple per-formances and extended engagement with the pilgrimage route. As such he became an early authority in the pilgrimage, able to influence others through his guidebook, his published collection of miracle tales, and his pilgrimage stone markers, all of which shaped how others experienced the pilgrimage. Later pilgrims also attained status and authority from similar immersion in and extended performances of the pilgrimage. Nakatsukasa, for example, achieved a high degree of authority because of his continuing unending pil-grimage. This enabled him to produce a guidebook telling others how to be-have on the pilgrimage, as well giving him an aura and reputation for being able to bestow healing and blessings on others.[37]

In more modern times this development has continued. Reader has previ-ously discussed the activities of Miyazaki Tateki, a retired futon maker (now deceased) from Matsuyama in Shikoku who initially walked the pilgrimage

[37] Mori 1986: 105–107.

in 1979 and, frustrated at the lack of information for walkers and the difficulty of finding the correct path, devoted his later years to researching the
route and erecting new signposts specifically for the benefit of walkers.[38]
In all, during the next thirty years, he erected over 2000 such signs around
the pilgrimage route, set up a walking pilgrimage support group, and produced a detailed guidebook for walkers, initially published in Japanese and
later translated into English. He also organised group activities focused on
clearing sections of the pilgrimage route where they passed through mountain and forest areas. Miyazaki viewed himself as an authority on where the
correct pilgrimage path should run, had strong views about the right way
to do the *henro* (by foot), and was critical of bus pilgrimage tours as well as
of the temples, which he saw as too ready to accommodate bus tours and
not supportive enough of walkers. He also identified with past figures in the
henro's historical landscape, regarding himself especially as following in the
footsteps of, and in a sense as being a latter-day representation of, Shinnen.[39]
Miyazaki died in November 2010 on the pilgrimage route; he had parked his
vehicle and set out into the hills to clear a section of path but did not return
afterwards. It was not until several days later that his body was found, and it
appears that he died, aged seventy-five, while working on the pilgrimage trail
that had become the focus of his life for the past thirty or so years.

We have earlier mentioned Tabuchi Yoshio, and he is another example of a
devout pilgrim who became a venerated pilgrimage authority figure. Tabuchi
was heavily involved in pilgrimage support societies, notably a confraternity
from Osaka, the Osaka Rakushinkai, and the Kansai Sendatsukai, the official representative body of Shikoku *sendatsu* living in the Kansai region, and
of which Tabuchi served as leader for some years.[40] He is now commemorated by a statue at Temple Two, Gokurakuji, that was erected by his disciples
after his death. Tabuchi had put up a stone marker at this temple in 1987 to
commemorate his 100th circuit; the stone records that he first did the *henro*
in 1929 and completed his 100th on 2 August 1987. After his death members of the Osaka Rakushinkai erected the statue and a metal plaque next

---

[38] Reader 2005: 259–262.

[39] These themes emerged in an interview Reader conducted with Miyazaki in April 2000 at
Miyazaki's house in Matsuyama, in which Miyazaki stated that he saw himself as a successor to
Shinnen because of his work in developing and revitalising the pilgrimage. He also said that in areas
where the older pilgrimage paths (there were often many such, rather than one single route) had disappeared due to modern developments, roads, and so on, he felt he had the authority to decide where
the path should run.

[40] Reader 2005: 88–92.

to it that provides a somewhat hagiographic account of his life. It states that 'Tabuchi *sendatsu*' was born in 1909 in Wakayama-ken and began doing the pilgrimage while young. He received Kōbō Daishi's blessing in his twenties while on pilgrimage and continued doing the *henro* for the next seventy or so years, completing well over 100 circuits, not on his own behalf but for the benefit of others whom he guided in various ways. Tabuchi, the plaque states, was sustained through numerous difficulties (illness, the sudden death of his eldest son, business difficulties) by his faith in Daishi and gained peace of mind and spirit through the *henro*; he was a lay believer who spread his spiritual virtue (*kudoku*) to ordinary people, giving them strength and guiding them in their lives. It was for such reasons, members of the Rakushinkai stated, that they had put up the statue in 2001 after his death.

Others besides Tabuchi who have been involved with, set up or led pilgrimage confraternities and associations have also become revered authority figures through their pilgrimage experiences. Naitō Kinpō (d. 1973) who founded the pilgrimage association the Shiga Shingyōkai and whose descendants continued Naitō's proselytising about the pilgrimage is another representative of this tendency.[41] In our fieldwork in Shikoku we have encountered other such leader figures who head pilgrimage confraternities and who have acquired a status and authority because of their continuing pilgrimage activities. The confraternity whose visit to Kōyasan was described in Chapter 1, and whose leader had done over 230 pilgrimages in Shikoku, is a good example of a social group focused on pilgrimage whose founder and leader has acquired special status and authority as a result. We will say more about this group in Chapter 5, but here note that we have met other pilgrimage groups led by individuals who had—in the eyes of their group—a special authority through his or her (albeit more often his) depth of experience as a pilgrim.

Individual authority figures

One need not be the leader of a pilgrimage confraternity or organisation to claim or attain authority status. The capacity or potential to become an authority figure is also enhanced by modern developments such as the internet

---

[41] Reader 2005: 92–93. See also the book produced by the Shiga Shingyōkai (Shingyōkai Honbu (ed.) 1981) that outlines its history and the role of Naitō.

and modern media that allow people to publicise themselves and their views in an unmediated way. Frequently we have met pilgrims who have become authorities (or, often, self-styled authorities), offering advice and operating as guides and leaders to others. For example, in March 2018 we met three men from Nishinomiya in Hyogo prefecture at Temple Thirty-Nine. One was dressed in the brown work clothes known as *samue* worn by Buddhist priests when doing tasks such as cleaning at temples; the other two wore white pilgrimage clothing. The man in brown led the others in chanting and reciting sutras at the temple and appeared to direct them in other areas as well. When we spoke to them the man in brown said he was not a priest and that his main focus in religious terms was on venerating the *kami*, the deities of the Shinto tradition. However, after falling sick with cancer and needing to have surgery, he had been called to do the pilgrimage by Kōbō Daishi, and so he went to Shikoku. This, he said, aided his recovery and led him to come back again and again for the sake of his health. On average now he has, over the past fourteen years, done the *henro* around seven times a year, and was close to 100 circuits. He does it by car and always takes one week, staying always at the same places each night. He does not now carry a *nōkyōchō* as he said he was fed up with the attitude of people at temple offices and did not wish to give them any money (as fees for the stamp). The other two men had done the pilgrimage respectively five and three times. They had been inspired to do the pilgrimage by the man they were travelling with and said that they were guided by him and followed his instructions. As such he was their teacher and the authority through which they experienced the pilgrimage. He, as is clear, had his own interpretations and orientations, and determined his— and their—way of doing the pilgrimage.

Ozaki, the businessman from Osaka discussed in the Introduction who goes to Shikoku every weekend and who sleeps in his car, is another example of self-determined authority. Happy to meet us for an interview, he presented his view of the pilgrimage (including, as we note later, criticising homeless pilgrims who live permanently on the route) and gave us a copy of a short self-published handbook for first-time pilgrims on foot, outlining what, in his view, are the appropriate ways to behave as a pilgrim. His instructions range from fairly standard comments about the appropriate ritual practices to be performed at the temples, to more personal views such as telling pilgrims not to put their rucksacks on benches in temple precincts since these benches are for the benefit of all and should not be cluttered up with backpacks. The handbook contains much useful practical information (e.g. lists of cheap and free lodgings, maps, and distances), but it also is an extension of his own perspectives on the pilgrimage, based in his view of himself as an authority.[42]

Some such self-styled authorities implicitly portray others as lacking legitimacy in the ways they do the pilgrimage. The businessman Ozaki, as we have said, was highly critical of pilgrims who relied on begging, while Nakagawa-san, who blogs regularly and whom we interviewed in his hometown of Imabari in Shikoku, told us about the correct ways (as he saw it) to do the pilgrimage. This, unsurprisingly, was the way that Nakagawa and his wife (both had made over fifty circuits) did it. They worked all week and visited the temples at weekends, driving to and from their home in Imabari. They did it carefully, spending significant amounts of time at each temple to pray, perform appropriate rituals, and venerate Kōbō Daishi. For Nakagawa the focus was clearly on the temples themselves, *Daishi shinkō*, and prayer. He stressed the importance of spending significant amounts of time at each temple, visiting all the halls of worship, reciting prayers and sutras, and doing what he considered to be the correct ritual activities at each. To do it this way—the 'correct way' he asserted—would take a minimum of nine and more commonly ten full days by car.

He portrayed his experience in the pilgrimage, based on his number of circuits and how he had done them, as special, above and beyond that of others. When we commented that others had done it many more times than him, thereby implying (and, to be honest, seeking to test what his reaction might be) that others were in reality more experienced authorities than him, he demurred, repeating that to do the whole pilgrimage by car properly would take between nine and ten days. Those who did it more quickly were not doing it correctly; as such he considered people who had done hundreds of pilgrimages and been round many more times than him to be less experienced and less authoritative than he was.

Of course, we have met others who have expressed different views and have told us about 'the' correct (i.e. their) way to do the pilgrimage and who have asserted their authority on the subject. When we asked Hara, the ascetic mentioned in the Introduction, about people who had done the *henro* many hundreds of times he expressed a lack of respect for them, since he saw the pilgrimage as a form of asceticism and paid no attention to numbers of circuits. Consequently those who went by car and focused on speed and

---

[42] Ozaki (pseudonym) 2018.

numbers fell outside his perception of how one should do the pilgrimage. This is a not uncommon attitude among pilgrims who go by foot and who regard their mode of travel as the most correct—a theme found repeatedly in studies of pilgrimage[43]—even as others (e.g. those who go repeatedly by car) might view *their* depths of experience as authoritative. Several of those we have interviewed or received completed questionnaires from who state that they do the pilgrimage by foot, have displayed a general lack of regard for very high numbers of circuits, often commenting that those who do it a hundred times or more are only travelling by car, and suggesting that they, as walkers, manifest a more authoritative mode of pilgrimage.

Multiple performers as figures of reverence

Some pilgrims not only acquire a sense of authority but also become a focus of reverence due to their extended pilgrimage activities. Tabuchi, whose followers put up a statue and a reverential plaque to him, is one such example. Another is Fukuda Shōnosuke, whom we have mentioned on several occasions already and who died in 2017 after having completed 648 circuits of the pilgrimage. Temple Six, outside which stands the stone commemorating Fukuda's 500th circuit, also has a glass case in which numerous of Fukuda's *fuda* are mounted. As he showed it to us, a priest at the temple narrated stories that highlighted what he saw as Fukuda's quiet self-effacing kindness and dedication. He portrayed Fukuda as a devout pilgrim well known for generosity and thinking of others. He told us stories of Fukuda giving alms to fellow pilgrims and of pilgrim groups excitedly reporting how they had met Fukuda and been blessed by him waving at them. Such stories were reinforced by newspaper articles about Fukuda's multiple pilgrimages, in which Fukuda explained how he began to do the pilgrimage as a memorial for fellow soldier friends with whom he had served and who had died in war, and for his deceased wife. Fukuda's repeated pilgrimages helped bestow on him an aura of sanctity, illustrated by the ways the above priest praised him. An article in the pilgrimage newsletter *Henro* from July 2008 further illustrated this point when it reported on the dedication of a new statue of Kobo Daishi at Temple Seventy-Three, Shusshakuji. As the article noted, once the

---

[43] See, for example, Frey (1998)'s discussions of attitudes among pilgrims on the Santiago Camino and about concepts of 'authenticity' there; see also Reader 2005 for further discussions on such issues in Shikoku.

statue was dedicated and the head priest had performed an act of veneration before it, Fukuda Shōnosuke led the lay worshippers attending the dedication service up to pay their respects.[44] He was, in such terms, viewed by
fellow pilgrims and temple priests as a special figure who could lead other
pilgrims in ritual services.

Similar levels of respect and veneration are found in blogs about the pil-
grimage; just meeting Fukuda appears to have been a significant event for several bloggers. One states that he was able to see a statue of Kannon at Temple
Seventeen that pilgrims cannot normally view—because it is a *hibitsu* (hidden
Buddha[45] that pilgrims could not normally see)—because he was there with
Fukuda, who spoke to the priest and got them access.[46] The radio personality
Taoka Hiroko, who accompanied Fukuda from Temple One to Ten during one
of his pilgrimages in 2014, writes that Fukuda was surrounded by 'fans' at the
temples he visited and received gifts of *settai* from them.[47]

We gained further insights into this veneration when we interviewed a
couple from Kobe in March 2018 at Temple Thirty-Seven. They told us that
they had full work schedules but managed to visit Shikoku every month for
two to three days to do sections of the pilgrimage. Thus far the man had done
the *henro* thirty times and his wife fifteen. They were devotees of Kobo Daishi
and also revered other pilgrims who had long histories of the *henro*. They
illustrated this by producing a photograph of the wife posing with Fukuda
and Nishiyama-san, a female pilgrim from Tokushima in her eighties, who
did the pilgrimage 309 times with her husband by car. We have seen *fuda*
from Nishiyama indicating that she and her husband used to do the pilgrimage regularly; their 306th circuit was in September 2017, their 307th
in October, and 308th in November 2017. It appears they managed one
more circuit before he died, sometime in early 2018 and that she no longer
did the pilgrimage as a result (and also, we were told, because she did not

---

[44] *Henro* 280, July 2006 p. 1.

[45] Some statues are considered especially powerful, kept hidden or enclosed on altars and are only
opened for public viewing very occasionally; see, for example, Rambelli 2002.

[46] Blog   of   Kagawa   Yūki   at   http://blog.livedoor.jp/sanmeigaku/tag/
%E3%81%8A%E9%81%8D%E8%B7%AF (accessed 9 December 2019). This blog also claims that
Fukuda did his first 300 pilgrimages barefoot—something that we have not heard from any other
source. We do know from every source we have read and everyone we have spoken to that he did all
his pilgrimages by car.

[47] Blog of Awaji Kyōiku Sabisu (Awaji Education Service), at http://blog.goo.ne.jp/goo623695/e/
a5dd5f4b6dda2dabf73491b6ec2daf00 (accessed 9 December 2019). Taoka's account is included in
this blog, in which she mentions being Facebook friends with him and uses the loanword 'fan'. She
also states this was his 648th pilgrimage.

drive).[48] She was, however, well known among pilgrims and temple officials and was often spoken about with reverence. This was the case with the pilgrim couple at Temple Thirty-Seven who showed us their photograph of Fukuda and Nishiyama, which they kept in their *nōkyōchō* along with the *fuda* of other famous pilgrims they had met. They said they hoped to follow in their footsteps by doing multiple circuits and that for them Fukuda and Nishiyama were not simply fellow pilgrims but holy people to be respected, revered, and emulated. Temple officials too, at times, can express similar views about well-known multiple performing pilgrims; at Temple Thirty-Nine, for example, the two ladies working there took out a bundle of brocade *fuda* left by various pilgrims and commented on what they saw as the striking 'aura' (one lady used the foreign loanword here) of a man who had done the pilgrimage over 200 times and who, they thought, was the most devout of all.[49] In Chapter 3 we will mention an itinerant pilgrim who appears to be revered by those who know him and who see him as a highly spiritual and unworldly figure.

Status and ambivalence

While doing the pilgrimage multiple times can bring pilgrims special recognition from the temples and respect (and sometimes reverence) from fellow pilgrims, one should not think that this is always the case. There are some who look at people with very high numbers in a different light. When discussing reasons why people might do the *henro* multiple times one priest, although discussing it with us in Japanese, used a single English word: 'status'. He elaborated on this by saying that in his view people gained status from fellow pilgrims from being able to say they had done the *henro* X number of times. He added that they generally had deep faith but nonetheless he thought that those who did it multiple times were motivated primarily by status.

It is rare to hear such views expressed so candidly. Moreover it is evident that not all who spend endless time on the pilgrimage are focused on status, as we have already suggested was the case with permanent homeless itinerant

---

[48] This was information gleaned from informants at a number of temples, although no one knew a precise date for the husband's death.

[49] This man was one we sent a questionnaire to but did not receive a reply. Our general sense—also from other conversations with people working at the temples who came into contact with him—is that he is someone who did not open up to others or discuss in any detail why he did so many pilgrimages.

pilgrims (see also Chapter 3). Nonetheless not everyone is impressed with those who do hundreds of circuits, especially by car. One Buddhist priest who runs a pilgrimage confraternity dedicated to walking the pilgrimage and who has himself walked it seventeen times was less than positive when we said a key focus of our study was on those who had done 100 or more pilgrimages, saying that such people were just going by car and indicating that he was not particularly impressed by such things. One of our questionnaire respondents, who had walked the *henro* many times, commented that people he met who had brocade *fuda* were very clean with spotless pilgrimage shirts. This he saw as the special nature of *kuruma henro* ('car pilgrims'); they have not got dirty, as happens when one walks. For him the pilgrimage was about following Daishi's footsteps and as such, not using cars. While he realised that some people could not—for reasons of time and bodily impediments—go any other way than by car, he was clearly unimpressed by numerical performances.[50]

The priest who earlier told us about Nakano and the man who lived in his locality and claimed to have done over 700 circuits, spoke about the diligence and determined nature of the former and of the devout sincerity of the latter, even as he was unsure about his numerical claims. At the same time, however, his comments, accompanied by a quiet shake of the head, indicated that, despite his respect, he did not fully understand this drive to constant repetition and that in many ways he found it disturbing and problematic. It was as if he recognised that both had got *Shikokubyō* and were 'addicted' to the pilgrimage, while not viewing such things in a wholly positive way.

Shikokubyō, henro 'senility', addiction, and obsession

The ambivalence indicated by the aforementioned priest is something that surfaces from time to time when discussing those who perform the pilgrimage repeatedly. This unease is hinted at by terms such as *Shikokubyō* and *henro boke* and by notions that the pilgrimage can be 'addictive'. In general those involved in the pilgrimage use such terms as *Shikokubyō* and *henro boke* in an endearing way, but some view them less positively. A small

---

[50] Such views recur frequently in pilgrimage literature, and not only about Shikoku; Frey (1998), for example, indicates similar (perhaps even more pointed) views expressed by walkers on the Santiago Camino to those who go to Santiago de Compostela by car, plane or bicycle.

number of pilgrims we have talked to or received questionnaire responses from, have expressed dislike of terms such as 'illness' (*byō*) because they associate it with something negative and reject the idea that, in doing the *henro* dozens or hundreds of times, there is something wrong with them.

The pilgrimage is also in some quarters referred to as the *Shikoku byōin*, 'Shikoku hospital', a place of healing that helps people psychologically and cures them of all manner of problems.[51] In earlier times, many people came to Shikoku to do the pilgrimage seeking cures not just for diseases in an era prior to the advent of modern medicine but also for emotional problems. As we saw with Nakatsukasa, he went there in emotional pain and to soothe his grief at being refused permission to marry his beloved, and in a sense Shikoku healed him and enabled him to get over that hurt. It also clearly got him addicted to a life of constantly circling the island on pilgrimage. While nowadays, thanks to Japan's modern health system, people no longer need to do the pilgrimage in a desperate search for healing, the view that it can assuage emotional grief and help people deal with other problems remains strong. For instance, a growth in the numbers of walkers and begging pilgrims in the 1990s was widely seen as a result of middle-aged or older men losing their jobs in the economic downturn and often finding their marriages collapsing as well, leading them to go to Shikoku to cure themselves psychologically.[52] Previous research into the diaries of troubled Shikoku pilgrims indicates that while some sort of soothing psychological salve is sought through the experience, it is often the unexpected rigours and challenges of the journey that are perceived as creating the desired mental transformations.[53] As such, the 'Shikoku hospital' sometime employs a decidedly unanticipated cure more akin to 'shock treatment'.

To the extent that there is any sense of ambivalence around the idea of *Shikokubyō* is because of an awareness that the addictiveness of the pilgrimage can have troubling dimensions. One respondent to our questionnaire (a man who had done the pilgrimage fifteen times, the first by car and the next fourteen on foot) said he knew three people who had done it multiple times; one had done it 518 times and the others 192 and 132 times respectively. He noted that they all smiled as they told him that they could not stay very long at home; they were clearly addicted in ways that set them apart from their actual physical homes. So, too, was the man from Matsuyama

---

[51] Hoshino and Asakawa 2011: 38.
[52] Reader 2005: 27–28; Shultz 2013.
[53] Shultz 2013.

whom we mentioned in the Introduction, who could barely stay a day or so at his home before wanting or needing to get back on the pilgrimage path. A pilgrim who had retired from work and who had done over 250 circuits, mainly by car, said something similar; he just could not stay at home for long before needing to get back on the pilgrimage. He also added that if he stayed at home he would do little apart from drink; the pilgrimage thus may have been a form of addiction but it also served as a way to avoid the damaging effects of another type of addiction. We have met several others who have said that their associations with the pilgrimage—their visits, as it were to the *Shikoku byōin* and their engagement with *Shikokubyō*—were similarly therapeutic and associated with avoiding another form of addiction. As a pilgrim—again a retired man—on his fourth circuit by foot told us when we met him at a roadside service area in Tokushima prefecture, when he was at home he would feel he had too much time on his hands and would start drinking too much. At such times he would need to go off on the pilgrimage again in order to break the drinking habit; the pilgrimage might have been an addiction, but it was a counterweight to an even more dramatic one he faced when at home. This has led to some commentators arguing that compulsive pilgrims are simply substituting one addiction for another, a point made to us by a community organiser in Tokushima, who considered that such people are not truly healing themselves or addressing their underlying problems.

We consider that in order to fully understand the issue we are dealing with—multiple, incessant performances of pilgrimage—we need to be aware of issues such as addiction and obsessive behaviour, and to recognise, as do the various people we have cited here, that repetition can be highly ambivalent. Those who wholeheartedly embrace their recurrent pilgrimages and respect or revere those who devote their lives to the pilgrimage, are often, we have found, conscious that such activities and behaviour are beyond the parameters of the normal. Frequently those who do repeated pilgrimages have recognised this in discussions with us. This ambivalence came through frequently in interviews with temple priests as well, several of whom simultaneously expressed admiration for the devotion of people who come repeatedly to their temples, while indicating that they find it strange and even disturbing.

We are not by any means saying that everyone who does the *henro* multiple times is obsessive or addicted. However, we do recognise that such themes are evident in at least some of the behaviour and intense and recurrent activities we describe in this book. Especially when considered alongside the question of whether pilgrims reliably report how many circuits they have done, we think this shows that there are often elements of tension and ambivalence in the pilgrimage. Such issues are evident, for example, in the case of Shimamura, whom we have referred to several times already. As we have noted, he claims to have done over 700 pilgrimages, while others, including a priest who knew him, have doubted this figure (see also note 28). We have asked about him at many temples around Shikoku (usually showing officials the brocade *fuda* that he had given us during an interview), but few temple officials have expressed knowledge of him, whereas they generally knew or knew of others who did the pilgrimage large numbers of times. At the same time, other people have assured us of his veracity. We were, for example, first introduced to him by the owner of a free lodge for pilgrims in southern Shikoku, who, on learning of our project, insisted we had to meet Shimamura who, he said, was a devout pilgrim who had indeed done 700 pilgrimages around Shikoku.

There is, in other words, an ambivalence surrounding this man in terms of how many pilgrimages he has done and whether or not he is exaggerating the figure. We cannot say either way. At the same time, and this perception permeates this entire study, we also do not consider if it really matters whether he and others who make grand claims about their pilgrimage activities are 'genuine' in the sense of being rigorously accurate about their number of circuits. We first spoke to Shimamura by telephone from the house of the aforementioned lodge owner and arranged a rendezvous with him at a shopping mall car park near his house. He told us he would be recognisable because he would be wearing full pilgrimage regalia and brandishing a flag with pilgrimage symbols on it. Indeed, as we perused the car park, in pouring rain, we saw him wearing a pilgrim's bamboo hat, a long white pilgrim's robe and white trousers, and waving a large flag inscribed with the ideograms of Kūkai's name. His van was covered with stickers and symbols about the pilgrimage and had a bed in the back, which he slept on during his pilgrimage travels.

We went to his house and interviewed him there, where he showed us his computer, on which he prints his *fuda*, along with scrapbooks of his pilgrimage activities and numerous photographs of him at various pilgrimage sites. He lives alone. The house is a de facto shrine to pilgrimage, full of pilgrimage items, from a pilgrim's shirt that is soaked in ink from having been stamped at multiple temples, to his Buddhist altar at which he makes offerings each day. He told us that he was introduced to the pilgrimage by his mother when he was fifteen (she also had done it several times) and had been doing it ever since, a span of sixty years. He had lost his job many years back and ever since had focused on going to temples virtually every day, while he used his redundancy and unemployment money and later his pension to support his pilgrimage activities. He always, he said, dressed as a pilgrim whether temple visiting or not; he had not dressed up specially when he drove to the mall to meet us. That was his normal daily wear, even when shopping. We met him briefly the next day as he was on his way to meet up with and take a group of neophyte pilgrims to some of the temples, something he said he did often. Whatever the facts about his number of circuits might be, it is clear that his life remains obsessively involved with the pilgrimage. To that extent, whether he had done 700 pilgrimages or not might be less relevant than the evident point that his life was one of total immersion in envisioning himself as, and acting as, a pilgrim.

This view was also expressed by the priest who said that a key motive for doing multiple circuits was to acquire status. We raised the question with him of people who might overstate their number of circuits for this reason and whether they might be potentially fraudulent. The priest replied by saying that he thought that any such potential improprieties were inconsequential. As long as they were out on the pilgrimage path, at or visiting the temples, it was fine. After all, it was up to each person how they engaged with the pilgrimage. 'Fraudulent' pilgrims (or, rather, those about whom some doubts had been raised) were, after all, still people engaged with the *henro*, whether just hanging around temples wearing *henro* clothes and claiming hundreds of circuits. They were in such ways demonstrating an absorption in the pilgrimage. We concur with this. Whether Shimamura has done 700 circuits is less important than the point that his daily life is permeated by issues related to the pilgrimage so that he, like many others, appears to have a form of addiction that falls within the remit of our study.

A spectrum of multiplicity and the idea of 'permanence'

Although we have used terms such as 'permanent pilgrims' and unending pilgrimage as framing devices for this study, it is clear that most of those we have spoken of thus far are not 'permanent' in the sense of living all the time without cease on the *henro* path. In reality the numbers of people who are fully 'permanent' on the pilgrimage are relatively few and far between. Beyond them are many others who exist on a spectrum of types of multiple performance, spending significant portions of their lives involved with the pilgrimage centred around not just multiple performances of but also an overarching absorption in the pilgrimage. They may be serial, perpetual, and/or professional in nature, in that they return again and again, often at set times, to the *henro*, and/or find it to be a source of economic support for them. Some such as Fukuda and Nakano who do hundreds of pilgrimages by car, living in them during their travels and spending thirty, forty, or more weeks a year on the route, are very close to being permanent while not living wholly on the route. Others like Ozaki, who go weekend in and weekend out to walk sections of the route and who embed pilgrimage into their life and work routines, along with those who do the *henro* on a regular basis, and those who join confraternities that make regular monthly visits to the temples, are all in varying ways *on the way* towards permanence. Because, too, they almost invariably say that they will continue doing the pilgrimage as long as they are able and will only be stopped by infirmity or death, they are also on an unending pilgrimage, one that frames and permeates the entirety of their lives.

When we began this study we discussed what parameters we should use to identify the people included within it. Initially we talked about a lower limit of forty pilgrimages by car or other forms of transport, or seven pilgrimages by foot. Each would take a considerable amount of time (250 or more days for forty car-pilgrimages, 280 or more for seven foot-pilgrimages). However, it became clear as we started doing interviews that beyond any numerical frameworks one also had to think about mental ones. We talked to people who had not yet reached the numbers we used as our original defining framework and found that mentally they already aspired to go far beyond such numbers and were already of a mindset that kept them involved in the pilgrimage even while at home. A man met at Temple Twenty-Four in November 2019 is one example. From Kyoto, he was seventy-two years old and on his twelfth circuit. He had retired five years earlier and since then had done the pilgrimage twice a year, each spring and autumn, driving and sleeping mostly in his car but sometimes stopping at hotels. He had originally come to Shikoku not as a pilgrim but to visit a former schoolmate who was a priest at a temple in Shikoku. He had become fascinated by Shikoku and as a result decided to do the pilgrimage to learn more about the place. It was not, initially, he said, anything to do with faith, but gradually he had become absorbed by this aspect of the *henro* and had become a believer in Kōbō Daishi; he also emphasised how good the Shikoku scenery was and that doing the pilgrimage was good for his health and kept him fit. As a result he now regularly did the pilgrimage twice a year and in between focused on doing extensive planning for the next trip. As such, he said, the pilgrimage was part of his 'life cycle' (*raifu saikuru*—he used foreign loanwords here). He also said that he would continue doing the pilgrimage until he was no longer able to drive, at which point he would go on pilgrimage bus tours until he was no longer able to get on or off buses. He clearly viewed the pilgrimage not as some distinct entity apart from his everyday life; it was something that was unending and integral and central to his very life and being.

The couple met at Temple Thirty-Seven who revered and carried a picture of Fukuda and Nishiyama similarly had an unending perception of pilgrimage. They not only wanted to do more pilgrimages but aspired to be like those they revered by doing hundreds of circuits. If Fukuda, as we suggested above, was on the way to permanence, so, were they. Likewise we met several people who have walked the pilgrimage a small number of times—such as the man who said it was his fourth time and that every so often he has to set off again on pilgrimage to stop himself drinking—but who aspire to do it again and who say they wish to keep it doing while they are physically able. For them, too, the Shikoku pilgrimage becomes a permanent element in their lives, something that surfaces repeatedly while at home and that they wish to do until they are no longer able. We will encounter many such examples in Chapters 5 and 6.

As a result we use the term 'unending pilgrimage' to refer to a wide spectrum of people, from those who live on the route to those who have done it just a very few times but who aspire to continue doing it again and again. For all such people there is a sense of absorption and unending engagement with the Shikoku pilgrimage that is close to (and may well be or become) an addiction. They may have *Shikokubyō* and recognise it as a form of welcomed addiction, feeling a sense of permanent association with the pilgrimage that they do not wish to ever end. As such, although we look at people across a spectrum in terms of actual performance, they share common ground in never really being away from Shikoku and its pilgrimage. It is always part of their lives, a central organising theme and focus, and a core source of meaning, identity, and belonging. At home they are still pilgrims. The spectrum of performance we have identified, the terms we have identified as associated with it, and the extent to which people talk of being addicted and happily stricken with 'Shikoku illness', all point to a single direction of being drawn towards doing it again and again, and of such an absorption that it may become the central organising principle of their lives.

This, we contend, is a form of permanence that helps each pilgrim develop a sense of uniqueness and self-identity. It enables them to fit into the wider pilgrimage tradition and show they are part of a continuing community–not just single voyagers on a one-time pilgrimage, and thus transient, but part of a continuum with Kōbō Daishi, the permanent ascetic pilgrims of the past such as Shinnen and Nakatsukasa, and of an unending future of pilgrimage. They incorporate the *henro* into their lives and emplace themselves recurrently or even permanently (via such things as commemorative stones) on the Shikoku landscape. It provides them with a special sense of being and meaning, as well as a continuing stimulus to further activity as a pilgrim, to match up to famous pilgrims of the past and to embed themselves in an elite category spoken of with awe. Like Yamba's 'permanent pilgrims' they mentally conceive themselves within the framework of pilgrimage. Unlike those discussed by Yamba, however, they are actively engaged in making frequent and repeated pilgrimages and in circling the route that forms the framework of their existence.

In order to flesh out these issues and give a clearer picture of some of the many people and groups engaged in such 'unending pilgrimage' activities and attitudes, we now turn in the remaining chapters of this book to case studies and examples of the people we have studied, met, interviewed, and surveyed, who have done the pilgrimage multiple times or who live as pilgrims on the route. This includes the small number who in many ways are most closely linked to the earlier history of the pilgrimage as a practice largely followed by itinerant ascetics and mendicants, namely those who in the present era remain permanently on the pilgrimage, have no set abode, and who often depend on begging for alms to sustain themselves. It is to such figures that we turn next in Chapter 3.

3

Living on the pilgrimage

Perpetual itinerancy and 'professional pilgrims'

Alms and negativity

In the Introduction we introduced Hara, the man who has lived for the past several years as a pilgrim in Shikoku and whose source of economic subsistence was *takuhatsu*, alms solicitation, a practice intimately linked with his identity as a pilgrim. As we indicated in Chapter 1, begging and the provision of alms (*settai*) for pilgrims are practices that have historically been part of the pilgrimage. They have roots in pilgrimage foundation stories relating to Kōbō Daishi and Emon Saburō, in the images conveyed in those foundation stories of the pilgrimage as a path of ascetic and incessant itinerancy, in the practices of Buddhist mendicants, ascetics and other practitioners who followed in their footsteps, and in the local culture of Shikoku. *Takuhatsu*, also, is a long standing practice for Buddhist monks meant to teach them humility. As Hara indicated, he viewed it as a religious practice and austerity that enabled him to develop spiritually. As such, alms solicitation and perpetual itinerancy would appear to be at the very heart of the pilgrimage. Pilgrims have been seen as worthy of support and alms, not just because of their associations with Kōbō Daishi but because it was recognised that some of them were in desperate need in earlier times. It was not just local people who gave *settai* to pilgrims to help them on their way; feudal authorities from the late sixteenth century onwards also took steps to provide some support for them by setting up shelters for pilgrims and assisting with the repatriation of the bodies of those who died.

However, there is also a negative connotation to the idea of pilgrims soliciting and subsisting on alms and living permanently as itinerants, based in the view that some of those who do this are not really 'genuine' pilgrims but freeloaders using the pilgrimage and local generosity to support themselves and avoid work. Historically in Shikoku a variety of terms have been used to allude to such notions, including *nise henro* (false pilgrim), *kojiki henro*

Pilgrims Until We Die. Ian Reader and John Shultz, Oxford University Press. © Oxford University Press 2021.
DOI: 10.1093/oso/9780197573587.003.0004

(beggar pilgrims), and *hendo*—a term that, as we noted in Chapter 1, plays on the idea of *henro* but implies a false and fraudulent person who is using the guise of a pilgrim for nefarious purposes.[1] Another related term we have previously mentioned is *shokugyō henro* or 'professional pilgrim', a label that appears frequently in contemporary accounts of the pilgrimage as well as historical studies and that may be elided with others that have negative connotations. Historically linked to ideas of 'false pilgrims' (*nise henro*) and those who have committed crimes and have run away to Shikoku to hide among the pilgrims, *shokugyō henro* implies that such 'pilgrims' are really dropouts who pretend to be pilgrims in order to avoid working or to flee earlier misdemeanours.[2]

As such, although people in Shikoku have historically given alms to pilgrims, and have recognised that *takuhatsu* is a legitimate Buddhist practice, there is also a long history of negativity towards those who seek alms.[3] Mori Masato outlines how pilgrims were in earlier times often beset by poverty, suffered discrimination, and fell by the wayside. He notes that many turned to the pilgrimage out of desperation; for example, some pilgrims had been driven out of their homes due to illness, notably leprosy, and had no choice but to subsist as a permanent itinerant pilgrim.[4] However, even those in desperate circumstances faced hostility and were seen as burdens on the local population; many died on their travels, causing problems for local communities and authorities, who had to deal with the corpses.[5] Furthermore, large numbers of pilgrims soliciting alms were a recurrent nuisance for those who lived on the route, while those with no money for lodgings were a recurrent problem. By the 1880s the newly developed news media not only complained of pilgrims stealing and spreading diseases, but called for government prohibitions of them as economically unproductive and antithetical to the ethos of the modern state. Concerns about 'false' pilgrims increased in the early twentieth century, with newspapers warning against giving alms to pilgrims, while the police were encouraged to conduct pilgrim round-ups (*henrogari*) of those with no money. Mori, who grew up in Takamatsu in Shikoku, also recalls how the term *hendo* was used as an insult in his childhood to imply

---

[1] See Reader 2005: 132–138; Maeda 1971: 254–270; and Hoshino 2001: 117–121 for further discussion of these issues.

[2] Shiragi 1994: 72 defines *shokugyō henro* as people who do the Shikoku pilgrimage living solely on begging and notes that they may also be viewed as *hendo* (1994: 155).

[3] Maeda 1971: 266; Shinno 1980: 217–231.

[4] Mori 2014: 118–137.

[5] Mori 2014: 120–121.

that someone was a malingerer, cheat, or beggar.[6] Asakawa Yasuhiro, another academic who grew up in Shikoku, recalls that local people used differential terms to distinguish pilgrims (*henrosan*) from those they viewed as dissolute figures seeking to live off the pilgrimage and local generosity, who were *hendo*.[7]

Such hostile attitudes have been reiterated in recent times. Several internet commentators and bloggers who record their pilgrimage experiences display negative views in the present day about *shokugyō henro*. Some cite historical antipathies to pilgrims who beg;[8] others cite specific examples to disparage all pilgrims who beg. One online commentator, for example, talks about being approached by someone dressed as a pilgrim who solicited alms but could not, when asked, recite the Hannya Shingyō (the most common sutra chanted by pilgrims), an anecdote that implies that the person soliciting alms was not really a proper pilgrim.[9] A blogger walking the pilgrimage in 2003 complained about pilgrims who made use of free lodgings but left them in a mess, or who begged aggressively and harassed homeowners for food.[10] Another blogger warned about fraudulent pilgrims by citing the example of a man in pilgrimage clothes standing outside a temple in Ehime prefecture. The blogger commented that this person had no luggage or belongings with him and looked remarkably clean, whereas someone walking the pilgrimage would have some belongings while their clothes would be road-soiled. Moreover, when no one was around he was reading a comic, which he quickly put away when he heard a bus full of pilgrims approaching. As such, the blogger complained, he was posing as a pilgrim in order to get *settai* from busloads of elderly pilgrims.[11]

Not all online comments are negative, for some do draw attention to the historical nature of begging for alms and emphasise its value as an ascetic practice representative of the values of the *henro*. However, at the same time, such online posts can (inadvertently) show why others are sceptical about begging for alms. One blogger who advocated alms solicitation, for example,

---

[6] Mori 2014: 125–129.

[7] Asakawa 2008: 43–44, 362–365.

[8] See, for example, the blog Ohenro no susume, available at www.maenaem.com/henro/sp.htm (accessed 24 Oct 2019).

[9] This blog, http://junitarou.blog95.fc2.com/blog-entry-188.html (accessed 24 Oct 2019) is no longer extant.

[10] This is in the blog of Yomifuji Nadashi, at http://www7b.biglobe.ne.jp/~karasumoridounin/sikokue3.html (accessed 24 Oct 2019).

[11] This is in the blog penned under the name Garagarahebi, at https://ameblo.jp/garagarahebi/entry-10013834408.html (accessed 24 Oct 2019).

suggested that there was little difference between professional pilgrims and businesspeople, since both are doing something to get money to maintain their lives.[12] Another blogger, who uses the blog name *henroseika*, has a history of doing pilgrimages in Japan by foot over many years, including several circuits of the Shikoku pilgrimage since 2009. He emphasises in his blog that although *shokugyō henro* have been viewed in negative ways, they have been historically important in the pilgrimage, while *takuhatsu* has roots in the pilgrimage's ascetic traditions.[13] However, his blog also indicates an interest in tallying up how much he has been able to get through soliciting alms. For example, he records receiving a total of 46 222 yen in the month of September 2009 while walking just over half the pilgrimage route; of this, 12 969 yen was from *takuhatsu* outside houses, 31 880 yen from outside supermarkets and 1373 yen from *settai*.[14] While one cannot explicitly say that his Shikoku pilgrimages are oriented towards soliciting alms, it is clear that the Shikoku pilgrimage is the central focus of his overall itinerancy and that he counts every yen received.

Overall, however, the predominant image of those who beg remains negative. Due to concerns that beggar-pilgrims were annoying other pilgrims and creating a bad image for the pilgrimage, the Shikoku Pilgrimage Temples' Association banned *takuhatsu* at and around the temples in 2007.[15] We also heard several people in Shikoku express negative views of itinerants who relied on alms solicitation and lived permanently on the route; one lady working in community affairs and supportive of the pilgrimage, expressed negative views about itinerant beggar pilgrims, complaining that they lived off rather than contributed to the local economy and that they were in her view work-shy and lazy. The businessman we discussed in Chapter 2 who spends his weekends on the pilgrimage was even more hostile. He thought there were around thirty people who were not really pilgrims but who assumed this guise to enable them to beg. They were, he said, dishonest, stole from others, spent all their money on drink, caused all manner of trouble and harassed women. He did not, however, provide us with any details to back up his views. Some temple officials we talked to also had negative views, saying

---

[12] The blogger's web name and domain name is Doroashi; the comments were accessed at https://doroashi.com/henro3-sadhu on November 2018 but no longer available.

[13] The blogger does not provide a profile but the contents of the blog imply a male, and we have been informed by another source who knows him that this blogger is an itinerant who lives much of the time on the pilgrimage.

[14] https://henroseika.exblog.jp/i8/5/ (accessed 24 October 2019).

[15] Hamaya 2009: 108; see also Reader 2014: 169–170.

there might be some people masquerading as pilgrims who stole from others and from the temples, although without giving any examples.

However, our encounters with itinerants who live more or less permanently as pilgrims in Shikoku—as well as those of Hamaya, who did field research in 2001–3 and in 2007 on alms-seeking by itinerant pilgrims—indicate that such negative portrayals are only one part of the picture and that they are often misleading.[16] Certainly there are examples of itinerants who behave dishonestly and have drink problems, and there have been cases of people with dark pasts who have subsequently lived on the road as pilgrims. In this chapter we will provide striking examples of both. However they should not be seen as indicative of all who live permanently on the route and rely on alms. We have also met itinerants who view the pilgrimage as a devotional ascetic practice, as well as permanent pilgrims for whom the *henro* provides a sense of personal freedom and liberation, who not only eschew alcohol but stay away from those who drink. In the following sections we provide accounts of a small number of people who live on the pilgrimage route; apart from two pilgrims (one of whom died recently and whose history we have reconstructed from documents and interviews with people who knew him, and the other about whom we acquired information from a number of different sources) these are all itinerants we have met personally. While few in number they reflect a broad diversity in terms of their attitudes and ways they view the *henro* and are, as such, an example of how a single pilgrimage can contain multiple variations.

Permanent itinerants: numbers and issues

It is difficult to know how many people now live as permanent itinerants on the Shikoku pilgrimage. Mori recently claimed that such people had disappeared entirely due to the development of a social welfare system that removed any need for people to live as itinerant beggars. He states that while such pilgrims could still be encountered in Shikoku up to the mid-1960s, they became increasingly rare thereafter and that by the mid-1970s *shokugyō henro* (a category in which he includes all permanent itinerant mendicants) had disappeared.[17] However, Mori overstates the

---

[16] Hamaya 2009.
[17] Mori 2014: 135–137.

case. Hamaya Mariko, discussing her field research between 2001 and 2007, identified sixteen people—all male—who were long-term pilgrims who usually slept out and were reliant on begging. We, too, as we indicate in the next sections, have encountered—at different points since the 1980s—a small number of people walking the pilgrimage who live on the route, sleep out, and are on an unending pilgrimage around Shikoku. It is clear that although there is a social welfare net these days, some people, by choice, have decided to avoid it, feeling that an ascetic path of self-discovery or the freedom they derive from being permanently on the pilgrimage are worthwhile reasons not to embrace the modern welfare system.

Hamaya's case studies

Hamaya uses pseudonyms to refer to the sixteen people she identifies as pilgrims reliant on begging. All were male. The oldest was in his seventies, while the youngest were in their forties. The time they had spent on the *henro* ranged from two years (for four of the pilgrims) to eight years (for one), with others in between. Seven walked the pilgrimage, seven went by bicycle, and two used a mixture of walking and trains. They did not all spend their whole time on the pilgrimage. Two, for instance, lived for extended periods in a park in Kōchi City; one had a cheap room he rented and used as a base; some stayed for long periods in the free or cheap lodgings (*zenkonyado*) found in various places in Shikoku for pilgrims.

Hamaya provides case studies of four of these pilgrims. The one who appears to have done the most circuits she calls Satō-san, whom she first met in 2002. Originally from Yokohama, he was sixty-eight years old and said he had first done the *henro* around twenty-five years ago when his wife was stricken with cancer. He walked it on her behalf, and after she died he began to live a life akin to that of a monk. He did the pilgrimage some fifty times in her memory, including by rental car, and then sold his house and came to Shikoku to live. In all he reckoned to have done over 100 circuits and had been living on the pilgrimage for seven years when Hamaya met him. He said he either stayed in *zenkonyado* with people he knows around island, or he slept out. Interestingly, although he told Hamaya that he had done over 100 pilgrimages, he also informed her that he no longer called in at the official eighty-eight temples and only visited the *bangai* temples associated with but not part of the official route. He also said he had a very cheap room in Ehime prefecture that he stops at on every circuit.[18]

Morita-san, aged sixty, was not going around the pilgrimage route when Hamaya encountered him but was living in a park in Kōchi. He had come to Shikoku three years earlier, initially to do the *henro* and then find work, but during his pilgrimage he ran out of money so did *takuhatsu* to support himself, and then carried on doing this thereafter. He said he had stopped going around the pilgrimage and now lived in the park, while doing some part-time work and spending his time reading about religion. He added that he sometimes, when he needed money, still went to pilgrimage temples to beg and that when he does this he chants sutras and regards it as 'work' (*shigoto*); he also said he chanted more ardently and with gratitude when someone gave him money. For him *takuhatsu* was a mechanism for survival.[19]

Himeji-san was in his sixties and had been on the pilgrimage for two years. He started doing it in despair when he felt suicidal. At this juncture he met an elderly woman who was chanting sutras and who told him to do the same and to stand in front of houses and temples to do this; this was the start of his life as a beggar-pilgrim. He begged outside supermarkets and in front of people's houses. It took him three months to do each circuit of the pilgrimage.[20]

The other person Hamaya describes in any detail, Fujimi-san, was, she said, the only one who lives solely on *settai*. She did not know how old he was or how many circuits he had done and stated that he would not divulge any information about himself to her. He carried a number of bags with him and looked homeless, wore patchwork clothes, and smelled unclean, which meant he was sometimes chased away by people and also was occasionally picked up by the police. Fujimi-san told her that he did the pilgrimage like this, as a mendicant, in order to express the religious nature of the pilgrimage. He does not beg for alms but relies on being given *settai*, and he keeps walking in the hope of meeting people who might help him in this way.[21]

None of Hamaya's case studies appear to resemble the itinerant pilgrims people we discuss. There are probable reasons for this. One is that we were doing our study on the pilgrimage route in 2018 and 2019, over a decade after Hamaya's research. People living more or less permanently on the road,

---

[18] Hamaya 2009: 109–110. Hamaya does not explain at what point in her field research she met this man or her other subjects.

[19] Hamaya 2009: 112.

[20] Hamaya 2009: 112.

[21] Hamaya 2009: 113–114.

homeless, and reliant largely on begging, especially those aged (as the majority of hers were) in their sixties and above, might well not have managed to survive that long on the road. Itinerants we talked to stressed to us the fragility of life on the road if one did not take care of oneself by eating healthily and if one drank. One of our itinerant informants, for example, spoke of a homeless pilgrim he knew who drank and died as a result. In other words, it is possible that some of Hamaya's interviewees might have stopped doing the *henro*, either through infirmity or death. Some, too, might have simply found somewhere to stay; as the earlier account shows, some of her case studies in fact appeared not to be always on the pilgrimage but had places—whether a park or a rented room—where they spent periods of times. And of course, a distinct possibility is that because of the transient nature of these people and the length of the pilgrimage route, we simply might not have met them on our field trips.

Contemporary numbers and our studies

Various people in Shikoku have made estimates (or rather guesstimates) on how many people live permanently as itinerants on the pilgrimage, albeit without providing any concrete evidence for the figures they cite. The community worker who portrayed itinerants as lazy shirkers suggested a figure or 100 or so and also indicated places where they could be found. However, when we visited these locations we encountered no such itinerants. In fact at none of the places where people in Shikoku said we could find itinerants hanging out (rather than actually walking the pilgrimage) did we find any. That suggested to us that the idea of a number of 'professional pilgrims' just lingering at certain spots was more akin to fantasy than reality. By contrast two men whom we interviewed who were long-term itinerant pilgrims suggested far lower numbers; one said (based on ten years of constant circling of the pilgrimage route) that there might be around ten or so, while the other said perhaps twenty and gave us the names of half a dozen people he knew who lived as perpetual itinerant pilgrims in Shikoku.

Priests and others working at the temples have been unable to offer any real information on this score, although we regularly asked about such pilgrims. There have been three common responses to this question. One is that it is often hard for those at temples to know if a pilgrim carrying a large rucksack is just a walking pilgrim or a homeless itinerant. Another is that permanent itinerants might not be noticed by those at the temples because they are unlikely to carry pilgrim books to be stamped and hence normally do not visit temple offices, something that the itinerant pilgrims we have interviewed confirmed. The third is that several officials and priests who have been working at temples for several decades recalled earlier times when there were pilgrims who lived on the *henro* route and pushed handcarts with all their belongings on them, but they all said could not remember recall seeing any such figures in recent years.

While we cannot say with any clarity how many people might be constantly circling the route and sleeping out, we are clear that the number is probably very small indeed and that the two pilgrims cited who estimated between ten and twenty such people are more likely than not to be reliable. Overall, in 2018 and 2019 we met and talked directly to three pilgrims who fell clearly into this category and who identified themselves as long-term perpetual pilgrims. We also encountered several others (all men) who, while not continually on the route, spend much or most of their walking it, occasionally returning to a home somewhere for brief periods, including one man who pulls a cart with some of his belongings in it and who informed us that as a rule he only spends a day or so at a time at his home and is walking the *henro* the rest of the time. He, too, will feature in this chapter, as will another itinerant about whom we heard a fair amount, both from the itinerants we interviewed and another informant who knew him well. In earlier years of research in Shikoku each of us has met other itinerants, including one whose case study appears later in the chapter. We will also introduce another man whose case we have studied in some detail, who walked around Shikoku as a pilgrim pushing a handcart for six years between 1997 and 2003 and who died relatively recently. We also know of one man who spends much (but not all) of his time on the *henro* and pushes a handcart; we think (from information passed on by a Shikoku resident who knows this person) that he is the blogger we mentioned earlier, who writes under the name *henroseika*. However, we have not been able to meet him despite continually keeping an eye out during our travels on the pilgrimage route.

We should also note that encountering, interviewing, and gathering information on permanent itinerant foot pilgrims is difficult and in reality reliant almost entirely on chance. As we noted earlier, we have visited various places where people said such homeless itinerant pilgrims could be found, but have not come across such pilgrims. They do not, as a rule, have any means of communication apart from in direct encounters; none of the pilgrims interviewed in this chapter had communication mechanisms or devices (email, phones, an address to which questionnaires could be sent) through which one could contact them or ask questions. As a result, interviewing itinerants has turned out to be a matter of serendipity rather than planning. During our visits to Shikoku we travelled around virtually the entire pilgrimage route three times by car (both clockwise and counter-clockwise) and occasionally also walked sections of the route. We stopped at every opportunity when we saw walkers to talk to them. The very small number who said they lived more or less permanently (by which we mean all but a very few days a year) on the pilgrimage route are cited in this chapter.

We should also note that all those who said that they lived on the pilgrimage appeared to have time to stop and be interviewed, even if, as noted in the Introduction, they also had schedules they wished to keep. They were certainly not hurried in the way that many of the pilgrims we met who had done dozens or hundreds of circuits by car were and who often wanted to rush on rather than stop and talk. In the following sections we present in as much detail as possible accounts of all the permanent pilgrim itinerants we know of, have interviewed or have managed to gather material about in recent years, and then discuss how the narratives of such figures indicate variations even within the small minority of those who live as permanent itinerant pilgrims in Shikoku.

Unkai the 'ascetic' drinker

The first example we introduce is one that conforms most closely to the negative images expressed about itinerants as *hendo* and as 'professional pilgrims'; it involves a permanent itinerant whom Reader and his wife met while they walked the *henro* in 1984. At the time this man was dressed in black priestly robes and was pushing a handcart loaded with all his possessions. He said that he had spent nineteen years living permanently on the *henromichi*, during which time he said he had done fifty-six circuits. On that occasion he said was doing the pilgrimage in reverse order (*gyaku uchi*) for a change. He gave his name as Unkai and said it was a Buddhist ordination name that he had received by being ordained at Kōyasan, a place he visited from time to time. The name Unkai combines the ideograms for clouds and sea, and hence conveys images of itinerancy and flux. He said that most of his time was spent circling the pilgrimage route, which was his de facto home. He was not in a hurry, and because he had just been given a load of cakes and sweets as *settai* he was happy to sit down, talk, and share them. He also gave Reader and his wife a gold *fuda* with his name on.[22]

He said he did not walk at a regular fixed pace but slowed down in the colder weather, spending most of the winter in Kōchi prefecture, the warmest part of Shikoku. Nor did he appear to be concerned about piling up the number of circuits. He said he initially had come to Shikoku to do the *henro* (although he gave no clear reason why), and became immersed in it; at the end of his first circuit he just carried on walking until eventually it became a permanent affair. As a result he had got to know people around the island, including temple priests, and had friends who would sometimes give him overnight accommodation, although mostly he slept out. He lived on the road, supported by *settai*. Unkai was very friendly and engaging and came across, at the time, as a devout figure committed to the *henro*—something also implied by his Buddhist ordination, robes, and associations with Kōyasan.

However, there is another side to his story, provided by Asakawa Yasuhiro, who paints a picture of a pilgrim with a drinking problem who resorted to theft, boasts, and dishonesty. Asakawa's account refers to a man whom Asakawa calls U-san and who, Asakawa considers, was the same person whom Reader met in 1984.[23] Asakawa also refers to Reader's comment about seeing, outside a house near Temple One on 30 January 1991, a handcart adorned with pilgrimage accoutrements including: a pilgrim's hat and staff; flags saying *Namu Daishi henjōkongō*; a Japanese flag (*hinomaru*); and a sign saying *Shikoku henro 126 kai* (Shikoku pilgrimage 126 circuits). Reader doubted that this could have been Unkai's handcart since it was only seven years since he had met him on his fifty-sixth circuit, and it seemed highly unlikely that he could have done an additional seventy circuits on foot pushing a handcart in seven years.[24]

However, Asakawa is almost certain this was Unkai's handcart. He confirms that U-san (or Unkai, as we refer to him here) went at his own pace and that those who knew and put him up never knew when he would show up. Asakawa's account also indicates that some disturbing aspects began to emerge in Unkai's behaviour during the mid- to late 1980s, including claims to have done more circuits than appeared possible. Asakawa bases

---

[22] Reader 2005: 257–258.
[23] Asakawa 2008: 400, n.36 and n.38.
[24] Reader 2005: 258.

his account on discussions with people who knew and had for long helped Unkai: a seventy-year-old lodge owner from Shikoku whom he calls Yamane-san (the name is a pseudonym) and a female worker at Yamane-san's lodge named Michihara-san (also a pseudonym).

According to Asakawa, Yamane initially met Unkai at Temple 43 in 1980 when he (Yamane) was aged fifty and himself doing the pilgrimage. At the time Yamane thought Unkai was an ascetic and a pilgrimage guide/leader (*sendatsu*). Unkai told Yamane that he had initially come to Shikoku to seek a cure for a bad foot and that his first pilgrimage took three years because of his infirmity. He then continued to walk the pilgrimage, and by the time he met Yamane had done around fifty circuits. Yamane gave Unkai his name card (*meishi*) and, some months later, Unkai contacted him to say he was in the area and had nowhere to stay; Yamane went to collect Unkai and his handcart, putting him up for free at his lodge as *settai*. After this Unkai began turning up from time to time to stay. Each time he stayed, the lodge people, besides providing free accommodation and food, would also give him some money. Unkai would give them his *fuda* in return.[25] Then, some five years after Unkai first appeared at the lodge (i.e. probably in the second half of the 1980s), Yamane received a phone call from Unkai asking for help, as his cart was broken. Yamane drove for an hour and a half to where Unkai was and found that one of the cart's wheels was broken. He contacted someone he knew who ran a bicycle shop and was able to repair the cart. As 'payment' Unkai gave the man a business prosperity amulet (*shōbai hanjō fuda*), rather than a pilgrim's *fuda*—the normal response to those who give *settai* to pilgrims. Yamane therefore asked Unkai to bring a gold *fuda* on his next visit for the person who had repaired his cart, but Unkai did not do this, thereby upsetting Yamane. After this, relations deteriorated; on his next visits, according to Yamane, Unkai started stealing small amounts of money and other things from his lodge. Yamane also said that he met the wife of a pilgrimage temple priest, who told him that U-san had stolen things from their temple, including Buddhist rosaries. Yamane noted that Unkai had become a heavy drinker, and Yamane's wife commented that he became obstreperous when drinking. As a result of such experiences Yamane said that although he initially viewed Unkai as an ascetic *sendatsu* figure he now regarded him as a *hendo*—a false pilgrim who was in reality a miscreant.[26]

[25] Asakawa 2008: 384–385.
[26] Asakawa 2008: 385–388.

Michihara-san corroborated these negative views. She had given Unkai *settai* on several occasions when he visited the lodge and had kept all the *fuda* he gave her, so that she was able to provide Asakawa with a record of Unkai's visits; it is a record that raises serious doubts about his honesty. Over a period of seven years from 1984 onwards Unkai turned up fourteen times at the lodge to get free lodging, receiving *settai* there roughly every two or three months.[27] The *fuda* he handed out during his later visits implied more circuits than it appeared physically possible for him to have done. In March 1986 his *fuda* said he had done the pilgrimage sixty-seven times; when he came in February 1988 his *fuda* said he had done it eighty-seven times, suggesting he had walked twenty times around the island pushing his handcart in under two years. Gradually Michihara, like Yamane, came to the view that Unkai was not a real pilgrim but someone using the guise to solicit alms. Besides noticing how every time he showed up he claimed more circuits than appeared possible, she felt that he became more and more troublesome and generally smelt of alcohol. She noted also how he adorned his cart with increasing numbers of decorations, such as headlights, mirrors, and signs. One sign proclaimed him to be '*gyōja Unkai*' (Unkai the ascetic), while others cited how many times he claimed to have done the *henro*. By 1991 his cart had a sign saying he had done 126 circuits—the same number of circuits as inscribed on the handcart seen by Reader in 1991. He also began to use brocade *fuda* even before he claimed to have done 100 circuits and changed the name on his cart from 'ascetic Unkai' to *Unkai hōshi* (Unkai the dharma/ Buddhist teacher). He was, it appears, by this time claiming to do the *henro* around fifteen times in a year.[28]

Asakawa's account depicts Unkai as someone who behaved in ways that correlate with popular negative images of itinerants in Shikoku; he stole, drank, turned up repeatedly seeking aid, was untrustworthy, and eventually caused those who knew him, and who had a record of helping pilgrims, to view him not as a sincere pilgrim but as a fraud and miscreant. Unkai thus serves as an example of the 'dropout' type who becomes problematic, drinking, making false claims, stealing, and abusing hospitality. One cannot say that he was always like this or that he from the outset assumed the guise of an itinerant pilgrim in order to live off others; he did not come across this way to Yamane in his initial encounter with him. Yamane's initial

---

[27] Asakawa 2008: 390–391.
[28] Asakawa 2008: 391–393.

impression—that Unkai was a sincere and devout ascetic pilgrim—also fits with Reader's view of a friendly person who was keen to share his cakes with two foreign pilgrims and to talk to them. However, it is clear that during his time as a pilgrim he had succumbed to bad behaviour, probably influenced by his proclivity to drink (something not evident in 1984), in ways that fed into Shikoku *hendo* narratives.

Hara the ascetic

Not all itinerants all like this. In 2018 we interviewed two pilgrimage itinerants, individually and on separate occasions, who displayed very different attitudes, notably with regard to money, drink, and numbers of circuits. Both made it clear that they did not drink at all, regarding alcohol as something seriously problematic that would undermine their health and pilgrimage way of life. Both also said that they were aware of itinerants who did imbibe and who also stole (from temple offering boxes and other pilgrims) but that they both kept away from such people. One of them (Shimada) said that alcohol was especially damaging to those who lived on the road and slept out; it not only damaged their health and shortened their lives, but made them untrustworthy and liable to steal. The other (Hara) also reiterated the problems of alcohol and why he kept away from it, mentioning an itinerant pilgrim he knew of named Okada-san who had died that summer (i.e. 2018) at Muroto and whose death, according to Hara, was due to drinking. He also said that drinkers were a problem for itinerants such as himself, and he emphasised that he never told such people if he had received any money when doing *takuhatsu* because he feared being robbed.

Neither Shimada nor Hara viewed all itinerants as problematic figures to avoid; Hara in particular mentioned a number of itinerant pilgrims he knew whom he regarded as good people and trustworthy fellow companions. Shimada was one of those he named. When one of us later met and interviewed Shimada and mentioned Hara's name, he (Shimada) was complimentary in return, indicating that he was one of a small number of itinerants he trusted and regarded highly. Both also referred to another pilgrim, whom we have not been able to encounter but whose reputation as a devout ascetic pilgrim was also affirmed by others, and whom we will introduce briefly later, in very positive ways.

We saw Hara just outside the gate of Temple Forty-Five, Iwayaji, late in October 2018. He was dressed fully in white—including white trainers—and was holding a Buddhist begging bowl and doing *takuhatsu*. He was not ostentatiously soliciting alms, however, but was just standing there, bowl in his hands, quietly reciting something to himself with his eyes half-closed and cast to the ground as if to avoid eye contact. When we approached him initially he appeared not to notice us, nor to hear our initial greeting, because he had earplugs in. As he later told us, one of the practices he followed regularly was silence (*chinmoku*) and when he begged, rather than directly looking at people or directly accosting anyone, he would stand quietly in prayer, remaining silent so as not to pressurise anyone to give him anything, and just accepting what (if anything) was put in his bowl. He took out his earplugs and agreed to talk to us, telling us that he was fifty-six years old, and originally from Yokohama. He had initially come to Shikoku aged thirty to walk the pilgrimage, and he had really liked it. He returned to Yokohama to work, but never married or had children, had no family, and thus was not constrained by social ties. When he reached the age of fifty he decided he had had enough of a worldly existence and felt impelled to return to Shikoku to live on the road as an ascetic; since then he had spent the last six years in this manner, walking the *henro* and doing ascetic practices in the mountains. He always sleeps out, no matter what the season or weather and said the toughest time was the hot summer period of July to August.

He regards the pilgrimage as asceticism (*shugyō*) and supports himself by begging, which he also sees as a spiritual and ascetic practice. He lives entirely on what he is given; if he gets no alms and has no money he does not eat. He does not drink alcohol and lives very cheaply on very basic foods such as ramen (noodles) and bread, both of which he described as cheap. When begging he sometimes receives money and other items; the most he has ever received in a day is 13 000 yen, but on many days he will receive nothing, and he tries to view each (being given money, not getting anything) with equanimity. He has taken a vow to always tell the truth—something he says he maintains in all but one context: when someone asks him if he has received any money from *takuhatsu*, when he simply stays silent.

He knew of a small number of other itinerants, including some he respected, even though he said it was possible they might have done bad things in the past and had left home as a result. One such was Anan-san, a man originally from Tokushima prefecture. Anan-san, Hara said, was a nickname related to the area of Tokushima he came from; no-one knew his real name. Hara said the feeling he and other itinerants had was that Anan had, or used to have, a family but that he had left because of some misdeed or other, although none knew what it was—or, indeed, if it happened at all. Although Hara thought that there might thus be a dark cloud in Anan's background that caused him to become an itinerant pilgrim, he was in Hara's eyes a trustworthy person who did the pilgrimage as an austerity. Anan-san, according to Hara, had been doing the *henro* for fourteen years and was one of several good people among the itinerants; along with him Hara mentioned a 'childlike' man named Shinohara who had been on the pilgrimage for some twenty-five years, and who was rarely seen, since he spent a lot of time alone in the mountains, an itinerant who goes solely by a nickname, Sankyū-san, and Shimada, who, according to Hara was another good person who had been doing the *henro* for some fifteen years. We will meet Shimada shortly. Here we note that Shimada says he has been doing the *henro* for ten, not fifteen years; it may be that Hara's grasp of time (at least in relation to the experiences of others) may not be exact. Others he mentioned included a pilgrim called Sakamaki-san and one named Koyoshi-san who, Hara thought, had done the pilgrimage over 100 times and was in his eyes a very good person—the most devout of all. Asked how many people lived as itinerants on an unending circuit around the pilgrimage he estimated perhaps twenty in all. But he was not really sure, especially since he keeps to himself, apart from the small number of pilgrims he had already mentioned, avoiding any whom he thinks might be drinkers or miscreants. Even if he does not see them often, he views Shimada and Anan as friends and especially respects Koyoshi.

When asked about well-known pilgrims who have done the *henro* many hundreds of times by car, he was less positive. For example, when we mentioned Fukuda as someone who was widely revered and had done over 600 pilgrimages Hara just indicated he had encountered him, said that he did not view doing the pilgrimage hundreds of times by car all that positively, and felt that those who did it like this were not friendly or sympathetic towards itinerants. In saying this he in effect drew attention to something that occurred frequently in our study: that different categories and types of pilgrim had little real contact with each other at a level that enabled them to develop mutual respect, and that walkers and car pilgrims in particular operated in seemingly different universes.

We also asked if he faced any problems as an itinerant, for example, from public authorities. He replied that he had not personally but he was aware that sometimes the police might pick up and interrogate itinerants and ask them to produce identification documents. He said this had become more common since the 2003 arrest of a famous itinerant named Kōgetsu-san, who had been living as an itinerant pilgrim for around six years when he was identified as a fugitive from justice and was arrested on charges of attempted murder; we will outline Kōgetsu's story later in this chapter. Since then, Hara said, the police had become more suspicious of pilgrims and more likely to pick them up, ask questions, and harass them. He said that he felt a general lack of trust emanating from ordinary people as well as a result, citing Kagawa prefecture in particular as an area that had become tougher for itinerants. However, despite such issues Hara said that he had had no problems or trouble with civil authorities during his extended life on the road. This is not especially surprising as, outside of begging, which he does quietly and without accosting passers-by, he maintains a low profile. In addition to sleeping out and away from others, his rucksack was neat and tidy compared to the sometimes ungainly belongings of other itinerants, and he could easily pass as a more commonly found walking pilgrim.

Hara has in many ways detached himself from the world; he has no way of accessing the news and displayed no interest in worldly affairs. He did not know, for example, that Fukuda had died and was not aware of current affairs. He also was not able to say how many times he had been around the pilgrimage and appeared unconcerned by numbers; when pressed on the matter he reflected and said he might have done around thirty circuits, but he was neither sure nor concerned about such things. He also added that sometimes he does it *gyaku* (i.e. counter-clockwise). He does not carry a *fuda* or pilgrim's book, is not a *sendatsu*, and does not exhibit any signs of status. He had not taken any Buddhist ordination and just follows his own path. When we asked if he viewed himself as similar to or akin to a priest (*obōsan*) he replied negatively; priests, he said, run temples rather than do austerities. He had a very mild, quiet, and withdrawn demeanour, spoke quietly, and bowed several times as he spoke. His aim, he emphasised, was to follow an austere life style, with the pilgrimage as part of an integrated life of asceticism that includes mountain practices and silence. To him the pilgrimage was an ascetic practice, although he recognised that for some among the itinerants who lived on the road it was more akin to a means of supporting themselves. We asked how long he thought he would continue as an itinerant pilgrim in Shikoku. He said, firmly, 'until I die' (*shinu made*).

Shimada the radio-carrying itinerant

One person Hara referred to as a respected fellow itinerant was Shimada, and we also were able to interview him. This also came about through a fortuitous encounter when one of the authors visited the Maeyama Henro Salon (see Chapter 2) in late October 2018 to investigate materials held there. It was a few days after our joint encounter with Hara. Over the road from the Henro Salon was a service area of shops and toilets, and when the author crossed over the road to buy some food, he saw a weather-beaten man with a pilgrim's staff and a large rucksack beside him, seated on a bench. We exchanged greetings and asked if the man was an itinerant pilgrim. When we received a positive response, we explained the research project, asked if he could interview the man, and received a positive reply.[29] The man had a rather leathery face and was missing a few teeth but otherwise appeared in good health—something he confirmed during the interview. He had a sweater over his pilgrim's shirt because there was a slight chill in the air, and he wore blue tracksuit-type trousers and blue trainer-type shoes. He gave his name as Shimada, a name the author in question recognised from the earlier interview with Hara; Shimada confirmed that yes, he knew and was indeed a friend of Hara, and asked after him, appearing pleased to hear that he was well when we had met him.

Shimada said he was sixty-nine years old (although to the observer he looked perhaps a little older) and had been constantly walking (*zutto aruite*) the pilgrimage for the past ten years. Initially he said he thought he had done twenty circuits but then commented that he was not really sure how many times he had been round in all; like Hara, numbers appeared to be of little significance to him. He always walked, he said, whatever the weather (even snow), although he qualified this by saying that if the weather was really bad he would, if he had some form of shelter, stay there until it improved. Asked why he was doing it he said he had no work, and that as a result he 'simply became homeless' (*kantan ni homuresu ni natta*). He comes from Yamaguchi prefecture and had worked there in a pachinko parlour doing manual jobs. However, he said, the pachinko business prefers to employ younger people, and when he was aged fifty-nine he lost his job. He had no family and because he had no work and income, was unable to pay rent and lost

---

[29] Shimada said he preferred not to be recorded but was happy for the interviewer to take notes and write down what he said as well as to clarify any points that were initially unclear. What follows is taken from the author's notes of the interview.

his accommodation. As a result he decided—in a manner not uncommon to those who lost jobs in Japan's economic recession and who turned to the pilgrimage as a way of finding themselves[30]—to go to Shikoku and walk the *henro*. The first time he did it, he said, he carried a pilgrim's book and got it stamped, but this is something he abandoned after deciding to become a permanent itinerant, as the stamps cost too much. He found it was 'easy to live on the pilgrimage path' (*henro no michi no seikatsu wa shiyasui*) and so, after finishing his first circuit he just carried on.

When asked about faith, he initially said that this was not really a factor for him, although he returned to this issue later. He said he was a friend of Hara's but had not seen him for a while; likewise he knew but had not seen Koyoshi, the itinerant whom Hara cited as really devout and whom we discuss shortly, for some time. He reiterated Hara's respect for Koyoshi. Asked how many similar *henro* (i.e. permanent walking itinerants) he knew, he said about ten people in all. When asked if this number included also '*nise*' (frauds, pretend pilgrims) and untrustworthy people of the types Hara mentioned, Shimada said no. Since he tried to keep away from anyone he felt might have devious motives, he had not been really had encountered any such people himself. Like Hara he does not drink alcohol, viewing it as a path to ill-health and other problems. Asked about health and what he does if he gets sick he said he simply avoids such things through his lifestyle. Being outdoors in the air and walking keeps him fit, and he tries to eat well and healthily. Interestingly he said that before coming to Shikoku and the *henro* he did not walk much at all. The pachinko business is not noted for its healthy lifestyles, and we wonder whether his working lifestyle in Yamaguchi may have contributed—along with being outside all the time—to his appearance of looking weatherbeaten and older than sixty-nine.

He said he supported himself by begging for alms in the traditional pilgrim manner, which he does both at temples and at supermarkets. When doing *takuhatsu*, he said, he receives money, food, and even occasionally lodging (though the latter is rare). When the interviewer asked if the temple ban on *takuhatsu* was a problem he said that it meant not being able to solicit alms inside temple precincts. However, some temples do not mind if one does it outside their gates; we should note that when we met Hara he was begging outside the gate of Iwayaji, Temple Forty-Five, with no problems. Shimada said that sometimes temple policies change; if a new head priest takes over

[30] Reader 2005: 27–28.

he might stop people begging at the gate or might rescind a previous ban. He also said that he noticed little difference between doing *takuhatsu* at temple gates and at supermarkets in terms of the alms he was given. People overall have generally been kind and helpful to him. There are places he particularly likes, including the Maeyama Henro Salon, as there is a hut there that one can sleep in. Although he was outside the Salon when interviewed, he was not going to stay there that night. It was before midday—too early to stop even though there was a good place to sleep—and so he would walk on. He was doing the pilgrimage this time in reverse order and planned to spend the night somewhere he knew near Nagaoji (Temple Eighty-Seven).

One practical question we asked was about shoes—clearly an important element in the life of a permanent foot pilgrim. How does he manage when the shoes wear out? Shimada said he simply does more *takuhatsu* than he needs to do for his normal everyday needs (i.e. food) and puts money aside bit by bit so he that he can save up enough to buy new trainers of the sort he was currently wearing—something relatively cheap but comfortable to walk in. He also—unlike Hara, who carried no electronic devices and seemed indifferent to what was going on in the wider world—kept contact with the world at large and had some knowledge of worldly affairs because he carried a small radio, which he showed us. He had a negative opinion, for example, of US President Donald Trump and knew he was widely unpopular, although he also knew Trump still had many supporters in the United States and that there were some 'strange' (*henna*) people in Japan who liked him as well.

He also seemed highly attuned to weather conditions. During the interview it grew overcast and cooler, and the interviewer wondered if it might shortly rain. No, Shimada said, looking up at the sky; the sky conditions and the westerly wind direction told him it would be clear and would not rain later. (He was correct in this forecast and informed the interviewer that in Shikoku westerly breezes generally meant good weather.) He said that because he has been doing the *henro* for a long time he has friends around the island—not just other pilgrims but people who live in Shikoku and particularly in Kōchi prefecture, which was the region he liked best, not just because it had the warmest weather but it was where he felt people were the friendliest. By contrast the area he liked least was Kagawa (*amari yokunai*). He did not wholly endorse Hara's claim that since the Kōgetsu arrest, itinerants had been subjected to increased police harassment, saying that as a rule they left him alone. However, he then added that just three days previously he had been stopped by the police in Tokushima prefecture late at night, asked where he was from, and ordered to provide details and documentation relating to his address. Since he still carried documentation from his last fixed abode back in Yamaguchi, this satisfied the police and they let him go. He did not appear to be discomfited by the experience but talked about it with equanimity.

Asked if things had changed in the time he had done the *henro*, he commented on the growth in numbers of non-Japanese pilgrims, saying that he sometimes walked with them for periods; he mentioned several nationalities, including French, Italian, Chinese, Korean, and Australians whom he had encountered, while noting that not many spoke any Japanese. He was also aware that there was a special guidebook (produced by Miyazaki Tateki) for walkers and was aware that the red signs indicating the pilgrimage path were also the work of Miyazaki and the society he had set up. He also knew Miyazaki had died.

Had his feelings changed in the years he had been doing the pilgrimage? Yes, they had. It was here that he returned to the issue of faith. Earlier he had indicated that faith was not really something relevant to his itinerancy but as the interview continued he started to open up about the issue more. Because people helped him and were kind, giving him *settai*, his sense of gratitude (*kansha no kimochi*) had grown, and he then mused about whether this could in a sense be seen as a form of faith (*shinkō*). He did not take the matter any further, however, and at no point did he mention Kōbō Daishi either in relation to faith or to his own pilgrimages.

Two related questions sought to ascertain whether he might at any stage stop his continual walking around the pilgrimage. How long did he think he would continue to walk the *henro*? Mirroring the words of Hara, he said, probably until death (*tabun shinu made*). What, however, if circumstances changed? He had initially said that he started doing the *henro* because he had lost his job, had no work, and no home. What if all that changed, and he was offered a job and a permanent place to live? Would he then give up the pilgrimage? He thought for a moment and said no; he probably would not do the work as he had become completely free (*tabun shigoto wa shinai; jiyū ni natte shimatta*). He was walking around a place he liked, and felt free; having a job and a home to live in would make him feel enclosed, shut in, and restricted. He was so used to being on the road and not having walls around him that he did not want to stop; clearly the freedom of the road trumped considerations such as the comfort and convenience of a settled home and financial security. It was at this point, having in effect affirmed his identity as a permanent itinerant, that he ended the interview, saying that it was past midday and time for him to set off again—something that indicated that even though a permanent itinerant, he also had schedules and routines. As he did so he told the interviewer that he hoped we would meet again somewhere, donned his rucksack, gave a big wave, and set off down the road.

Koyoshi the saintly ascetic

While Hara indicated that he steered clear of some itinerants for fear they might steal, he was also fulsome in his regard for other itinerants he knew, as we indicated earlier. One person in particular he spoke about in such terms was Koyoshi-san; as we noted previously, Shimada had similar views on this pilgrim. Although we have not met Koyoshi we have talked to three people—Hara, Shimada, and a lady who, with her husband, runs a small hall of worship and *settai* place near Temple Eighty-Five—who know Koyoshi, speak highly of him, and whose accounts all paint the same picture of a humble pilgrim-itinerant who leads a life of devout asceticism. Hara, had said Koyoshi was the most devout, dedicated and humble pilgrim he knew, and this was reiterated by the aforementioned lady, who described Koyoshi as a lovely and devout man who always called by her *settai* place when he was passing by. She said that he had done more than 100 pilgrimages on foot and showed the interviewer a handwritten copy of the Hannya Shingyō (Heart Sutra) that Koyoshi had inscribed for her. She said that he always sleeps out, will not accept lodgings in temples or anywhere else, does not carry *fuda* (despite having done over 100 pilgrimages), and always acts humbly. His pilgrimage is his life (*seikatsu toshite* is the term she used). She said he is from Kagoshima and at one point went back there for five years to care for his ageing mother until she died, at which point he came back to the pilgrimage route again. Nor does he have any money or actively solicit support. When asked how Koyoshi subsisted, the lady said that he does not do *takuhatsu* and that he says anything he gets to support his itinerant pilgrimage lifestyle 'comes from the heavens' (*uchū, ten kara*). We know no more about Koyoshi than this, but the accounts all three interviewees gave us produced the same picture of a pilgrim who lives a life of pilgrimage wholly focused on itinerancy, austerity, devotion, and simplicity, and does not draw attention to his number of circuits or time spent as an itinerant.

Noguchi: an itinerant avoiding his home

We met Noguchi-san, from the Matsuyama area of Ehime prefecture, early one afternoon in March 2018 on the coastal road near Cape Muroto. He was walking briskly along the roadside, pulling a luggage trolley behind him on which was draped a white pilgrim's shirt. The trolley was stacked with items, including a backpack, various bags, coats, bottles of water, and an umbrella. He wore a bamboo pilgrim's hat and carried a pilgrim's staff. We stopped to talk to him and ascertained that he, more or less permanently, now lived on and walked the pilgrimage, although he also had a home in Shikoku as well. He had been doing the pilgrimage for about ten years incessantly, but had no idea about how many times he had done it. He told us he was retired and that he had a house and family in Ehime prefecture; he occasionally, he said, goes there to visit them but never for more than a day or so. His grandchildren and the house in general, he said, were too noisy and troublesome (*urusai*) to be around, so he sets off again almost immediately. The life of an itinerant pilgrim was preferable to the noise of settled family life.

Noguchi was suntanned and looked fit and healthy. He did not seem to be put off by stopping to talk to people; we first saw him while we were driving along the road, and we had to find a convenient spot to pull over so we could get out and talk to him. As we did so we then had to wait while he first stopped to chat to a passer-by who was going in the other direction. He was happy, when we approached him and explained our research, to talk. He told us that he liked walking and that growing up in Ehime he became used to seeing pilgrims passing by on foot. This led him to think he might like to have a go at the pilgrimage. When he did so he found he enjoyed it. He carried a pilgrim's book and got it stamped at the temples, not just the first time, but for his first seven pilgrimages. After that he stopped carrying a pilgrim's book and also gave up carrying *fuda*. On his first pilgrimage he stayed in local lodges and inns, but it was not enjoyable compared to sleeping out; in subsequent pilgrimages sleeping out (*nojuku*) became his standard pattern. Although he does stop off to visit his family and has a home he can live in, he considered himself a full-time itinerant. When asked, he said he had no clear idea of how many others like him were there but estimated that there were probably just a few.

Noguchi told us that he knew exactly where he would be staying that night—a spot around two kilometres away from where we encountered him. (Given the time when we met him it would appear that he was allowing himself plenty of time to get organised before it became dark.) He planned out every day, knew where he was going, where he would stop and so on. The only caveat was that if the weather was really bad he would, like Shimada, cited previously, shelter and wait until the weather got better. It normally took him around two months to walk the whole route. Although he had a fair amount of belongings, he does not take everything up the steep steps of temples or up to temples in the mountains. Instead he leaves the bulk of his things down below and comes back to collect them after ascending temple steps or going up to mountain temples.

While he was extremely cheerful when we talked to him and appeared ready to chat to those he met along the way, he also was keen to keep to himself in many respects. He did, not, he said, have people along the route to stay with, nor did he appear to seek such relationships. As with his wish to leave again soon after calling by his family home and his feeling that staying in lodges where he would meet other people was less preferable than sleeping out, he was not inclined to get into situations that involved spending time under someone's roof and putting up with the routines and noise of others. He told us he was not interested in receiving *settai* and that he was financially sound and not reliant on alms. Nor did he express any particular orientation or motivation related to faith; when asked about this he just replied that his family Buddhist sect was Jōdo (Pure Land) Buddhism. When asked about his views on Kōbō Daishi (whom he had not mentioned at all when talking about his interest in the pilgrimage) he simply said that he saw no difference between Kōbō Daishi and Pure Land Buddhism. The *henro*'s main attraction was that it gave him freedom and allowed him to engage in something—walking—he really enjoyed. One could also suggest that the pilgrimage provided a helpful structure for his itinerancy, one that allowed him to maintain some contact with his home and family yet maintained his freedom from them.

Itinerant artist, drinker, and Daishi devotee

At the end of October 2019 we drew up to Temple Eighty-Three in Kagawa prefecture late one afternoon; it was the last place we visited that day before the temple gates shut. On the small road leading up to the temple from the temple car park sat a hunched over and extremely thin man with an ink brush and several sheets of paper. He was mainly drawing devotional-style

Figure 3.1 Itinerant artist drawing on pilgrim's shirt near Temple Eighty-Three

pictures of Buddhist figures such as Kōbō Daishi and various Buddhist in-scriptions in Sanskrit. He was extremely adept at drawing, As pilgrims passed by he beckoned them over and skilfully drew pictures of Jizō, the popular Buddhist figure of worship, on their pilgrim shirts.[31] He had a flair for cap-turing the attention of pilgrims walking from the car park to the temple; just about every pilgrim he beckoned to came and squatted down to let him draw on their shirts without him having to say anything. None objected to their shirts being drawn on (see Figure 3.1). Although he indicated that he was not asking for money for the pictures he drew (in fact he gave us all his day's drawings without seeking anything in return), the pilgrims whose shirts he drew on all put monetary offerings in the small bowl he had in front of him. In less than half an hour he received some 4500 yen in donations, including from one man who had been told, after his wife had given the man 1000 yen for drawing on her shirt, that he (the drawer) would do one for the husband for nothing.

The man doing the drawings was not wearing any *henro* clothing and was extremely hunched over and thin. He told us his name was Kurosawa, that he lived on the pilgrimage route and had been doing so for thirty-five years, during which time he said he had done it 219 times. (He was, we should note,

[31] One of Jizō's roles is as guardian of those in transient states, and hence his statues and images are often found in places associated with travel, such as mountain passes and along pilgrimage routes.

the only person who said he lived permanently on the pilgrimage route who gave a precise figure for the numbers of times he had done the *henro*). It took him, he said, twenty days—something that seemed far too fast, especially as he said 'walking' (*aruite*), until we found out as the conversation developed that he had a bicycle and rode the pilgrimage on that.[32] We later saw his bicycle, which was quite new and onto which a variety of possessions had been loaded. He also said that he was currently sleeping in a wayside hut (*henro koya*) close to Temple Eighty-Three and that he planned to spend the next day there, just resting rather than moving on. He would not, he said, do any drawing the next day because he was 'tired' (*shindoi*). He also said that besides drawing he also sometimes did *takuhatsu* to support himself in places such as shopping arcades; money, he said, was not a problem for him. When he did not have any he simply visited people who did and asked for some. He also was clearly savvy in terms of shopping, saying he would go to supermarkets late in the afternoon (when they sell off the remainder of that day's prepared food) and buy two pre-prepared packed meals (*bentō*) at a time. He knew various places where one could sleep, notably *tsuyado* (basic overnight shelters), which were free. He also slept out from time to time and knew some people who let him stay overnight as well. He also said that some pilgrims did bad things such as stealing, and hence he was wary of others. He told us he did not know any other itinerants; when we mentioned several by name including Hara and Shimada, he first said he did not know them and then said Shimada had been arrested some time back; as he did so, however, he indicated that the person arrested had a long white beard. Since Shimada was clean-shaven we were fairly sure Kurosawa was referring not to him but to the pilgrim known as Kōgetsu, who had a long white beard, had been arrested many years ago and whose story, widely known in Shikoku, we will discuss shortly.

One reason for his vagueness in response to some questions was evident from the carton of liquid he clutched and from which he sipped through a straw; it contained *shōchū* (an alcoholic drink). He was very thin, while his hands were marked, scratched and swollen, as if he had recently fallen over; overall he appeared to not be in good health. He was not easy to talk to; his diction was mumbled, and the alcohol was clearly taking effect, although it

---

[32] Sometimes we have found that people use *aruite* (walking/on foot) to refer to any means of travel not using one single means of transport for the whole route. People might say they are 'walking' (*aruite*) the pilgrimage when they use a mixture of walking and local transport. See also Chapter 2, note 13.

appeared to in no way affect his drawing; his hand remained steady even as his answers to questions became more incoherent. He said he had started to do the pilgrimage because he liked Kōbō Daishi; his drawings also reflected this point. It was not possible to ascertain, though we asked, why he had continued to do so, although he did answer when asked if he would give up doing the pilgrimage at any stage. Yes, he said, giving a precise date the next year but one that indicated this would be a temporary cessation. He did not like the summer period so each year, he would go into hospital when it got too hot to be outside. He added that he feigned illness to do this and that in hospital he would get three meals a day, enabling him to recuperate, get strong again, and be ready to go back on the pilgrimage as the weather got cooler. At that point he began to pack up his drawings, handing them all to us, before ending the conversation. When, a few minutes later, we came back from a visit to the temple, he had his bicycle with him and was sitting beside it sipping his *shōchū*, paying no attention to anyone who was coming or going.

Kōgetsu-san: poet, criminal, fugitive, and charismatic pilgrim

Our last case study is that of a man known as Kōgetsu, whose name has already come up in this chapter, mentioned by Hara as an example of a pilgrim whose arrest and subsequent imprisonment for criminal activity had cast a negative image over itinerant pilgrims in general, while Kurosawa and Shimada also indicated they were aware of his case. Indeed, his name cropped up a fair amount in our investigation, for Kōgetsu's is a remarkable story, one that shows that pilgrims can have complex and riveting back stories and that highlights some of the ambivalent perceptions of itinerant pilgrims. Kōgetsu's real name was Tanaka Kōjirō, but he was known to all and sundry as Kōgetsu.[33] He first began walking around Shikoku in around 1997, when he was seventy-four, and over the next six-and-half years he pushed a handcart around the pilgrimage and became a well-known sight. He had a round smiling face and a white beard, which, according to one informant who knew him well, might have been dyed. The informant told us that Kōgetsu was image-conscious and that once his beard began to turn

---

[33] This name combines the first ideogram of his given name (*kō*) with the ideogram *getsu* (moon). We have found no indication of when or how this nickname developed.

grey (he was already balding) he began to dye it white to make it look better. Kōgetsu told those he met that he was engaged in a 1000-day pilgrimage—one that he extended for another similar period after completing the first one. He wrote poems, and in July 2003, when he was eighty, a book of his poetry was published through a pilgrimage association in Hiroshima.[34] It included colour photographs of Kōgetsu the pilgrim with a long white beard and smiling face and, in one photograph, doing cold-water austerities. In an introduction to the book Matsuzaka Yoshimitsu (a man who is also listed as the book's publisher) recounts first meeting Kōgetsu on the pilgrimage in 1999, speaks of Kōgetsu's ascetic cold-water practice, talks of how a newborn baby beamed when cuddled by Kōgetsu, and generally portrays him as an avuncular and kindly pilgrim who cared for others.[35] Around the same time, Kobayashi Shinji, a photographer from Shikoku who had encountered and followed Kōgetsu around the pilgrimage route, published a book of photographs of him in various poses, pushing his handcart, cuddling a small dog, stooping in full pilgrimage regalia to scoop a handful of water from the sea, and encountering people along the way. Kobayashi's brief introduction to his book talks of Kōgetsu (who certainly was highly photogenic, generally displaying a warm smile) as earnestly (*hitasura*) walking the pilgrimage and giving energy to other pilgrims.[36]

Matsuzaka's description and Kobayashi's photographs projected the image of a warm-hearted itinerant who engaged in some ascetic practices and whose kindly demeanour captivated those who met him. This was a feeling many people had; Kōgetsu received support from numerous people around Shikoku during his peregrinations. He also clearly enjoyed such attention; a man who knew him well, and who said Kōgetsu used to stay with him whenever he passed through western Ehime prefecture, confirmed this in an interview in November 2019. Indeed, this informant said, Kōgetsu appeared to seek publicity and success; he even suggested that some of the things Kōgetsu did (such as posing for a photograph under a waterfall doing austerities) were for display purposes.

Although Kōgetsu clearly welcomed publicity, it also brought him infamy and imprisonment. Around the time that the previously mentioned two books were published he featured in a documentary made by NHK, Japan's national broadcaster. He had come to the attention of NHK through his

[34] Kōgetsu 2003.
[35] Matsuzaka 2003.
[36] Kobayashi 2003.

pilgrimages, and as a result a camera crew followed him around and shot a documentary centred on him.[37] It was aired on national television on 27 June 2003 with drastic results. A policeman who saw the documentary recognised Kōgetsu as a fugitive from the law, wanted for attempted murder in Osaka. It transpired that Kōgetsu had been a leader of a group of day labourers in Nishinari ward, Osaka (an area where many people live precarious lives dependent on day to day jobs), when he got into dispute with a fellow worker and stabbed him on 5 November 1991. Although the man recovered within one month, the attack was deemed attempted murder, but Kōgetsu had already fled, initially not to Shikoku but elsewhere (notably the Sanya area of day labourers in Tokyo). He had been on the run for some six years before arriving in 1997 in Shikoku as a pilgrim. He then spent six-and-a-half years as an itinerant pilgrim before being arrested in July 2003, twelve years after the crime. He was tried, found guilty, and sentenced to six years imprisonment. He served the whole sentence and, on release, aged eighty-six, returned to Shikoku, where supporters helped him get accommodation; he was no longer able to walk far and did not do the *henro* again, although he occasionally visited some temples. He spent much of his time playing *shōgi* (Japanese chess) at the local *shōgi* club and enjoyed talking to people and drinking in the evenings. He died in Niihama, Shikoku, in February 2018, aged ninety-five.

His arrest, the disclosure of his crime, and the subsequent prison sentence amply fed into narratives about false pilgrims, something that permeated Japanese media coverage of the events. Magazine and newspaper articles in general portrayed him as having adopted the guise of a pilgrim to evade justice and living a lie, and they contained comments from people who said that, far from continually walking the pilgrimage, Kōgetsu would often stop somewhere for weeks on end, drink every evening, and just used the pilgrimage as a means of support.[38]

The reality is more complex; many people who knew Kōgetsu from his period as a pilgrim rallied to his side. Over 1000 people signed a letter of support for him, petitioned for leniency, and contributed donations to a fund to help fight his court case and also to try to persuade the man he had stabbed to drop the case. People who had given him support and lodgings during his pilgrimages also attended court sessions to support him and kept

---

[37] One of NHK's remits is to feature aspects of Japanese culture, and in this context it has produced several features on the Shikoku pilgrimage (Reader 2014: 109–110). The documentary was NHK 2003.

[38] See, for example, *Shūkan Shinchō* 2003 No 28, July 24 pp. 50–51.

in touch by mail. When he was released they helped find him somewhere to live in Shikoku and enjoyed his company until the end of his life. One man who knew him well described him as a 'charismatic pilgrim' (*karisuma no henro san*) in an interview. Various bloggers, too, have provided positive accounts of Kōgetsu that countered the media portrayal of him as a fraudulent pilgrim.[39]

Beyond such dualistic responses—the negative media portrayals and the positive accounts and support of those who knew him as a pilgrim—there is a more complex picture of someone who appears to be both a charismatic, ardent pilgrim and someone who lived a life of chance, tumult, and crime. Here we outline the basics of his life along with his reflections on what happened, which we have reconstructed based on materials, including letters he wrote to supporters, provided to us by those who knew him in Shikoku, and also from materials provided in the court case.[40] As mentioned earlier, his real name was Tanaka Kōjirō. He was born in rural Fukuoka prefecture in 1923 to a poor family; his father was a miner. He ran away when aged twelve, then again at fifteen. On the second occasion he went up to Tokyo where he sought but could not find work and instead lived precariously, relying on what he could steal. This brought him money but drew attention because when he had it he indulged in lavish spending on clothes and geisha. As a result he was arrested and sentenced to three years' incarceration in a young offenders institution. He was released three months early on the condition of going into military service; Japan was at this point embroiled in World War Two. In 1943, aged twenty, he was sent to New Guinea, serving not on the frontline but in a supply unit. However, the war campaign in New Guinea was dreadful for all concerned, and vast numbers of Japanese died there; several of Kōgetsu's subsequent poems, written while a pilgrim, reflect on his experiences in New Guinea and its horrors.[41] When the war ended Kōgetsu (like some other soldiers) initially escaped into the jungle rather than surrender; he had a rifle and appears to have been a good shot, able to survive for a year by hunting wild boar, before returning to Japan.

---

[39] See the blog of Kondō Chieko at http://taiyohanasaku.waterblue.ws/chieko/wordpress/tag/%E9%81%8D%E8%B7%AF%E5%B9%B8%E6%9C%88/ and the website of the Kikusui Henrokan at http://www.kushima.com/henro/news/030517.htm (both accessed 11 Dec 2019).

[40] We thank Ugawa Fumio for sharing his knowledge and extensive collection of materials of Kōgetsu with us and the Director and staff at the Maeyama Henro Salon for allowing us to study the collections of materials (including letters Kōgetsu had sent to supporters whilst he was in prison) about Kōgetsu that the Salon holds.

[41] Kōgetsu 2003: 19.

His existence, in a Japan ravaged by war and its aftermath, remained hand-to-mouth as he moved around the country, returning for a while to his home area in Kyushu, back to Tokyo and then to Kyushu again. Again, lacking work, he lived on the margins, relying on theft and probably also the black market. Aged twenty-four, he was arrested again, this time in Kyushu, and again was sentenced to and served a three-year prison sentence. Released at the age of twenty-seven he again turned to a life on the margins. Reports indicate he had a wild lifestyle, got involved in fights and thefts, particularly targeting American Occupation forces, and again got caught and imprisoned for three years. It was while in prison that he heard, in January 1953, that his mother had died at the age of fifty-two. He was unable to attend the funeral, due to being in prison. Apparently he was deeply attached to his mother, and her loss affected him strongly; it comes through in several of his poems.[42]

He was released when aged thirty-two and returned to his home village in Kyushu, where he married a woman named Kimura Sachiko; they had two daughters, but shortly after, probably in 1958, Sachiko left and then divorced him. This was likely because Kōgestu had taken up with another woman—Tajiri Keiko, aged eighteen, with whom he had a child. Around this time he was imprisoned again for three years for being involved in a fight with a yakuza (gangster). On release from 1963 he ran a shoe repair business in Kyushu (he was apparently, according to an informant, highly skilled with his hands and good at repairs of all sorts) and in 1964 got married again, this time to Kanagawa Tamiko, though he divorced her the year after because of her drinking. He married again in 1971, this time to Matsumoto Chiyoko; he also, during this turbulent period of his life, maintained connections with Tajiri Keiko, although there appear no records of a marriage. What is known is that in 1978, at the age of fifty-four, he had incurred heavy debts after borrowing money because of gambling and that he then absconded to escape his debts, leaving his family to face the consequences. After this he travelled around but spent much time in Nishinari ward in Osaka, where he became a leader figure of a group of around thirty day labourers. It was here that in 1991 he got involved in a fracas with a former member of his work gang, who was trying to set up a rival group, and stabbed him.

He fled the area and went to various places, mainly Nagano and Tokyo, where he worked as a labourer until 1997. He then went to Shikoku to do the pilgrimage,

---

[42] We thank Kaneko Nachika for making this observation on reading Kōgetsu's poems. We heard something similar also from an informant who knew Kōgetsu.

sleeping out as he did so. He initially did one circuit of the pilgrimage before returning to his wife on the Japanese mainland, but he then sold off their furniture, took the money, and left again for Shikoku. After that he remained as an itinerant until his arrest. It appears that his reason for becoming a pilgrim was not to conceal himself and evade the law (his later courting of publicity certainly shows this as well) but to do the pilgrimage as a memorial for his dead parents—something his defence lawyers stated at his trial[43] and that an informant confirmed to us. The lawyers also said that he did austerities in order to reflect upon his crime, although this may have been more of a defence case mechanism aimed at getting his sentence reduced than a genuine statement of fact.

It is clear, then, that Kōgetsu had a turbulent life and that he lived on the edges of society from the outset. He committed various crimes and was imprisoned several times. His private life was tempestuous, with several marriages and wives left in the lurch. His daughters apparently disowned him. Even those who were supporters after his 2003 arrest have indicated that they felt he was primarily concerned with himself; one said to us, when asked why Kōgetsu appeared to have courted publicity while a fugitive, that he thought that Kōgetsu had just forgotten about the incident. This informant mentioned Kōgetsu's vanity (dying his beard) and ambition—qualities that led him to publish his poetry book and cooperate with Kobayashi's book and the NHK documentary. Kōgetsu's interest in fame emerged in a letter he wrote in prison to the informant in question; in it, he wrote that now (due to his arrest) the name of *kusa henro Kōgetsu* (the pilgrim Kōgetsu who lives in the wild)[44] had been inscribed into the history of the Heisei era.[45] The informant thought that whatever regrets Kōgetsu might have had over the stabbing related not to the victim but to himself and the prison sentence it brought to him.

Yet, despite all this, the fact remains that many people who encountered him through his time as an itinerant pilgrim pushing his handcart around Shikoku came to his support at his arrest. Even those who expressed their shock that such a smiling and kindly figure (as they saw him) could have done anything so bad[46] remained supportive. They petitioned for mercy, gave money for his

---

[43] This is reported on the Gajetto Tsūshin news website at https://getnews.jp/archives/2084645 (accessed 11 Dec 2019).

[44] This is the title of Kobayashi's book of photographs of Kōgetsu.

[45] Letter to supporter, dated 21 November (year unclear but shortly after his arrest) kept at the Maeyama Henro Salon in Kagawa and read by us, 31 October 2019. Heisei is the Japanese era name of the period between 1989 and 2019.

[46] See, for example, the comments by people who knew him that are reported in *Josei Sebun* 2003 July 31 pp. 52–53.

defence, stood by him during his imprisonment, and helped him on release. The informant who said that Kōgetsu thought of himself above all, also was deeply attached to him and was perhaps his closest supporter. We have heard one story in which he abused hospitality; shortly before his arrest, Kōgetsu had used bad language when staying at the home of a lady in Tokushima who was known as a spiritual healer. He was asked to leave as a result. Other than that, however, those who helped him and put him up remained positive about him (see Figure 3.2).

Figure 3.2 Kōgetsu the poet-pilgrim, as depicted on the cover of his book

He was never educated formally, but those who knew him said he was erudite, and his poems indicate a deep knowledge of language. There are also indications that he did reflect deeply on the troubles of his life and experiences, and that in later life, from the time of doing the pilgrimage onwards, issues of death and memory concerned him. His poems, for example, indicate the pain and experiences of his time in New Guinea and talk of the occasional hardships of life as an itinerant pilgrim who sleeps out. He talks of the discomfort of sleeping on the ground, of sleeping on a bed of leaves, of simple, even sparse meals eaten by torchlight, and of not being able to cook rice because his bottle of water had frozen. The poems also show a concern for his family and children (something his life until then had seemingly not done), his love for his mother and, strikingly, recurrent thoughts about death and other pilgrims. He talks of burning incense for an unknown dead pilgrim and of making memorial offerings at the grave of another pilgrim, for example. He probably also venerated Kōbō Daishi; one poem talks of how at the end (of life) the *kusahenro* (i.e. Kōgetsu) would enter into the arms of Daishi.[47]

His letters from prison also indicate some form of self-reflection and suggest he saw the pilgrimage as a way to come to terms with his life. He wrote that the *henro* was a 'route of repentance' (*zange no michi*) and 'a training ground for practice and enlightenment' (*shugyō to bodai nehan no dōjo*), and that he had decided that it was a place to walk until he died. He had no idea how long that would be but he just intended, he said, to keep walking. He saw the pilgrimage as a connection to the next world as well as a way to live in this one. Through the pilgrimage he had discovered good feelings for people and experienced their warmth. There are some reflections on his crime; one letter, from December 2006, for instance, refers to the hand that carried out the stabbing being the same as the hand that prayed (at the temples). The general tenor is of someone who, even if his main concern was for himself, was also reflecting on his position in the world and of someone who had lived a fraught life on the margins of society where trust was in short supply, but who had through the pilgrimage, found the good side of people and felt enriched as a result. Although he was unable to walk the pilgrimage again when he came out of prison, the

---

[47] Kōgetsu 2003: 123.

letters indicate that his wish was to keep walking and remain a pilgrim for the rest of his life.[48]

The ambivalence of perpetual pilgrim itinerancy

The stories and accounts outlined in this chapter indicate that, even within what is a very small minority within the wider pilgrimage world in Shikoku—those who spend many years or the rest of their lives endlessly going around the *henro*—there are multiple variations. For example, they had varying attitudes to or associations with the idea of faith. Hara was the most overt in this context, with his view of the pilgrimage as a path of asceticism and his focus on doing austerities. From accounts we have heard, Koyoshi, too, appears to be of this ilk. Kōgetsu, too, appears to have been motivated in his first pilgrimage by the wish to perform a memorial for his parents, while his poetry and letters indicate themes of repentance and self-searching, as well as reflecting on death and entering Daishi's embrace. Even Unkai, despite seemingly going off the rails, appeared devout to those who met him in the early 1980s. Shimada, who initially refuted the idea of faith, reflected on the kindness of others and his sense of gratitude to indicate that he might also have some feelings in this context. Kurosawa at Temple Eighty-Three referred to his feelings for Kōbō Daishi as a reason for being involved in the pilgrimage, and his drawings of Kōbō Daishi and other Buddhist figures reflected a continued engagement in this area. The four case studies Hamaya outlines all manifest religious elements, from Satō's initial pilgrimages in memory of his dead wife, to Morita's interest in reading about religion, to Fujimi-san's motivation for appearing unkempt. Only Noguchi, who mentioned that he belonged officially to the Pure Land sect, appeared to have little real sense of faith as a factor in his pilgrimages.

Their stories also indicate that portrayals of perpetual itinerants that write them off as 'professional pilgrims', affix pejorative labels such as *hendo* to them, and claim that they only take on the mantle or guise of the pilgrim in order to have an easy life and leech off others, are superficial. Clearly some of those cited earlier exhibited some such aspects: Unkai, with his drinking and

---

[48] This is a very brief summary of themes we were able to draw from the cache of letters Kōgetsu sent from prison to a supporter and that are stored at the Maeyama Henro Salon, where we were able to examine them, with the consent also of the person to whom the letters were sent.

dishonest behaviour; the itinerant at Temple Eighty-Three who drank and said he feigned illness to rest up in hospital from time to time; and Kōgetsu and his case history of crime, family desertion, and self-centredness. Yet there are counter-examples: Hara, living an ascetic life, avoiding bothering people, and striving to always be honest; Shimada, eschewing alcohol, taking care of himself, and constantly walking; and Noguchi, who has no need of begging and yet chooses to walk and sleep out. Some such as Hara and Shimada only appeared to use alms solicitation to provide basic support for themselves and nothing more. Rather than having an easy life, these itiner-ants appear to prefer the freedom of being on the road and living without walls to home comforts.

In her article, Hamaya shows that each person she talked to had their own methods of soliciting or acquiring support, and they all found meaning in soliciting alms and in living their lives on the road.[49] Our studies reiterate this point; those we interviewed, and whose cases we report, similarly found meaning in their pilgrimages that validated their lifestyles as itinerants. No one appeared to be doing any of this—sleeping out, relying on begging, or alms—simply to avoid work or to have an easy life. Even those who appeared to have issues with alcohol such as Unkai and Kurosawa also seemed actively engaged in pilgrimage activities. Unkai, even with his exaggerations of status and circuits, was (certainly when both Reader and Yamane first met him) walking the pilgrimage pushing a handcart and clearly solicitous of other pil-grims. Kurosawa at Temple Eighty-Three admitted that for part of the time he pretended to be ill in order to avoid the summer heat and get a hospital bed and food. But he also had (according to his testimony) done multiple cir-cuits, and he certainly had a skill in drawing pilgrimage-related pictures that he used to good effect to support himself. Nor did he at any time when we ob-served him do anything to promote himself or coerce pilgrims into donating money to him.

Kōgetsu in many ways is the most intriguing case of all. Seen as charis-matic, able to charm people, and displaying a skill in poetry, he attracted (and seemingly sought) attention. Yet he also had a dark past that he concealed from his pilgrimage associates until his arrest—and it was a past not just of crime and self-centred actions but of deserting wives and children and run-ning from debts. Yet while mass media portrayals after his arrest seek to de-pict his turn to pilgrimage as a 'lie', those who knew him well saw other sides

---

[49] Hamaya 2009.

to him, while his writings show a more complex picture. His poems reflect a sense of engagement with thoughts about death, and indications of faith, as well as reflections on his past life. His letters indicate that he was aware of his earlier life of criminality and showed that the pilgrimage had given him a way to find meaning in his life. All the materials we have seen related to Kōgetsu, along with the reflections of those who knew him, indicate that he initially did the pilgrimage as a memorial for his deceased parents. That (and the tenor of some of his poems) suggests that by his mid-seventies, when he became a Shikoku pilgrim, he was beginning to think of his own death and reflect on his life. His wish to keep walking until he died also suggests that he became captivated by the way of life on the pilgrimage route. We should also note that as far as we know and from what we have been told by those who knew him he did not beg. Rather, he used his practical skills to work from time to time (we were told he used to work occasionally for a car repair garage) to get money to support his itinerant lifestyle before moving on.

It may be, of course, that some of his reflections arose after he was arrested. He was clearly ambitious before that and interested in self-promotion. The reference to his name being 'etched into the history of the Heisei era' certainly implies that. Yet he also reflects that via the pilgrimage he came to find people interesting (a statement that suggests beforehand he was only interested in himself) and that he had been fortunate and blessed to find a way via the *henro* and to receive warm feelings from others. Such comments suggest that the Kōgetsu of old—the Tanaka Kōjirō who committed numerous crimes, stole, ran away with borrowed money, married, and then left his various wives for other women, causing problems for his family—may have died and that a new person had emerged. One cannot tell; what one can say is that Kōgetsu in many ways encapsulates much of the ambivalence and many of the contradictory perceptions surrounding those who live (or lived) on the road as permanent itinerant pilgrims.

Concluding comments

While the numbers of permanent itinerants on the pilgrimage route may be small, they are a significant case study for several reasons. One is that they encapsulate most clearly the point we have made throughout this volume, that pilgrimage can be an unending enterprise and that people may spend their entire lives involved in its practice. Another is that in many respects the itinerants of the modern era are following in the footsteps of the itinerants of earlier times who went on foot, were peripatetic, lived on alms solicitation and formulated and developed the pilgrimage in Shikoku. Although at times maligned (unfairly, for the most part, as we have suggested) as malingerers and seen at various times as false rather than proper pilgrims, they are in a sense those who come closest in their lifestyle to those who initially gave rise to the *henro*. They are a reminder of how the pilgrimage first really developed and of the point that for all of the modern developments that have continued to shape the *henro* and give rise to new modes of practice and engagement, such as car pilgrimages, there is also a continuing thread of itinerant mendicancy that has permeated the pilgrimage and that remains present still in the twenty-first century.

Such pilgrims are not the only ones who do the pilgrimage repeatedly however. Beyond the small number who spend their lives on foot in Shikoku there are myriad others who spend large parts of their lives circuiting the pilgrimage as well as spending much time preparing for their next pilgrimage. Some do the pilgrimage mainly or always by car, while others walk regularly, and others use a number of different means of performing the *henro*. Many of them also do other pilgrimages as well, although Shikoku is invariably the main focus of their pilgrimage activities. It is to such issues that we now turn, in the next chapter, where we outline the results of a detailed questionnaire sent to pilgrims who we knew to have done large numbers of Shikoku circuits, as well as looking at the schedules and patterns of pilgrimage that such unending pilgrims have.

4

Attitudes, practices, schedules, and triggers

Addictive patterns and the intensity of performance

Permanent and unending pilgrims: a general overview

While the itinerants discussed in Chapter 3 may constitute the only group of pilgrims who are permanently present on the pilgrimage route, there are many others who have an incessant engagement with the pilgrimage, spending large parts of their lives on it, performing it dozens of times a year, and doing it so regularly that it becomes an intrinsic part of their life routines. We have touched on some of these figures in earlier chapters. In this chapter and the two that follow it we look at them in greater depth, outlining their modes of travel and practices, their schedules and patterns of pilgrimage, what motivates them, and how the pilgrimage is so embedded in their lives. Some lead pilgrimage groups and are involved in confraternities whose purpose is to do the pilgrimage. Many go on pilgrimage alone, while others travel with one or more companions, commonly a spouse. Some only ever travel by car, while others have experienced the pilgrimage by a variety of means: on foot, by car, and perhaps also on bus tours or even by bicycle. Some always walk, at times expressing scepticism towards those who do it other ways. Some have developed highly efficient (or, to some eyes, highly speeded up) ways of doing the pilgrimage that enabled them to complete a whole circuit in a week or less, and thus to complete dozens of pilgrimages in a year, while others may take weeks to go round on foot, limiting themselves to a circuit or less a year. There is, in other words, no definitive pattern or mode of travel that is intrinsic to the lives of unending pilgrims. What binds them all is that their continuing involvement with the pilgrimage and their sense that it is not a once and only event but part of a continuing practice, one that they hope to be unending or only ended by death or infirmity.

Pilgrims Until We Die. Ian Reader and John Shultz, Oxford University Press. © Oxford University Press 2021. DOI: 10.1093/oso/9780197573587.003.0005

In this chapter we present a broad picture of those who do multiple pilgrimages by introducing responses from an extensive written questionnaire that asked pilgrims about their background, ages, reasons for doing the pilgrimage, and much else. The questionnaire allowed space for respondents to express opinions and to elaborate on various issues. As such it served as a form of written interview. After outlining the responses to the questionnaire and providing an assessment of predominant themes that emerged (themes that, as we indicate later, broadly replicate those that emerged in other parts of our fieldwork) we look at the schedules of pilgrims who do large numbers of pilgrimages in Shikoku in order to further highlight just how intensively some people become involved in this practice.

Methods, questionnaires, and interviews

Although we were able to meet and talk to numerous people with extensive pilgrimage histories during our field research, we also wanted to expand the study by sending questionnaires to people we otherwise might not have been able to meet. We used several sources for this endeavour. One was from brocade *fuda* on which pilgrims had included their names and addresses, made accessible to us by temple priests and others who had collections of such items. These formed the main group of questionnaires we sent out. We also found addresses from online sources of people who had done multiple pilgrimages. On occasion, too, while visiting the temples we encountered people who had done large numbers of pilgrimages who said that since they had demanding schedules to keep they could not stop to answer questions then, but they would be willing to fill out a questionnaire later. An article about our research published in *Henro* also elicited responses from pilgrims who indicated they were willing to be interviewed or complete a questionnaire.

Using the addresses thus gathered we sent out a detailed questionnaire with thirty-four questions, ranging from basic questions about age and employment to ones about pilgrimage practices and issues related to multiple performance. We included a covering letter explaining that this was an academic project funded by official Japanese academic research agencies and conducted under the auspices of the Japanese university where one of the authors worked, and that we would maintain confidentiality by not disclosing respondents' names. We also included a stamped addressed envelope for respondents to send their questionnaires back in.

As a result we got twenty returned questionnaires—a relatively small number, representing about half the questionnaire letters we had sent out, but a return that contained detailed answers that helped us develop a broader understanding of those who do the pilgrimage multiple times. In general the responses we received from the questionnaires bore many similarities to responses and views that we heard in fieldwork interviews. We should note two further points before outlining the responses. The first is that those who responded to us after reading about the project in our *Henro* article and saw themselves as fitting into the category of unending pilgrims were people who had mainly done the pilgrimage by foot. They self-identified as pilgrims perpetually involved in the pilgrimage and thus relevant to the study even if they had done the pilgrimage fewer times than our original conceptualised framework of seven times by foot or forty by motorised transport. They in effect reaffirmed the point we have made earlier, that a large number of pilgrims view themselves as being on an unending pilgrimage even without having done it multiple times.

The second point is that not all those we sent questionnaires to replied; anyone who has done surveys and questionnaires knows that response rates never come close to 100%. One can never, of course, know why someone (including those who asked us to send them questionnaires as they did not have time to talk when we met them and who said that they would respond) did not do so. What did stand out was that non-respondents included several people who, we knew, had done several hundred pilgrimages in Shikoku. Of the twenty who replied nine had done it over 100, including two with more than 250 circuits each and one with over 700. These were all people whose names we had come across from information passed on to us by temple officials and others who know the pilgrimage well. Others we knew about who had done many hundreds of circuits did not respond, however, and they included one person with around 700 circuits, two people who had (according to their *fuda*) done the pilgrimage over 400 times, several who had done it over 200 times, and some who had done it over 100. We tried via numerous means to contact those we knew had done the most circuits, from questionnaires mailed to their home addresses (sometimes more than once) but not responded to, to attempts to contact them through intermediaries. At two temples where officials said they knew the man mentioned in Chapter 2 who has probably done the most circuits (over 700 as of late 2019) we also left messages asking if he could contact us, and left telephone numbers for that purpose. One temple official who knew this man took details of our project, plus one of our name cards and telephone numbers, saying she would explain our project to him when he next came to the temple and ask him to get in touch with us. He did not do so. The temple officials who knew him told us he was reserved and did not give much indication as to why he was doing it so often. Similar reticence also emerged with some of the others whose *fuda* indicated they had done several hundred pilgrimages; temple officials who encountered them frequently as they stamped their books commented that such people rarely said much about themselves. While generally we have found that pilgrims tend to be willing to talk about what they are doing and why, there are those who are less so and who preferred to remain private.

Responses: provenance, age, home situation, and sectarian affiliation

Here we summarise the basic themes that emerged from the questionnaires. The majority came either from Shikoku (eight in all) or prefectures adjacent to it, such as Hiroshima (four) and Okayama (two). Proximity to Shikoku was thus a factor in doing the pilgrimage, as it has been historically.[1] The other six came from farther afield, two from Aichi prefecture (an area that has traditionally been a stronghold of pilgrimage activity), and one each from Tottori, Tokyo, Ishikawa, and Miyagi prefectures. Respondents were largely above Japan's formal retirement age. The average age of respondents was seventy-two-and-a-half; the youngest was aged thirty-eight, the second youngest sixty and the oldest eighty-four. Only two were under the official retirement age of sixty-five, and one of these two indicated in a formal interview that he had moved to Shikoku after doing the pilgrimage in order to run a lodge catering to pilgrims and other visitors to the island. Most said they were now unemployed, a category that includes being retired, although some said they occasionally did part-time work to bring in extra money that they used to support their pilgrimages. Two listed their profession as Buddhist priests, and both indicated that they were involved in spiritual healing activities. Some indicated that they occasionally worked in a professional capacity as pilgrimage guides.

It is unsurprising that they were mostly retired, given that the pilgrimage is time-consuming. Many only were able to focus their energies on and

---

[1] Reader 2005: 174; Osada, Sakata, and Seki 2003: 226–229.

immerse themselves in the pilgrimage after ceasing work. For some a stated reason for getting so involved with the pilgrimage was that they were looking for something to do that could fill their time and keep them active after ceasing work.

The occupations they had prior to retirement were multiple, from owners of small businesses such as shops, noodle restaurants, and electrical businesses, to company employees, professionals, and white-collar workers. Although we did not ask about gender, all respondents gave their names, which indicated that they were all male. This does not mean that all those who do multiple pilgrimages are male; we have already in Chapter 2 mentioned some females who have extensive pilgrimage histories, and in Chapter 5 will introduce some more. However it is fair to say that for the most part those who do the *henro* large numbers of times and who tend to get obsessed with it and especially with numbers of circuits, are male. Responses, however, indicated that several questionnaire respondents at times did pilgrimages with their wives; this exemplifies a pattern that we also touched on in Chapter 2, of couples doing the pilgrimage multiple times together. It perhaps says something about issues of gender in Japan that invariably when we contacted or met couples doing the pilgrimage multiple times together, it was the male who sought to respond to our questions or who filled in the questionnaire. When we met Nakagawa (see Chapter 2), the man from Imabari who had done over fifty circuits by car at weekends, and who presented himself to us and online as a pilgrimage authority, it was only in the course of the interview that we discovered that his wife had done more or less the same number of pilgrimages as him and that normally they did pilgrimages together. We also should note that quite frequently during interviews with men who spent a lot of time on the pilgrimage, it would emerge that they were married and that their wives remained behind at home while they travelled around Shikoku. When asked if their wives minded their absences, the response was that they did not seem concerned at all or that they appeared quite happy at their husbands' absences—and often appeared to encourage them. This is an issue that we will see especially in Chapter 6 when we talk about older men who walk the pilgrimage regularly.

Eight of our questionnaire respondents were in a household of two people, usually with their wife, though two were living with a son, having lost their wife or been divorced. Three were in extended family units of three generations. Two did not respond to this question. Seven respondents lived alone because they were unmarried (three), divorced (two), or because their wife had died (two). One of the two bereaved men said he took his wife's mortuary tablet (*ihai*) on pilgrimage with him, a practice that we have discussed in earlier work on the pilgrimage.[2] Bereavement, especially of a female spouse, along with performing the pilgrimage as a memorial service (*kuyō*) for deceased partners, emerged also (as we discuss later in the chapter) as something of a recurrent theme among those who had completed the most pilgrimage circuits of all.

There was no dominant sectarian orientation among those who responded, and this accords with the general profile of Shikoku pilgrims. As we discussed in Chapter 1, although there are close associations between Shingon Buddhism and the pilgrimage, the *henro* is not a sectarian practice. Not only is Kōbō Daishi viewed as a transcendent figure who has gone beyond sectarian confines, but the pilgrimage is seen as a Japanese (rather than a specifically Buddhist or Shingon) pilgrimage associated not only with Buddhism, but with the folk tradition as well as Japanese cultural identity. Nonetheless eight respondents (the largest number) had a Shingon sect affiliation; this may well be because Shingon is dominant in Shikoku, where the largest number of respondents came from. One of the eight was brought up Christian but converted to Shingon through an interest in the pilgrimage. Jōdo Shin (the True Pure Land) sect affiliation was next with four, followed by Tendai (two, both of whom were priests), and Rinzai Zen, Sōtō Zen, Jōdo (Pure Land), and Shinto, with one each. Two did not answer the question about religious affiliations. Three of the respondents indicated that they had taken a Buddhist ordination, two as priests. The third took a lay Buddhist ordination, something that, as we have seen with the earlier examples of Fukuda Shōnosuke and Nakatsukasa Mōhei, is not uncommon among long-term pilgrims who develop close links with particular temples.

First pilgrimages, reasons, and means

Since we were interested to find out what it was that started these people on their extended engagement with the pilgrimage we asked how and when they first did it. This produced a mixture of answers that did not always directly

---

[2] *Ihai* (mortuary tablets) are commonly used in Japan as part of the process of memorialising dead kin. They represent the spirit of the deceased and are normally kept in a family Buddhist altar; sometimes pilgrims carry *ihai* with them both as a memorial service for the dead and also to let their dead kin 'do' the pilgrimage with them (Reader 2005: 80–82).

respond to the question. Some told us how old they were on their first pilgrimage and said with whom they did it (normally family members and often parents), while others (reflecting a point we made in an earlier chapter that pilgrims are not always precise with dates and such things) were rather vague about when they did their first pilgrimage. Others, rather than citing when, only talked of how, most commonly by car. The youngest age cited by a respondent for a first pilgrimage was fifteen and done with his parents; this respondent indicated that he was now aged seventy-four and hence had a pilgrimage history of almost sixty years. Such extended histories were more common than not, and several others had pilgrimage histories going back thirty, forty or, in some cases, over fifty years. The most recent first pilgrimage was ten years previously in 2009, while the oldest first-timer was a man whose first circuit was at the age of seventy.

Our question about the reasons for first doing the pilgrimage produced, as expected, diverse responses as did a corollary question about whether their reasons for doing the pilgrimage had changed as they did it more times. Many were first introduced to the pilgrimage by family members; for the man taken on the pilgrimage by his parents at the age of fifteen, it was to thank Daishi after he had recovered from a grievous accident. One person said his great-grandfather had done the pilgrimage, and this served as an inspiration for him; another stated that his mother had wanted to do the pilgrimage but died before she could, so he did his first pilgrimage to fulfil her wish and had been doing it ever since. Others said that friends had done the pilgrimage, and this inspired them to follow suit. Several mentioned a wish to seek or pray for worldly benefits (*goriyaku*), a common theme of pilgrimage motivation that has deep resonances in Japanese religious practice in general.[3] One man, for example, did it to pray for the success of his son's business and another for his wife's recovery from illness. Such people stated that they felt their prayers had been answered, leading them to do the pilgrimage again and again, to seek further benefits or to express gratitude to Daishi for benefits received. Several cited an interest in travel and tourism as an initial reason that led to repeated pilgrimages because they sensed a deepening of interest and faith that drew them back, or because, as one respondent put it, he found that doing the pilgrimage helped keep him healthy and prevented senility. Some also said that they began doing the pilgrimage after retirement because, as one put it, he had nothing else to do, with the result that it became part of his life (*seikatsu*

---

[3] Reader and Tanabe 1998.

no ichibu) and identity. Several mentioned retirement as something that now enabled them to do the pilgrimage regularly when previously work had been a barrier.

Asked how they usually did the pilgrimage the most common response was by car, although with some variance depending on season; some also at times travelled with pilgrim groups by bus. Seven always went by car; five always by foot; one indicated he did it once alone each year by car, once also in a large tour group, and twice a year with a small *sendatsu*-led confraternity. One said the first time he went on foot but thereafter always by car. Most did it the 'normative' way (i.e. clockwise) with the majority (twelve) doing a whole circuit at a time, usually, if going by car, taking seven or eight days. Some said that they had previously always done it in one go but as they got older they now preferred to do it in sections. Some at times, besides their personal individual pilgrimages, also led groups as a *sendatsu* with their method of travel varying depending on the group. Those who mainly walked said that it all depended on when they had time, although one indicated that he had a very regular schedule of doing it each year around the same time. Unless they were leading a group, the general pattern was to travel alone; eleven of the twenty normally went this way, while another respondent one wrote '*dōgyōnin*' here, implying simply with Daishi. Fifteen of the twenty had a *sendatsu* rank and eleven of these were at a rank above the basic *sendatsu* level. Several also held *sendatsu* ranks for other pilgrimages as well.

Times, places to stay, and means of support

The number of times they had done it varied considerably. The lowest number was four circuits, all by foot, by a man in full-time work, who stated that he does it in stages due to work schedules, but that he spends three to five days every month on the pilgrimage. The highest number was 708, claimed by the man who did his first pilgrimage aged fifteen and who had the longest history of pilgrimage of all respondents. We have mentioned him previously (see Chapter 2) amid doubts at his claims, but here we note that we have accepted the numerical statements of all respondents equally. Those who did it by foot unsurprisingly had lower numbers than those by car. In all, seven respondents indicated that they had done it on foot, with some of these also having made circuits by motorised transport as well. The numbers cited by each person are as follows (all by vehicle unless otherwise indicated):

four (all on foot); seven (all on foot); ten (all on foot); thirteen; fifteen (all but one on foot); nineteen; twenty; twenty-two; twenty-five (five on foot, twenty by car); eighty; 101; 115; 125 (ten on foot, 110 by car); 127; 170; 176; 230;[4] 265; 278; 708 (eleven on foot)

The average number of circuits for the twenty respondents was 124.4 times. While this average was boosted by the man who had done 708 circuits it was also influenced by the numerous walkers who responded and had low numbers. We should add that had some others who had done over 200 circuits, along with those with 400 or more and Nakano, the man who also has claimed over 700 circuits, replied to the questionnaire, the average number of circuits would have been even higher. As it stands, fully half—ten—of the respondents had done over 100 pilgrimage circuits each and seven had done more than the average total for respondents. These figures indicate that not only is there a corpus of pilgrims who do the *henro* multiple times, but that such practices are found both among walkers and those who go by car. While those who drive are clearly the ones who accrue the highest number of circuits and who thus carry brocade *fuda*, there is a not insignificant body of walkers who perform the Shikoku pilgrimage—a journey that takes forty days or more on foot—many times. We will see this again in Chapter 6 where we discuss pilgrims we have interviewed who have walked the pilgrimage several times and in some case well into double figures.

One more thing to note here in passing is that one respondent (the one who gave the figure of nineteen pilgrimages) said he was actually on two different pilgrimage circuits of Shikoku at the same time, doing one by himself and one with a confraternity. This is something we encountered from time to time as well: the idea that one can be in effect making two different pilgrimages on the same pilgrimage contemporaneously.

All respondents stated that they had their own abodes; none were homeless. They tended also to follow special (often self-determined) rules when on the pilgrimage. Having one's personal set of rules (something that, as we noted in Chapter 3, was the case with permanent homeless itinerants who, for example, avoided alcohol or had made vows about how to conduct themselves) appears to be important for virtually all the

---

[4] This person did not give a number but wrote that he had a brocade *fuda*. He also gave his name and address, from which we realised it was a man we had met some months previously who said he did not have time to talk then, but who had given us his *fuda* indicating he had done 230 circuits and who said he was willing to be sent a questionnaire.

multiple performing pilgrims we met, enabling them to construct their own individual pilgrimage identities and to find meaning in and through them. While six respondents said they had no special rules but did the pilgrimage the normal way, fourteen indicated that they had developed their own special rules or practices that they adhered to and that were centred on making them better people. One said that he carries the ancestral memorial tablets of his deceased wife and family ancestors around the pilgrimage twice each year. Several who travel solely by car said that they had taken a vow to give alms to any walking pilgrims they encountered. Most (especially those who stated that they were registered *sendatsu*) said they sought to guide others and pass on information about the pilgrimage. Some (but by no means all) refrain from alcohol, while most emphasised generating a good atmosphere and interacting well with others; trying to maintain a pleasant disposition, being friendly, showing gratitude to others, and not causing problems were near-universal responses. Most indicated that they did various religious practices, such as copying sutras (*shakyō*) and/or reciting sutras and mantras (notably the Hannya Shingyō); some also said that they made use where possible of *shugyōba* (ascetic practice places) that can be found at some of the temples.[5]

They stayed in a variety of places, from temple lodges to *minshuku* (Japanese guesthouses) to business hotels. Those who walked used the widest variety of places, including, for one person, sleeping sometimes in a tent or, as was mentioned as an occasional practice by three respondents, sleeping out. One respondent who always walks had no fixed plans or pre-determined schedules, letting destiny shape his pilgrimages. As such on some occasions he might be somewhere with no lodging, when he would sleep out. This was something of an outlier in terms of responses, not just among those replying to the questionnaire but more generally; overall we found that the vast majority of those who do the pilgrimage multiple times have set routines and very clear ideas of where they will stay each night. This was also evident in another questionnaire response, with several people saying that they had connections with various people in Shikoku whom they tried to see on each circuit and sometimes stay with, while one mentioned souvenir shops and

---

[5] *Shugyōba*, commonly also known as *gyōba*, are locations designed for ascetic training. Often found especially at mountain temples and associated with the mountain ascetic tradition, they include waterfalls under which cold-water austerities can be practiced, caves and other underground passages, and various climbing challenges that often include ladders and/or chains embedded in mountainsides in order to make steep ascents of rock faces.

bars (*izakaya*) he always stopped at to see friends in the four main cities on the island.

Overall, though, the most commonly cited place to sleep was in their own vehicle (*shachūhaku*). Nine respondents said they slept in their cars; these were the nine people with the highest numbers of circuits. Generally it appears that the more times one does the pilgrimage the more likely it is that one will do it this way—something that came out not just through this questionnaire but in our interviews in general.

We asked how these people supported their pilgrimage activities. All were self-financed. Only one, who had taken a priestly ordination, mentioned *takuhatsu* at all, although he emphasised that he supported his pilgrimages with his own money and did not rely on alms. For all retirees their pensions were a prime source of support, though several noted that if relying just on their pensions they needed to be frugal in their everyday lives in order to have enough money to support their pilgrimages. Some also had part-time work that helped supplement their pensions, and several also mentioned savings built up during their working lives that they used for the purpose. Those still in work (one a full-time employee and one a man who runs a lodge in Shikoku) use their work income to finance their pilgrimage activities. For all, pilgrimage was a central element in their personal economies, which were to a significant degree oriented towards supporting their lives as pilgrims.

Views of others, veneration, and social interaction

We asked if there were special pilgrims (both historical and contemporary) they respected; we cited Nakatsukasa as an example in order to clarify the question. His name unsurprisingly cropped up in some replies, as did that of Shinnen, mentioned by some and referred to in one response as a 'pioneer' of the pilgrimage. A small number of others were also cited, mainly deceased pilgrims such as Fukuda Shōnosuke and well-known *sendatsu* of earlier times, as well as Miyazaki Tateki, the man cited in Chapter 2 who produced a walkers' guidebook, erected signposts, and cleared pilgrimage paths. Unsurprisingly the person who cited Miyazaki was himself a walker. Several respondents either mentioned no names or simply indicated that there were no pilgrims they specially respected. Two people, who both said that they always walked the pilgrimage, used this question to state that they were not impressed by people with very high numbers of circuits. One, for instance, said that unless one did austerities, doing pilgrimage hundreds of times was meaningless.

Our question asking how they viewed Kōbō Daishi showed that faith in Daishi and views of him as a spiritual transcendent figure akin to a Buddha or deity guiding the living were important for some, but that this was by no means an overarching view. Many respondents saw Kōbō Daishi as a highly relatable human figure, speaking of him as a multi-talented human figure who was a guide, inspiration, and teacher; two respondents also referred to him as a friend with whom they felt a sense of kinship. In essence they focused on the achievements of the human figure Kūkai rather than the legendary miracle-working figure Kōbō Daishi; one person, for instance, specifically mentioned Kūkai's work as an engineer and calligrapher, while another said Japan would be different if he came back now, and a third referred to Kūkai's social welfare work that made him stand out among all the Buddhist sect founders in Japan.

All, when asked about relationships with other pilgrims, said that they interacted with fellow pilgrims, although this was usually a case of passing the time when meeting them on the route. Several said they did not talk much to other pilgrims, and even those who said they might sometimes walk for a few days with another pilgrim indicated that more commonly they travelled alone. That confirmed a general observation that doing the pilgrimage was primarily an individual practice, even if this was located within a potential context of social engagement. There were nonetheless some degrees of sociability evident among these multiple performers. One respondent, for example, said one of the pleasures of the *henro* was walking with others (an attitude that, as we will see in Chapter 6, can often be found among those who have walked the pilgrimage many times), while another stated that he maintained longer-term links with pilgrims met along the way, for example, by exchanging New Year's cards with people he had met on pilgrimage tours. Those who at times did the pilgrimage in the company of others (e.g. with a confraternity, or when acting as a guide) also noted the social dimensions of such occasions. Some of those whom we interviewed who slept in their cars and did multiple pilgrimages, also wrote of a sociable atmosphere that sometimes developed at night at places such as *michi no eki* when a number of pilgrims were staying overnight in their cars there (see also Chapter 5). However, the broader picture is one in which multiple performing pilgrims were more focused on following their own paths than on engaging socially with others, commonly spending significant amounts of time on their own.

Settai, numbers, and competition

Asked how important *settai* was, all without exception emphasised its significance for the *henro* and as evidence of the warmth of people in Shikoku. All also expressed the important of showing gratitude when receiving it. Several used the word *arigatai* (thankful, something to be grateful for) to describe *settai*. However, none relied on it or saw it as essential to their own pilgrimages, and all said they could manage without it. Overwhelmingly they stressed that one should not expect to get *settai* and that they did not do the *henro* in order to get it. *Settai* (which one person said included kind words as well as more material things) was seen as a blessing and a way for donors to symbolically accompany the pilgrim and take part in the pilgrimage, but it was not something pilgrims should expect or seek out.

We asked if the number of times one goes around Shikoku mattered and whether it is important to do it more times than someone else. This produced a very clear across-the-board response, rejecting the idea that the number of times one does it is important; a near-universal response was that one should not judge others (i.e. make value judgements based on the number of times people had done the pilgrimage). One person (who throughout emphasised the importance of doing the pilgrimage in order to eradicate the sins of one's ancestors) thought that the number of times one did it depended on the deeds of one's ancestors, although he was the only person who in any way related numbers of circuits to karmic issues. Several respondents indicated that they were not impressed by people who cited the numbers of times they had done the pilgrimage. One person, for example, stated that those who write how many times they have done the *henro* on their *fuda* are simply boasting. Yet there was also a recognition that numbers were in some way important, which is unsurprising given that each person who replied to the questionnaire had done multiple pilgrimages and had made this known in some way. One pilgrim replied, for example, that pilgrimage was part of his life and he was very aware of how many times he had done it, while another said his (positive) feelings about the pilgrimage were strengthened by meeting those who had done it many times.

At the same time there was a general rejection of any thoughts about creating pilgrimage records for the number of circuits completed. Every respondent stated that they not think about such things, and all rejected the idea of records. Most respondents said they were not competitive and that the *henro* was not a contest, while the person who said he had done it 708 times was adamant that numbers were unimportant and that he paid no attention to records. Two others, however, even as they appeared to repudiate the importance of records and numbers, also managed to emphasise the number of times they had done it, one saying that he had no interest in records, but that thanks to Daishi's grace he had been able to do it 278 times. Walkers appeared more overtly critical about numbers. One stated that those who emphasised numbers were turning the pilgrimage into a 'stamp rally' (*sutampu ra-ri-*, a term widely used in Japan to indicate the practice of collecting stamps from famous places).[6] Another walker said that whenever he met pilgrims with brocade *fuda* they were travelling by car and were clean with spotless white pilgrim shirts, unlike walking pilgrims. He thought that pilgrims should be following in Daishi's footsteps and that going by car was not the same—although he also recognised that some people can only do it by car due to constraints of time and their physical state.

There is, in other words, a negative feeling to saying too much about numbers; one respondent even commented that while there were people who did it hundreds of times who were good people, there were others who were not. Despite such critical comments, however, there was a total consensus on attitudes towards modes of doing the pilgrimage. All respondents, asked whether it mattered how one travelled, were adamant that it was up to each pilgrim how they did it. It was commonly agreed that it was the pilgrim's attitude and spiritual view that were important, not their means of conveyance. One commented that while walking was the original way there are all manner of ways to do it; he even mentioned helicopter tours (which were offered for a brief period in the 1990s but no longer exist) and said they were acceptable because the pilgrims who did them wore white pilgrim's clothing. Another even (without evidence, it has to be said) claimed that Kōbō Daishi had said there was no special way to do it. Another stated that originally everyone walked and that he felt this was the correct way to do it, adding that he walked just like Kūkai did, though he also accepted that nowadays there were many ways one could do it. Another walker emphasised that it was only on foot that one could follow some parts of the old route, while adding that the best part of the *henro* was meeting local people and getting *settai*—something

[6] Normally 'stamp rallies' centre on famous tourist sites; thus, for example, one of the authors was visiting a famous hot spring resort in Yamaguchi prefecture in 2016 during a the annual dolls' festival, in which a number of exhibition displays of Japanese dolls were shown at different locations throughout the town; those who visited each display could stamp a specially provided booklet and collect all ten stamps as a souvenir. This event was publicised as a stamp rally.

car pilgrims do not really experience. As such just walking once provided, in his view, a greater sense of achievement than doing it 100-plus times by car.

However, this view was not widespread, and even those who felt that walking was best nonetheless also felt that the benefits of doing the pilgrimage were the same for all no matter how they travelled. To that extent, although those who walk do make distinctions between their methods of doing the pilgrimage and those of others who go by car, one does not see the levels of criticism of those who go by means other than foot that are evident in the Santiago de Compostela pilgrimage as reported by Frey or that emerge in the accounts of walkers on that route.[7] That may be because, unlike the Santiago Camino, which attracts a lot of younger people, most of our respondents were in their sixties or above, as are the bulk of Shikoku pilgrims in general, and hence they (walkers and those who go by car or bus) have more of a degree of empathy for each other. Moreover, as many of those who walk the *henro* have acknowledged, they are aware of their own growing physical limitations and that there may come a time when they are no longer physically able to walk the route. As such they are conscious that it may be necessary for themselves in the future, if they wished to keep doing the pilgrimage, to make use of cars and buses. For all, doing the pilgrimage was paramount, and the means by which it was done was secondary.

Miracles, experiences, *Shikokubyō*, and continuing engagement

Our question about whether they had experienced miracles (*reigen*) or received benefits (*goriyaku*) via doing the *henro* produced varied responses. A very small number expressly said they had received miracles, while a couple of respondents bluntly said no. Some cited stories they had heard about others who had benefitted from miraculous events through doing the pilgrimage, such as a childless couple who were able to conceive and produce a healthy child as a result of their pilgrimage, and a wheelchair-bound schoolgirl who was cured and able to walk thanks to having done the *henro*. These

---

[7] See Frey (1998: 125–136) for a discussion of how walkers on the Camino create a notion of authenticity about their way of doing it and how they are critical of those who use other means of travel, while Hoinacki (1996) is a good example of the disdainful comments walkers on the Camino make about other types of pilgrims. See also Reader (2014: 10–11) for countervailing comments on this issue.

responses did not make it clear whether these were people the respondent knew or whether they were just repeating stories they had heard and that commonly circulate among pilgrims.[8] One respondent stated he had experienced miracles three or four times along with various worldly benefits; he added the comment that if one believes, dreams come true (*shinjereba mune hiroku*). Another said that through the pilgrimage the bad deeds of his ancestors had been eradicated and another talked of sensing his dead mother's spirit while he was walking one early morning on the *henro*. Some also stated that doing the pilgrimage had enhanced them spiritually; one, a former company employee who became a priest, claimed he had developed spiritual powers thanks to the *henro*. There was a general feeling that one gets worldly benefits from doing the pilgrimage, and several specifically mentioned health. Being able to continue doing the pilgrimage at an advanced age (something said by one person aged eighty-three and another who was seventy-four) and still be healthy was cited as a clear benefit (*riyaku*) of the *henro*. As such our respondents felt a variety of benefits, both with relation to health and to spiritual development, accrued from doing the pilgrimage repeatedly.

Overall respondents heartily embraced the idea of *Shikokubyō* or Shikoku 'addiction' (*chūdoku*) when asked their thoughts on such matters. They thus reiterated the views expressed commonly in our fieldwork interviews. Several said straightforwardly that they had *Shikokubyō* and were, or were on the way to being, addicted. Two used the term *Daishibyō* (Daishi illness), one adding that this was a blessing. One said his family used to refer to his obsession as *Shikoku baka*, 'Shikoku stupidity', or *henro boke* 'pilgrimage senility', but they now have just come to terms with it and no longer use such phrases. One said that while he used to have *Shikokubyō*, this was not the case at present; it transpired that he was taking a break from doing the pilgrimage while he concentrated on developing a lodge in Shikoku where pilgrims and others could stay, although he also indicated he still visited some pilgrimage temples from time to time.[9] Two respondents rejected the idea of having *Shikokubyō*, one saying that doing the *henro* was part of his life, so it was neither an addiction nor an illness, while the other was annoyed about the question because we had used a term (*byō*, illness) that to him had negative

---

[8] See Reader (2005: 56 and 237–238) for more on the ways in which miracle tales circulate orally in the pilgrim community.

[9] Besides the comments that this person made in the questionnaire we also conducted an extended interview with him in November 2018 in which he also talked about *Shikokubyō*.

connotations, when clearly for him any enduring association with the pilgrimage could only have positive meanings. The man who said he had done it 708 times in nearly sixty years, whose van was covered in pilgrimage stickers, and whose house was effectively a shrine to pilgrimage, was also emphatic that he did not have *Shikokubyō*, although he did not reject the idea that some people might have this condition. The rest of our respondents embraced the term positively; a representative comment was from the man who said that certainly he had *Shikokubyō* but added that 'this type of illness is a good illness' (*kono byōki ha yoi byōki da*).

This sense of immersion and addiction—and of it as being something positive—also came out in response to the question about why they kept doing the pilgrimage. Respondents recurrently said it was part of, or embedded in, their lives (*seikatsu no ichibu*) and several mentioned their relationship with Kōbō Daishi, talking about being helped and guided by him. Some said they continued doing it for benefit of their body and mind, because it made them feel calm and purified, and/or because they viewed it as a religious practice (*shugyō*). Two said they did it to give thanks and express gratitude (to the Buddhas), while another respondent also alluded to transcendent meanings by stating that he liked walking and the sense of non-attachment it gave him. One said he continued to do it because of a belief in transmigration (*rinne*) and the need to acquire good karma to attain a better rebirth. One simply said he kept doing the pilgrimage to help other pilgrims.

Only one respondent spoke of goals when asked why he kept doing the pilgrimage; initially, he said, he wanted to do it 100 times, but now (having reached that number) he had a new goal to do it 108 times. The man referred to earlier who said he did the pilgrimage initially to fulfil the wish of his deceased mother hoped that in continuing to do the *henro* he would meet her spirit. He also had a practical wish; he has a photo of his daughter and grandchild taken on the pilgrimage (at Dōgo hot springs, a popular overnight resting place for pilgrims) and wanted to have one of his great-grandsons (now aged three) there, presumably when he was old enough to do the pilgrimage. One respondent indicated that he felt he was starting to understand the meaning and aim of life as a result of repeating the pilgrimage while another simply responded to this question by saying 'I don't know, I don't understand why'. This latter response is one we heard quite often when we asked pilgrims why they were doing it again and again. It also relates to the idea, often expressed by pilgrims, that doing the pilgrimage is a constant learning process and that the more one does it the more one can understand its meanings and learn about why one is doing it.

Other pilgrimages, cessation, and time

We asked whether they had done other pilgrimages besides Shikoku and all but three—one of whom had done Shikoku 170 times—had. Most had done significant numbers of other pilgrimages, notably the Saikoku Kannon thirty-three-temple pilgrimage and some of Japan's regional eighty-eight-stage pilgrimages, such as the Chita Hantō, Shōdoshima, and Sasaguri pilgrimages, all of which are focused on Kōbō Daishi and are based on the Shikoku model. They are all much shorter than the Shikoku pilgrimage and especially in earlier times served as ways for those unable to get to Shikoku to do the pilgrimage in their local area.[10] It was common for respondents to have done some of these regional pilgrimages, in some cases many times each; one, who lived in Aichi prefecture, said he had done the Chita Hantō pilgrimage (located in Aichi) 188 times. One respondent cited twelve different pilgrimage circuits, mostly centred on the bodhisattva Kannon, that he had done; this was the most by any of those surveyed, though several others had done half a dozen or more different pilgrimages. Two had done several pilgrimages in Hokkaidō, the northernmost island of Japan. One person stated that he had not only done the 100-Kannon pilgrimage (a combined pilgrimage involving the three prominent Kannon pilgrimages of Saikoku, Bandō, and Chichibu) but had also walked the length of the main islands of the Japanese archipelago, from Sōya Misaki in northern Hokkaidō to Sata Misaki at the southern tip of Kyushu in Kagoshima prefecture. Another pilgrimage commonly performed was the Shikoku Bekkaku pilgrimage—a pilgrimage group of twenty temples in Shikoku with connections to Kōbō Daishi and that are often seen as having links to the Shikoku pilgrimage temples. Several respondents indicated that they were *sendatsu* on this pilgrimage as well as Shikoku. Two respondents mentioned pilgrimage visits to a temple in China (Seiryūji) where Kūkai had trained; they also referred to this as Temple 0, a term that indicates a view that this is an 'origin' temple for the Shikoku pilgrimage, given Kūkai's connection with Shikoku. One had done a large number of walks to various

---

[10] See Reader 1988 for a discussion of regional small-scale versions of the Shikoku pilgrimage.

shrines and temples in his home prefecture (Okayama) that he referred to as pilgrimages (*junrei*) and that involved hikes of thirty or so kilometres each.

We asked our respondents if they thought they would ever stop doing the Shikoku *henro*. This elicited uniform responses: either a straightforward no or a reply along the lines of 'as long as I can / as long as I am able to still do it' or 'as long as my body is able'. Sometimes respondents conflated both answers. One person did say he might stop at some point and another (aged eighty-three) said he felt he was going to have to do so as his legs were now too weak to carry on. Another said also that he hoped the time would never come when he would have to give up. One respondent, who always walked, did not answer this question directly but had said in reply to an earlier question about whether numbers matter, that he wanted to continue doing the pilgrimage as long as his body and money allowed. He also said that each year after finishing he says 'not next year' but when November comes around he always starts planning again. Such responses reflect the views we cited in earlier chapters—by the time people have done several pilgrimages they have become immersed in an unending pilgrimage path that they wish never to end and that will only be terminated by death or physical incapacity.

In response to how much time they spent each year on the pilgrimage, all said it depended on their circumstances. Everyone spent a significant amount of time each year, although some added that they were now having less time to spend because of age and weakening bodies. One pilgrim summed up this issue of ageing by saying that he had been doing the pilgrimage ten times a year taking seven days each time and thus spending seventy days a year on pilgrimage. Now, however, he was down to shorter three-day, two-night trips. Another respondent also said he used to do it ten times a year but was down to two or three. The one who appeared to spend the most time now on the pilgrimage replied that (save for January, August, and December) he spent nearly all his time on the *henro*. Other respondents spent respectively, one-third of their time and two-and-a-half months annually on the pilgrimage. Walkers, who often broke their journeys up into shorter sections, tended to spend between forty and sixty days a year on the route. One did it in around fifty-five days each year, while another now makes ten visits a year to the pilgrimage route, walking for four or five days each time. Two respondents, while not answering the question directly, expressed aspirations; one simply wanted to spend half his life 'with Daishi' while the other, instead of saying how long he spent on pilgrimage, simply urged us to do the pilgrimage.

Other observations

Even this small number of responses—like the small number of long-term itinerants discussed in the previous chapter—demonstrates that there are many variations and attitudinal differences among those who do multiple pilgrimages in Shikoku, even as there are also many themes that draw them together. These themes also came through in our interviews and will emerge in more detail in the following chapters.

At the same time, alongside the multiple variations, some clear themes emerged. Our respondents were almost all retired, with pensions and in most cases savings that enabled them to do the pilgrimage. They also remained well enough to still do the pilgrimage even as some recognised that they were ageing and slowing down. The responses certainly underline the point made by the interviewee cited in Chapter 2, who said that having free time, health, and money were the prime factors in facilitating multiple pilgrimages. It is clear, too, that expenditures on the pilgrimage formed a significant element in their personal economies; several, indeed, indicated that they took on part-time work to help support their pilgrimage interests.

Most lived in or near to Shikoku. This does not mean that all those involved in unending pilgrimages in Shikoku are retired people living in the vicinity of the island; some of our respondents (and many of those whose stories we tell in the next two chapters) come from farther afield and many are in work, fitting in their pilgrimage activities around their work schedules. Proximity is certainly an aide to multiple performance but not a necessary element in it; the allure of Shikoku reaches far beyond its immediate geographical area. So too is retirement an aide to doing multiple pilgrimages but not a necessity.

In practical terms walking and going by car were the most prominent ways of doing it, and several used both; while some who went by foot indicated that they thought this to be the best way to do it, none thought that it was the only way. This again reflects the views we have heard throughout our studies of Shikoku: that doing it whichever way one wishes is acceptable, that not everyone can walk, and that more important than the manner of doing it is the fact that one does it. We also should note that several respondents had done the pilgrimage by car and on foot, and sometimes also by bus tours (or had led pilgrimage tours), and that this hybrid nature of doing the pilgrimage may well have helped develop a tolerance for all manner of pilgrimage performance.

It is clear also that there are ambivalent feelings about numbers. All our respondents refuted the idea of competition and records, dismissing the importance of numbers, while some expressed a degree of cynicism about emblems such as brocade *fuda*. Yet at the same time, our respondents were very aware of numbers and showed respect for those who did it multiple times. Such attitudes reflect what we found among pilgrims in general; as we indicated in Chapter 2, many pilgrims are excited to meet a pilgrim who has a brocade *fuda* or wish to attain that status themselves. They were also very aware of how many pilgrimages they had made—something that we found throughout our research, save for permanent itinerants and, just occasionally, one or two car pilgrims. Walkers, even when critical of those who used other means or piled up high numbers, were nonetheless invariably aware of their own number of circuits. In other words, there is an ambivalence towards numbers, with everyone saying they are not interested in numbers and records. They say that these are not relevant while simultaneously being highly aware of them, whether displaying this via public manifestations such as brocade *fuda* inscribed with their number of circuits or talking about how many times they had walked the route.

Faith in some form or other plays a part in the allure of the pilgrimage, notably expressed through feelings of respect or reverence for Kōbō Daishi. Coupled with this was a feeling shared by many respondents that through their pilgrimages they received various benefits, sometimes miracles, and certainly a sense of spiritual amelioration. Yet faith was not unquestioning or universal, with some, notably walkers (something we found also in our interviews that are reported in Chapter 6), being less focused less on ideas of faith than on seeing the pilgrimage as a walking route that helps keep them fit. For some the idea of benefits was grounded in the highly practical view that doing the pilgrimage was good physical exercise. It was also striking that many respondents viewed Kōbō Daishi as human in nature, portraying him as a friend, a practical worker for good, and a historical figure whose influence resonates to this day. This also fits with interviewees cited in earlier chapters who spoke of Daishi as a friend or said they were 'fans' of his. Only one respondent mentioned notions such as transmigration and rebirth, despite these being proclaimed as important symbolic elements in the pilgrimage.[11]

---

[11] See Reader 2005: 63–64 for a discussion of this issue.

A striking finding was that for the most part these serial pilgrims did not limit themselves to Shikoku. While the *henro* was their core pilgrimage focus, they did not ignore other pilgrimage routes, with many of Japan's well-known pilgrimages (from the nationally known Saikoku pilgrimage to prominent regional pilgrimage routes) featuring in the lists of other pilgrimages they had done. Nor did they do these other pilgrimages just once; several respondents listed a number of other pilgrimages they had done numerous times. Some held *sendatsu* ranks at other pilgrimages besides Shikoku—something that we came across not just among questionnaire respondents but from other multiple performing pilgrims we met or whose *fuda* we were able to examine. Thus one pilgrim whose *fuda* we found in the scrapbook of brocade *fuda* held at Temple Twenty-Four's lodge (see Chapter 2) who had done the Shikoku henro 111 times, not only held a senior *sendatsu* title in Shikoku, but listed five other Japanese pilgrimage circuits on which he was also a registered *sendatsu*.

In other words, addiction to pilgrimage is not specifically limited to Shikoku, which is to an extent a manifestation of a wider association with, or addiction to, pilgrimage in general. This was not something limited to the questionnaire respondents, for pilgrims we met and interviewed often also indicated that they had done several pilgrimages besides Shikoku. Even Nakatsukasa Mōhei, perhaps the most engrossed pilgrim of all in Shikoku terms, twice left Shikoku during his fifty-six years peregrination to do other pilgrimages. However, for him as for our serial pilgrims in general, Shikoku remained the central factor in an unending engagement in pilgrimage.

Questionnaire responses highlighted a theme that emerged repeatedly in our interviews, namely that there is a special condition or addiction, referred to most commonly as *Shikokubyō*, but with other variations including *Shikoku chūdoku* and *henro boke*, that keeps pilgrims associated with the Shikoku *henro*. This remains central to the wider theme of unending pilgrimage. Most respondents affirmed that they had a form of *Shikokubyō* but one that was not something to be complained of, and they rejected the idea that it was in any sense a real illness. Rather, it was something pleasant, to be welcomed and embraced. Nor did they see it as something they ever wanted to stop. Pilgrimage might be addictive, but it was a welcome addiction, an unending lifelong process and a state of permanence that was not just physical but mental as well.

Schedules and speeds

Two questions we did not specifically ask were how many days they took for each pilgrimage and how often they did the pilgrimage each year, although the responses we received contained some information on these issues. We also were able to gather data via interviews and the *fuda* that pilgrims left at temples, while earlier research on the pilgrimage further helped us develop an understanding of such matters.[12] All these sources indicated that schedules and patterns of pilgrimage vary from pilgrim to pilgrim and that each pilgrim determines his or her ways, speed and schedules. This is a major attraction of the Shikoku pilgrimage in that it offers scope for every person to determine their own itineraries and engage with the pilgrimage in the ways they think most appropriate to them. While those who walk the pilgrimage take much longer and do less circuits than those who go by their own transport, we also found, both from what walkers wrote on their questionnaires and from interviews with walkers (see Chapter 6) that many regular walkers did one circuit per year, with a very small number saying that they might do it twice a year. By contrast, those who went by car, usually with their vehicles serving as their peripatetic home while on the pilgrimage, did many more circuits and tended to do spend far longer actually on the pilgrimage each year.

There are factors that can constrain pilgrim schedules or facilitate speedier performances. One is the opening times of the temples themselves; the Shikoku Pilgrimage Temples' Association has determined that the temples should maintain standard opening hours for the offices that stamp pilgrim books and scrolls.[13] This standardisation was instituted because pilgrims complained that they might arrive late in the afternoon at a temple only to find it closed and hence were unable to get their books stamped. Nowadays the temples open from 7 a.m. to 5 p.m. (open 8 a.m. in winter). This limits the amount of time each day that people can do the pilgrimage if they wish to get their books stamped. However those who do not wish or need to get their books stamped—something not uncommon for those who have performed hundreds of pilgrimages and whose books are already wholly red—are less

---

[12] See, for example, Reader 2005; Hoshino 2001; and Osada, Sakata, and Seki 2003.

[13] This has caused disputes at time, and for a while one temple, Temple Sixty-Two, had different opening times, leading to a split with the Temples' Association. However as of 15 December 2019 this dispute has been resolved and Temple Sixty-Two now follows the same hours and rules as all the other pilgrimage temples. See this report in the religious newspaper Chūgai Nippō https://www. chugainippoh.co.jp/article/news/20190802–001.html (accessed 10 December 2019).

constrained and can visit some temples out of hours. Not all temples are open all hours, however, for many temples have gates that shut at night; the authors have at times arrived at temples too late to enter. We have heard that some pilgrims stand outside the gate and perform their rituals even if the temple is closed, and then move on, thereby (in their minds) having performed the act of visiting that temple; a priest who knew one of the pilgrims with the highest numbers told us that this man extended his pilgrimage day well beyond temple opening hours through this method. Indeed this priest suggested that the pilgrim in question sometimes spent eighteen hours a day on the pilgrimage. Although we have not directly interviewed anyone who says they do this, several informants at the temples have reported that this is not an unknown practice, and we will cite one example shortly.

For those who perform the pilgrimage hundreds of times, being able to spend very long hours each day and to move around swiftly are important. Various pilgrims have told us that they have set routines and fixed numbers of days in which they do the pilgrimage, such as the couple in Chapter 2 who said it took them six days to do the whole circuit. For some this appears too quick, as was the case with the example of Nakagawa, who claimed anyone who did it in less than the nine or so days he took could not be doing it properly. As with so much in the pilgrimage, such views are highly personalised; pilgrims we have talked to who do it in six days or less are as adamant that their way is correct and legitimate as is Nakagawa with his contrary claims. Certainly there is no regulation stipulating a minimum time one has to spend on each circuit or at each temple. There are various rituals and activities that are commonly done at each temple that feature in guidebooks to the pilgrimage and are cited in official instructions and guidelines for *sendatsu* produced by the Temples' Association;[14] one is supposed to go to the main hall of worship and then the Daishi hall to make offerings and recite sutras, invocations, and prayers. These actions take several minutes at least and should be done before going to the temple office to get one's book or scroll stamped. However no-one at the temples is likely to refuse to stamp a pilgrim's book because they have not done sufficient rituals and invocations. We have sometimes been at temples when pilgrims who have clearly come straight to the temple office have been asked to first visit the halls of worship before bringing their books to be stamped, but we have never heard any official ask pilgrims what prayers and rituals they have done or refuse to stamp a

---

[14] See *Shikoku Hachijūhakkasho Reijōkai* 1965, which is the standard guidebook for *sendatsu*.

book because they felt insufficient acts of worship had been carried out. And certainly, too, we have seen pilgrims do only the most cursory activities—perhaps a simple bow and little more—at the halls of worship before getting their book stamped.

Many people we have interviewed have spoken about how they managed to make their circuits more efficient and quicker. Sleeping in one's car equipped with the means to prepare one's own food helps in this respect. As several pilgrims have told us, they can keep travelling until late rather than needing to check in to a lodge and can get moving again very early. Some plan their travels with almost military precision, as was the case with one man who told us he has walked the *henro* fifteen times and who showed us the meticulous records and spread sheets he has drawn up of his pilgrimages, detailing how long it takes (or will take) for each section of the route and so on. Those who are not worried about getting their books stamped—and who thus can call by at the temples after their official closing time—can reduce the amount of time for each circuit significantly as well. Of course, doing it multiple times helps as well. Along with the advantages that GPS navigation systems provide for finding the quickest route between temples, experienced pilgrims also get to know shortcuts and the places where they can go faster and develop skills in accessing such place, which is very important in Shikoku, where some roads (especially up to some of the mountain temples) can be steep, narrow, and difficult to navigate. Several temples have very narrow and single-track access roads; in some places one might have to wait until a car coming the other way has cleared the way, or reverse to a convenient passing place—something that, as we found repeatedly when driving around the route, eats up time. A lady working at one such temple with a very narrow access road commented that people with very high numbers of circuits tended to visit it very early in the morning, when there were rarely any other pilgrims or cars around to impede their progress. As a result, we have come across examples of people—invariably the most experienced pilgrims with the highest numbers of circuits—getting their pilgrimages down to four days or even perhaps less. Being able to do it quicker of course means being able to do more circuits per year.

As we have said previously, those who do the most circuits usually go by car and drive themselves. The importance of this was emphasised to us by a man we met at Temple Eighty-Five in late October 2019. He said he had done twelve circuits on foot and forty-six by car. He had initially walked the *henro* four times but in so doing had met other pilgrims who had done it over fifty times and who had handed him their gold *fuda*. He realised he also wanted to be like them, carrying gold *fuda* to hand out to fellow pilgrims, but he also recognised that he would not be able to achieve this goal by walking, since each circuit on foot took six weeks or so, and he had to combine his pilgrimage activities with full-time work. So he turned to driving and did forty-six circuits by car so as to get to fifty circuits and qualify for a gold *fuda*. After that, however, he went back to walking, which he preferred because going by car did not really challenge him and did not provide the spiritual feelings and experiences he felt when walking.

Like him many pilgrims we have interviewed or surveyed have done the *henro* a multiplicity of ways; it is not uncommon for those who have done dozens or hundreds of circuits by car to also walk it at least once as well, as was evident also in the responses to our questionnaire. However, car pilgrimage remains the predominant (if not only) means for those we have met who carry brocade *fuda*. Most such pilgrims, too, have developed routines and schedules that enable them to do the pilgrimage in a relatively short space of time. To illustrate this and to give a flavour of how doing the pilgrimage hundreds of times can lead to extremely intensive levels of performance, we will outline some examples of the schedules of multiple performers, along with what we know of their backgrounds.

Speedy pilgrimages and intensive performance

In Chapter 2, where we drew attention to the collection of brocade *fuda* held at Temple Twenty-Four's lodge, we cited examples of pilgrims whose *fuda* indicated that they had done multiple pilgrimages in relatively short times—from the woman who in a space of eighteen months did nine pilgrimages, to a man who, over seven years, did sixty-five circuits, thereby averaging over nine pilgrimages in Shikoku a year. Even these are relatively mild levels of performance intensity by some standards however; during a field trip from October to November 2018 we saw two *fuda* left by an eighty-one-year-old man from southern Shikoku; one was from May 2019 from his 150th pilgrimage and the other was from July of that year from his 157th circuit—indicating he had done seven pilgrimages in the space of two months, an average of not much more than a week for each pilgrimage.

Even this is less intensive than some pilgrims whose names and practices emerged frequently during our studies and in interviews and conversations with people at the Shikoku temples. A noodle restaurant owner who had done 230 circuits, whom we met and talked to at a temple in Kōchi prefecture in March 2018, and who also filled in a questionnaire for us, told us on a separate occasion that he was doing around eighteen pilgrimages a year at the time—something that temple officials who knew him confirmed. Others we heard of but were unable to meet were also doing the *henro* at similar or higher levels of intensity. Thus Harayama-san, a pilgrim from Nagasaki prefecture, had done some 223 pilgrimages by late 2019. He also left his brocade *fuda* not just at the temples but at the Maeyama Henro Salon to commemorate special circuits. Such *fuda* have helped us establish his general schedules and regularity of pilgrimage.[15] Temple officials we have talked who knew him invariably considered him to be an especially devout pilgrim who spent much time performing rituals of worship at each temple. They also noted that he did not open up much if at all to them or indicate why he did the pilgrimage so many times, although a lady at one temple office said that she thought he started doing the pilgrimage as a memorial (*kuyō*) for his deceased wife. However, we were unable to discover much more about his motives than this.

We know from materials he left at the Henro Salon that he went there on 9 September 2012 to leave a brocade *fuda* commemorating his 100th circuit, which had been completed in June 2012. He visited again on 27 September 2017, aged seventy-four, leaving another brocade *fuda* (this time commemorating his 200th circuit) to be put on display. His June 2012 *fuda* states, in handwritten Japanese, that it had taken him eight years to complete 100 circuits. This suggests he started doing the pilgrimage in or around 2004— when he would have been around sixty-one—and that he was averaging just over twelve circuits per year. He was quicker from 100 to 200, accomplishing this between June 2012 and September 2017, i.e. just over five years and close to twenty circuits per year. Two *fuda* we have received from his 196th and 199th circuits, the first in May 2017, the second in June 2017, indicate that he was at times doing three circuits within the space of a month. However after his 200th circuit he slowed somewhat, as the *fuda* from his 206th circuit is dated September 2018 and the date on the *fuda* from his 207th circuit is October 2018, indicating that he had done seven circuits in just over a year

---

[15] We were not able to interview or survey him directly, however. He was one of those who did not reply to the questionnaire sent to his home and whom we were never able to come across during our travels in Shikoku.

since September 2017. He appears to have speeded up after this, because we then came across a *fuda* for his 223rd circuit in October 2019, meaning that he had done sixteen circuits in one year since October 2018. None of his *fuda* indicate how many days he took for each circuit but at a minimum estimate of four days for a circuit or a more common six, seven, or more days by car, he would have been spending anything from around sixty-four to well over 100 days in a year on the pilgrimage.

Such examples of multiple circuits, however, pale beside our last two examples, both of whom have done well over 600 and in the second case now 700 circuits, in both cases in less than twenty years. The first is Fukuda Shōnosuke, whom we have already referred to several times, whose stone commemorating his 500th circuit stands outside Temple Six and who, according to an article in the *Henro* newsletter, spent as many as 340 days a year on the pilgrimage (see Chapter 2). Fukuda initially began doing the pilgrimage in 1998 after retiring from work as a truck driver and head of a transport firm in Osaka; he travelled with his wife and daughter, but the next year his wife died. After that Fukuda (whose daughter thereafter ran his company) devoted himself to the pilgrimage, which he did to pray for happiness in the next world for his wife and for colleagues who died in the war. By 2011—fourteen years after he started—he had done the *henro* some 560 times according to a newspaper article,[16] all by car. Economically he was supported by income from his business, which he had bequeathed to his daughter. Eventually he died after completing 648 circuits.

We gathered information on the regularity of Fukuda's pilgrimage circuits from a collection of eighty-two brocade *fuda* that he left at Temple Six and are kept in a display case there. The *fuda*—on each of which Fukuda recorded his age and the number of his circuits—run from his 100th circuit, when he was aged seventy-five, to his 646th, in 2016, when he was ninety. Thus in around fifteen years he did 546 pilgrimage circuits, an average of thirty-six circuits each year. Between the ages of seventy-five (his 100th circuit) and eighty (his 300th) the figure rose to closer to forty pilgrimages per year. According to the priest at Temple Six who knew him, Fukuda took around one week per circuit, which meant he spent roughly forty weeks per year in his retirement years on the pilgrimage. Several priests we talked to who knew or were aware of Fukuda also said that he would regularly do several circuits in a row before returning home for short periods.

---

[16] *Tokushima Shinbun*, 22 July 2011.

Another pilgrim whom we have referred to before as having possibly done more circuits than anyone else and who is currently (at least as of our last fieldtrip to Shikoku in November 2019) still going around the *henro* route regularly, is Nakano, the man who has done over 700 circuits and who has been mentioned in earlier chapters. He is one of those pilgrims we were aware of from early in our research and whom we tried repeatedly to meet, always without success. In the time we were in Shikoku our paths never crossed. Attempts to get in touch by various means met with silence. He is the person cited earlier whom we tried to contact by leaving telephone numbers and messages with temple officials, and to whom we sent questionnaires on two occasions (including times when we thought he would not be on the pilgrimage route) to his home address. We never received any communication in return, possibly because (as several temple officials and priests said to us) he was a very reserved person who, even if he called by at their temples and talked to them, appeared not to reveal much about himself. A priest who said Nakano sometimes stopped to talk to him thought he did not even have a phone.

We made a habit of asking at every temple office and with every pilgrimage temple priest we meet on the circuit whether they knew him, whether he had been seen recently, and whether he followed regular routines. The responses were multiple and varied. He is, we were told by various officials, a farmer who has a fruit business in his home prefecture of Okayama. A lady working at one temple office said that outside of the short summer period when he went home to cater to his fruit business, she thought he was constantly on the pilgrimage. However, at another temple a priest told us that he came three times a year to Shikoku and each time spent around three months constantly circling the island.

It is certainly the case that he has for many years spent much of his time travelling around the pilgrimage. Sometimes priests and temple officials would say to us that he had been at their temple 'just the other day' or that they thought he might call by in the next few days. Some temple priests said he came regularly, at a particular time of day, to their temples, yet other officials at temple offices said they have not seen him for some time and wondered whether he was still doing the pilgrimage. Others still were not aware of him at all, suggesting that if he visits their temples at all he either avoids talking to anyone there or does not go to the office to get his book stamped.

We certainly heard confirmation of this latter point from sources who said that he no longer gets his book stamped at every temple. However, and indicative of how one hears so many divergent stories on the pilgrimage, one priest insisted that Nakano always stopped to get his book stamped even though it was already saturated in red, while a lady working at another temple office told us that he had come there to have his (wholly red) book stamped on his 698th circuit and had said then that he would return again for his 700th—a circuit which he was apparently commemorating by getting stamps at more temples than usual.

Some of those who know him or have talked to him have said that Nakano now has reduced mobility—a result, according to one priest, of having done the *henro* so many times and spent so long in his car that he has damaged his health. Because of this he does not climb up to the halls of worship at temples that have steep steps, instead standing below at the gates to do his various prayers and rituals there. This has helped him do the circuits quickly as he may no longer stop by every temple office or be bound by temple hours. At one temple in Kōchi prefecture, where the main hall of worship is up a steep flight of steps but the Daishi hall and temple office are close by the temple entrance, on the same level as the temple's car parking spaces, a lady at the temple office said that he came there regularly and, unable to climb the steps to the main hall, would just sit on a bench before the Daishi hall and perform his rituals and prayers for both the Daishi and main hall of worship there before getting his book stamped.

He does appear to hand out brocade *fuda* fairly regularly at the temples and at times to fellow pilgrims he meets. This and the information written on them has helped us establish some details of his travels. It appears that in 2019 he was eighty-one years of age and that he started doing the pilgrimage in or around 2002 when he was about sixty-four. An online blog by a pilgrim from Miyazaki in southern Japan writing under a pen name, states that on 11 April 2014 while walking the pilgrimage he met Nakano at Temple Sixty-Three and that Nakano gave him a brocade *fuda* that indicated he was on his 385th circuit. He told the blogger it had taken him twelve years to do this.[17]

Brocade *fuda* of his that we have been shown or been given at temples show that on 17 February 2016, he was aged seventy-eight and on his 445th circuit; on 23 November 2016 on his 488th; and on 10 November 2017, on his 550th pilgrimage circuit. The period between this first dated *fuda* we have and the

---

[17] This is on the Ohenro Pōtaru website where pilgrims discuss pilgrimage experiences: https://www.ohenro-portal.jp/doucyu/193/201404/2209.html (accessed 14 January 2020).

one from his 550th circuit is 633 days (ninety weeks and three days) during which time he had done 105 circuits, indicating an average of just over one circuit per week for the whole period and over fifty circuits in a year. On 26 October 2018 we were shown a *fuda* he had left at Temple Sixty-Five dated 8 October 2018 stating he was on his 625th circuit and that he was aged eighty. The priest there, however, thought Nakano had called by at least three and perhaps as many as five times since then and that he might actually now be on his 630th circuit. Since he said this eighteen days after Nakano had left the aforementioned *fuda*, this suggests at least three and perhaps as many as five circuits in that period, with each circuit taking four or less days. The priest commented that Nakano told him he used to do the whole circuit in three days but now, due to his age, it took four. He also confirmed that Nakano slept in his car. A year later, on 31 October 2019, we met a pilgrim at Temple Eighty-Five who said he had recently, on 26 October 2019, encountered and received two *fuda* from Nakano (one of which this pilgrim passed on to us) that indicated he was on his 698th circuit, and shortly after at Temple Twenty-Eight we were shown the *fuda* he left there on 5 November 2019 while on his 700th circuit. In other words between 8 October 2018, when we saw a *fuda* for his 625th circuit, and 5 November 2019, he had gone from 625 to 700 circuits—a total of seventy-five in thirteen months, or six-and-a-half circuits per month. At four days per circuit that would mean around twenty-six days per month on the pilgrimage averaged throughout the year (around 312 days in a year).

From our discussions with those who knew him it appears he first did the pilgrimage to pray for his wife's health; this was what Nakano told the man who passed on one of his *fuda* to us at Temple Eighty-Five in October 2019. Temple officials and priests also thought his initial motivation related to his wife's poor health and then to perform a memorial (*kuyō*) pilgrimage for her after she died. They also ventured other possible reasons for his continuing pilgrimages; one temple official said he developed close links with a small number of priests around the island and liked to call by and talk to them regularly. One such priest thought that Nakano aspired to attain some form of awakening through multiple performances of the pilgrimage, while another said that self-fulfilment, self-discovery, and praying for his personal future (*jibun no shōrai*) played a part. Several of those we talked to felt that the pilgrimage had become so embedded in his life that it was simply natural for him to keep going on pilgrimage—and that numbers and perhaps records might have become a motivation as well.

Trigger points, memorials, and intensity

We also will make a further suggestion that is another possible factor in some of the cases we have outlined here. The last three examples we have cited, Fukuda, Harayama, and Nakano are all (as are most of those who do the pilgrimage many hundreds of times) men. All three, according to sources who know or knew them, appear to have done the pilgrimage early on as a memorial for a deceased wife and may have continued doing it in part for the same reason. This point was made to us by two ladies working at one temple office who said they thought that those who did the *henro* many hundreds of times had, in their experience, generally had some special 'trigger' (the term they used was *kikkake*—trigger or motivating factor) that drew them into the pilgrimage, and that this was the death (or initially the illness leading to death) of their wives. As a result the bereaved men then set out, as have many pilgrims in Shikoku over the ages, to do the pilgrimage as a memorial rite for their wives. They then returned home to an empty house that made them feel lonely and unhappy because their wife was no longer there—leading them to go back again to Shikoku where they had found people to talk to while on their pilgrimage. As a result they began to find a sense of community or comfort there that countered the emptiness and loneliness of their home; for some, they might even feel the presence of their departed loved one there.[18] As such, the ladies at the temple suggested, they became increasingly focused on the pilgrimage, where they could feel more at home and at ease than at their actual homes, where they were more acutely aware of their bereavement.

While we cannot specifically say that the cases cited here are specifically sparked by bereavement and loneliness, all three appear to be of men at or near retirement age who lost their wives, did the pilgrimage as a memorial for them, and then became immersed in the *henro*. As we also noted earlier in our summary of replies to our questionnaire, several respondents cited doing memorials for a dead spouse as a factor in their engagement with the pilgrimage. Doing the Shikoku *henro* as a memorial for a deceased relative has been a common motivating factor for pilgrims, and many of those we

---

[18] In earlier research on Shikoku pilgrims we encountered such feelings, with pilgrims feeling the presence of their deceased kin while doing the pilgrimage as a memorial for them (Reader 2005: 80–82; see also Araki 1990 and Yamamoto 1995: 13). Moreover, in November 2019 one of us met a woman from Tokyo who was doing the pilgrimage on foot, for the first time, as a memorial for her deceased brother and her parents. She told the author in question she felt happy and at ease on the pilgrimage because she felt she was walking 'with' her brother's spirit and those of her parents.

met during our fieldwork cited this as a key element in their pilgrimages. For example, an eighty-two year old man from Ishikawa prefecture met at a wayside temple in Kōchi prefecture who was walking the pilgrimage for the fourth time told us that he first did the pilgrimage nine years earlier, aged seventy-three, after his wife died, as a memorial for her. He added that *Daishi shinkō* played a small role in his pilgrimages, but he was mainly motivated to do it again as a memorial rite for his wife and because, when doing the first pilgrimage, he met so many people who were kind to and supportive of him. Moreover it kept him fit, active, and motivated to keep doing memorial rites for his wife. Thus he came back to walk it again when aged seventy-seven, when eighty, and now eighty-two, although he wondered whether this might be his last pilgrimage; he wanted to keep going as long as he could, and he knew he was slowing down and was not sure he could manage another pilgrimage. Bereavement and the wish to perform memorial services for a deceased relative or spouse thus were factors in his starting to do the pilgrimage and in causing him to return.

Fukuda and Nakano's initial engagement with the pilgrimage also appears to be of a similar ilk, sparked by bereavement and leading to an intensity of performance that is quite extreme even in the context of a pilgrimage that people do many times. While not itinerants in the sense of the pilgrims we encountered in the previous chapter, who have left their homes behind to live and sleep permanently on the *henro*, they are (or were, in Fukuda's case) virtually itinerant in spending so much of their time circling the island. Their main abode was on the pilgrimage and in their vehicles, while their actual homes in effect became marginal and even transient places of existence. They are also, somewhat akin to itinerant walkers, highly individualised, usually travelling alone and maintaining some sense of distance from others. They thus represent in an extreme form the types of pilgrims we have introduced in this chapter who do the pilgrimage many times. They also show how motorisation can intensify the practice of pilgrimage. We now turn, in the next chapter, to other aspects of the world of motorised pilgrimage and, in particular and in some contrast, to the individualised modes outlined here, its social dimensions, and how these contribute to the culture of repetition.

5

Pilgrims and their cars

Sociability, scenery, faith, and enjoyment

The importance of motorised pilgrimage

A man who had done over 250 pilgrimages around Shikoku, sometimes with a pilgrimage confraternity but mainly in his car customised for sleeping overnight, commented to one of the authors about the significance of motorised transport in the pilgrimage. It was the most common form of pilgrimage in modern times and yet was largely neglected in academic studies and popular accounts; by contrast, he complained, those who walk the pilgrimage got all the attention. He in effect made a plea for a study of motorised pilgrims to remedy what he saw was an imbalance in discussions of the contemporary Shikoku *henro*. In this chapter we address his plea by looking at what is now the largest sector of the Shikoku pilgrimage community: those who travel by motorised transport and who also make up the majority of those who do multiple pilgrimages there.

The Shikoku pilgrimage developed, as we discussed in Chapter 1, as a pilgrimage on foot, and there remains a tradition of doing the pilgrimage multiple times on foot, as we indicated in Chapter 3 and will return to in the next chapter. However, despite a tendency in some quarters to claim walking as the 'authentic' way of doing the pilgrimage[1] there is no stipulation evident in the pilgrimage's history that one should do it this way. Certainly it was for centuries the only viable way to do it, but this effectively meant that many people were shut out from the possibility of doing the pilgrimage for reasons of gender, age, and health. As we discussed in Chapter 2, it was the advent of modern transport and its accompanying support structures that enabled many people to become pilgrims in Shikoku. Indeed, for a prolonged period from the 1950s, when bus pilgrimage tours in Shikoku revived what

---

[1] See Chapter 4, especially note 7, and also Reader 2005 and 2014 for discussions and criticisms of the idea of 'authenticity' and of the idea that walking is 'the' correct way to do the Shikoku pilgrimage.

Pilgrims Until We Die. Ian Reader and John Shultz, Oxford University Press. © Oxford University Press 2021.
DOI: 10.1093/oso/9780197573587.003.0006

was at the time a partially defunct pilgrimage, until the 1990s, walkers were few and far between, especially compared to those who used buses.[2] Even though walker numbers have increased since then, this segment of the pilgrimage population remains small compared to those who travel by motorised means. Walking remains only one aspect—a minority one in terms of overall pilgrim numbers—of the contemporary pilgrimage.[3]

While bus tour pilgrimages were dominant until the 1990s, in more recent times, as we noted in Chapter 2, there has been a shift towards more individualised pilgrimage by car. Now bus tour groups, and notably large coach-size groups, are comparatively rare; during our field visits from 2018 to 2019, we barely saw any bus tours, even in the high pilgrimage seasons of early spring and autumn.[4] Temple officials and priests on several occasions mentioned the rapid decline of bus tours in recent years to us and confirmed what we and others had observed, that pilgrims travelling in cars or vans, whether individually, in couples or occasionally in small confraternity groups, now are the most visible part of the pilgrimage numerically. They also constitute a significant group in terms of the patterns of repeated intensive pilgrimage in Shikoku.

We have already seen this in earlier chapters, where we drew attention to practices such as *shachūhaku*, sleeping in one's car or van, and to the speedy and intensive schedules of some motorised pilgrims. In this chapter we develop these themes by focusing on motorisation as a driving force in unending pilgrimage and by looking at contexts in which people become involved in recurrent circuits of Shikoku. Notably this relates to the social dimensions that contribute to this phenomenon, including membership and involvement in organised confraternities or in informal social groups. We also examine one of the most striking manifestations of social multiple performance—that of husband and wife couples doing it together, very often sleeping in vehicles adapted for the purpose—as well as those who travel on their own but who often find a sense of community with others who travel in similar ways. One theme also evident in this chapter is that many such

---

[2] These issues have been explored in depth by Reader (2005) and Mori (2005) for Shikoku specifically and by Reader (2014) in more general terms. Maeda (1971), referring to the era when bus tour pilgrimages became prevalent, and Satō (2004), also illustrate this development.

[3] Mori 2005; Reader 2005, 2014.

[4] A survey of pilgrims published by the Shikoku Keizai Rengōkai (the Shikoku economic federation) in 2019 showed a general decrease in pilgrim numbers in the period since 2010 but with bus pilgrimages showing significantly the greatest decline (Shikoku Araiansu Chiiki Keizai Kenkyū Bunkakai 2019: 55).

pilgrims are female; by the latter part of the twentieth century, thanks particularly to the rise of motorised transport, females had changed from being a
minority into the largest segment of the community.[5]

Pilgrimage groups, leaders, and the social sides of pilgrimage

In recent years Kawamura-san, the man who commented that motorised pilgrims had been neglected in comparison to those who walk, has averaged
around twenty circuits a year, mainly on his own and sleeping in his car.
He also has a close association with a pilgrimage confraternity based in his
home prefecture of Ehime in Shikoku and does pilgrimages also with them.
The association he is linked to, the Sanwakai, is run by Hirose-san, a man
aged seventy-two from Saijō in Ehime who had (as of 2019) done over 230
Shikoku pilgrimage circuits as well as having a full-time job. In 2018 one of
us met him and his confraternity at their base in Ehime and also took part in
one of their pilgrimage outings. Hirose had established the Sanwakai around
twelve years earlier in order to encourage others to follow in his footsteps and
become ardent pilgrims. He himself appears to do a whole circuit of the pilgrimage every two or so months; his brocade *fuda* from his 100th pilgrimage,
dated August 2005, is in the collection of brocade *fuda* at Temple Twenty-
Four's lodge (see Chapter 2), while later *fuda* that we have seen show he was
on his 225th circuit in March 2018 and his 232nd in June 2019. In just under
fourteen years, in other words, he had done 132 circuits, an average of nine or
so per year; like several others we have met in this book, his pilgrimages have
been fitted into and around his work schedules, and he has mainly doing the
henro in stages, over weekends, and sleeping in his car.

Besides his own pilgrimages he leads the Sanwakai on a regular basis, doing
two full pilgrimage circuits a year with them. Each circuit by the Sanwakai
consists of six weekend trips, each of two days and one night. During the first
five they complete, in stages, a circuit of the eighty-eight Shikoku temples.
For the sixth they go to Tōji, the famous Shingon temple in Kyoto founded by
Kūkai, and Kōyasan. The weekend pilgrimage outings are spread throughout

---

[5] See also Chapters 1 and 2. Studies indicate that while Shikoku had more female pilgrims than
some other routes in pre-modern times, they constituted less under a third of all pilgrims, whereas by
the late twentieth century they represented well over sixty per cent of all pilgrims (Reader 2005: 77–
78; Satō 2004).

the year, one each month, so that the group has a continuous schedule with an outing every month; when one of us accompanied the group on their visit to Tōji and Kōyasan to complete one circuit, members were talking about and already looking forward to the next month's pilgrimage trip when they would start a new circuit. There was, as such, no sense of a break or end point to their pilgrimage but instead a feeling of continuity and of the pilgrimage as a constant activity rather than a singular finite event. Moreover, it became clear from talking to members that once they started a circuit with the group they were committed to seeing it through and not missing any of the monthly outings. The group's social dynamic thus reinforced a sense of continuity and unending engagement.

This schedule suits those who are, like Hirose himself, working; around half of the confraternity's members were employed and half were retired. There was (when we met the group) only one couple involved, and a slight preponderance of women; many were widows who became involved after losing their husbands. However, from conversations with them it appeared that their involvement was not related to doing memorials for their deceased husbands but more about developing social contacts and doing something to get them out of their homes. In all the confraternity has some ninety members from all over Japan, with the large majority coming from the area where the leader lives. Others are from more distant places such as Osaka, Ishikawa prefecture, and the southern island of Kyushu. Some thirty of the ninety are considered to be active members (i.e. participating regularly in their pilgrimage activities), while around sixty are registered *sendatsu*, with the rest usually working towards, and encouraged to acquire, that status. Members were keenly aware of their *sendatsu* registration number and respected the status of *sendatsu*; those who were not yet *sendatsu* appeared, in meetings and pilgrimage outings, to be of junior status and were given orders about what to do and tasks that they had to look after. It was they, for example, who had to carry the group members' pilgrim books and get them stamped.

The significance of status and what it meant to members came through in a curious incident while drinking with confraternity members in an *izakaya* (Japanese style restaurant and drinking establishment) in Hirose's home town of Saijō. It also demonstrates how pilgrimage experiences can fit into an even wider social dynamic on the island. While dining at the bar with Hirose, Imai-san, a woman who, as we discuss later, is a leading light in the group, and Mizuno-san, a nurse who works with Imai and who is enthusiastically rising up in the organisation, a briefly tense situation developed. Three working men, their skin darkened from hours in the sun, were quaffing co-pious amounts of drink and generally enjoying themselves when the man nearest to Mizuno began teasing, flirting, and speaking somewhat inappro-priately to her. The man aside of him eventually struck him playfully and said that he should stop doing this as the ladies were *sendatsu* and thus deserved respect. The third man on the far side agreed completely with this assertion, while the two ladies seemed to straighten up with pride, acknowledging that they were, in fact, a special case. The inappropriateness ceased immediately. The brief episode showed part of the attraction of a confraternity with an em-phasis on pilgrimage guides; members were endowed with a certain status that even non-pilgrim locals in Shikoku hold in regard.

Hirose is both the founder of the group and its unchallenged leader. The group has no formal rules or written guidelines, although there appeared to some common practices engaged in by all members. To all intents and purposes their activities are overseen and directed by Hirose, who refers to members as his *deshi* (disciples, followers) and supports and encourages their endeavours to acquire *sendatsu* status. They all, according to Hirose, carry a pilgrim's book (see Figure 5.1), and all members also have a white pilgrim's shirt (*hakui*) that they get stamped at the temples and that will be used as a funeral garment when they die. On the occasion of the visit to Kōyasan two of the group were getting their *hakui* stamped (the others having already had their funeral *hakui* fully stamped by all the temples on earlier pilgrimage circuits).

Although Hirose is the leader he also defers to and accords respect and even reverence to the aforementioned Kawamura, who has done more pil-grimages than him and is treated by Hirose and all the others as an elder whose experience of the pilgrimage makes him an authority whose views are always listened to. Other group members, too, have acquired status and re-spect due to their engagement with the group. Thus Imai, who is aged seventy and is still in full-time work, appears to all intents and purposes to be Hirose's lieutenant, overseeing the group's activities. Well organised and efficient, she is head of a large care centre for the elderly in her hometown and shows no signs of quitting work. She has been involved with the group for around ten to twelve years and was, when we talked to her in June 2018, on her nine-teenth pilgrimage circuit. She had been introduced to the Sanwakai by Kataoka-san, a ninety-year-old man who was viewed as an elder statesman within the group; other members treated him with respect and looked after him during the pilgrimage to Kōyasan. At the time of our meeting he had

Figure 5.1 Pilgrim's shirt (*hakui*) with temple stamps on it

done sixty-nine circuits but had only started doing the pilgrimage when aged seventy-six, averaging around five circuits a year since then. As of June 2018 he had also visited Kōyasan and got his pilgrim's book stamped there sixty-seven times. His family background is in Shingon Buddhism, and he recalled his excitement at first visiting Kōyasan when he was aged fifty-five, although it was not until two decades later that he began doing the *henro*. Kataoka was keen to increase his number of circuits and informed us that besides the two circuits a year he does with the Sanwakai he also does three tours per year on organised bus pilgrimage tours. He was one of the few people we met who had done over fifty pilgrimages that had all been done with parties of pilgrims and in organised tours.

We were able to glean information from several others with varying levels of experience during our interactions with the group. One woman, aged eighty, whose husband had died in 2005 and whose offspring had long since left home to live in Tokyo, said she had initially been alone at home spending her time mourning her husband. Then she encountered the Sanwakai and got into doing the pilgrimage as a result, around 2006. Since then she has done the pilgrimage with the group around twenty times, usually twice a year, and she intends to keep doing it as long as she is able and well enough. She was one of the few who was not a *sendatsu* (even though she had done the pilgrimage enough times to qualify), and she appeared uninterested in the idea; nor did she evince any sense of veneration for Kōbō Daishi or indicate any faith-related reason for doing the pilgrimage. For her being with a supportive group that got her out of her home was a paramount factor in her engagement with the *henro*.

Another female who lived in the same area as Hirose and who was in her seventies said she had done the pilgrimage eleven times and intended to continue doing it as long as she was able; she mentioned costs as a limiting factor in this respect. While not giving a clear reason why she started doing the *henro*, she did express a sense of reverence for *o-Daishi-san* (honourable Daishi) as she called him. What was interesting about this was that she had also stated that she was the most 'non-religious' (*mushūkyō*) of the group; moreover, she said, her husband had been explicitly hostile to religion (*shūkyō*). However, he had died in 2007 and she started doing her pilgrimages after this. Even though she was overtly 'non-religious', some sense of feeling for Kōbō Daishi, alongside a social sense of interaction with the group, played a role in keeping her involved in the confraternity.

Another woman involved with the group was aged seventy-six and originally from Niihama, in the part of Ehime where the Sanwakai is based. She now lived in Nishinomiya, a town between Osaka and Kobe on the main island of Honshu. She had done the pilgrimage five times, the lowest number of all those we met in the group, and regarded all other members as her *senpai* (seniors). She first did the pilgrimage with the group three years previously and now does it once or twice a year with them depending on circumstances. She said she originally met 'sensei' (teacher, i.e. Hirose) through one of the group members and via her social contacts in the area. She stated that she initially did the pilgrimage some twelve or thirteen years previously with a women's group she was in that decided to do the Shikoku pilgrimage together as a social activity. It was not, she said, anything related to faith but primarily a social matter of a group of people wanting to do something together. She also indicated there was a clear tourist dimension to that journey. Then her husband died and she thought of doing the pilgrimage again, especially as her son was then aged forty-two, the traditional Japanese male 'unlucky age/year' (yakudoshi), which has often been cited as a reason for doing the pilgrimage.[6] Subsequently, she was introduced to the Sanwakai by contacts in her home region and she now does pilgrimages with them. She also referred to her background as a native of Shikoku, opining that if one lives or comes from Shikoku one should do the henro at least once. She expressed a sense of reverence for o-Daishi-san and said that making requests (onegai) to him was a motivation for her, but she also emphasised the social dimensions of doing pilgrimages and spoke about the 'pilgrimage friends' (ohenro no tomodachi) she had made through the group. Another group member, Iguchi-san, a male from Niihama who became a sendatsu four years ago, further emphasised the social dimensions of pilgrimage, saying that his experience of the henro was wholly related to the Sanwakai and to its members who were 'friends' (tomodachi). While he also mentioned Shikokubyō he especially cited the social dimensions of the group as a factor in his continuing involvement with the pilgrimage. This, indeed, was something that came through in all the conversations we had with members.

Hirose's standing as a committed leader and guide has spread beyond the immediate confines of the Sanwakai, as was evident when a woman from Osaka, Okuno-san, joined the group at Kōyasan after driving from Osaka. Although she had previously done a pilgrimage with the Sanwakai she was actually affiliated to another pilgrimage confraternity based in Osaka. It was, however, about to lose its leader. As a result, she said, she was receiving advice and training from Hirose so that she could assume a leadership role in her Osaka confraternity. At the same time, because she was not really a member of the Sanwakai, she appeared to keep a distance from group members and appeared not to mesh too well with them. Her presence, however, indicated

---

[6] Reader 2005: 15, 45.

how Hirose sought to aid others and to develop support for the pilgrimage through confraternity networks.

The Sanwakai is a good example of how ardent pilgrims and the social groups they form can encourage commitment to and increased practice of the pilgrimage. Hirose has built up his own extensive knowledge and experience through repeated pilgrimages fitted into his work schedule and life, extending this into further performances leading the Sanwakai. In so doing he has aided others to do recurrent pilgrimages. The group's annual schedule of two circuits a year done over weekends spread across the whole twelve-month cycle has created a sense of continuity and unending engagement among all who take part. Members who join in with the group's activities are spurred to do repeated pilgrimages and acquire *sendatsu* status, and in so doing, are very much on the way to becoming like their mentors, pilgrims with long histories of multiple performance.

While faith is important for Hirose and Kawamura and at least some of the others, there is clearly also a strong social dimension to the Sanwakai; several members, as we have indicated, said that their involvement was primarily related to this. As we have seen, too, members socialise by going out together to eat and drink. They were drawn to the Sanwakai primarily through social connections, for example, by being introduced to Hirose's group by someone who was a local contact from the Niihama area. The group thus expanded its network via social interactions, offering members a way to get out of their homes, travel, bond and do something with others. Especially for those resident in or with community links to Shikoku, it helped reinforce their sense of local culture and identity.

The deeply interpersonal social aspects of the group were evident during the final stage of their pilgrimage circuit, the aforementioned visit to Kōyasan in June 2018. There was a great degree of social bonding and encouragement on display throughout, with members putting their hands on each other's shoulders, occasionally slapping backs, and giving spontaneous hugs. The group engaged in serious prayer and worship rituals at each temple and site visited, but outside of these moments the overall atmosphere was quite light-hearted and playful. While group members refer to Hirose as *sensei* and respect him immensely, there was little talk amongst them about matters of faith. Even when they talked about Kōbō Daishi and referred to prayer requests (*onegai*) that they made to him, they tended to talk about him mainly as a friend and a familiar figure who is 'there' and able to help one if one wants.

Confraternities, encouragement, and reinforcement

Confraternities such as this have been a significant element in the development and performance of pilgrimages in Japan and they provide both a faith-oriented and social dimension to the pilgrimage.[7] Other confraternities associated with the Shikoku *henro*, such as the Shiga Shingyōkai, have also been instrumental in facilitating long-term engagements with the pilgrimage. The Shingyōkai was established by Naitō Kinpō, who initially walked the pilgrimage in 1923, and it was run after his death by his son and descendants. Over several generations it has supported and encouraged people in the Nagahama area of Shiga prefecture to do the *henro* through its regular meetings and group pilgrimages there.[8] It remains active albeit smaller than in decades past, according to a man we met in March 2018 at Temple Thirty-Eight who told us he was in the Shingyōkai. Aged seventy-six, he told us that it was due to the Shingyōkai that he first began walking the pilgrimage in 1995; since then he had come to Shikoku many times. He always walked it in short sections, usually two nights and three days at a time, and sleeping out; interestingly, unlike most walkers we met, he could not recall how many circuits he had done and nor did he have a pilgrim's book that could serve as a reminder. He indicated also that his association with the pilgrimage would continue, through the Shingyōkai and walking, as long as he was able.

Another example of how involvement with a confraternity or similar faith-based organisation along with the inspiration of a powerful individual figure can spur people to become ardent pilgrims and reinforce their beliefs came in an extended interview we did with a woman named Terao Noriko in October 2019. In her mid-seventies, she is widowed, although she stated that she communicated regularly with her deceased husband's spirit and that he was spiritually always with her and accompanied her on her pilgrimages. She also said that she receives messages from various spiritual figures, ranging from Shinran (founder of the True Pure Land sect in Japan) to the bodhisattva Kannon and Kōbō Daishi. Her entire life has been framed by spiritual encounters and feelings that the world is populated by spirits that influence and co-exist with humans. Born in Kagoshima in southern Japan, her family

---

[7] There is an extensive literature on this topic both in Japanese and Western languages. See, for example, Shinno 1980, 1991; Shinjō 1982 passim, but esp. 776–787; Bouchy 1987; and Kouamé 2001, esp. 241–247.

[8] On this confraternity see Reader 2005: 92–96.

background was steeped in folk traditions and religious associations. Her father was born into a Buddhist temple family while her grandmother was a *reinōshi* (spiritual healer), and the family had a strong association with spiritual healing, pilgrimage, and prayer. Terao recalled that when young she and her siblings were taken to spiritual healers not doctors. She continues to eschew medicine, relies on doing pilgrimages and getting blessings from religious figures to keep her healthy, claims she never gets ill, and last had any illness almost half a century ago. She thinks all illnesses (including cancer) can be cured through spiritual means.

Terao visits numerous shrines, temples, and pilgrimage circuits. She makes annual visits (*Ise mairi*) to the Ise shrines,[9] and is devoted to the bodhisattva Kannon. She started doing the thirty-three stage Saikoku Kannon pilgrimage in 1983 and in all has done it thirteen times, always as a series of day (*higaeri*) trips from her home near Osaka. She has also done several other Kannon pilgrimages. She also venerates Kōbō Daishi, has done the Shikoku pilgrimage seven times, starting in 2011, and visits Kōyasan regularly; when we interviewed her in October 2019 she had been there 219 times. She always carries scrolls and books to be stamped there; as she said this she produced two pilgrimage scrolls that were filled entirely with the stamps (*shuin*) of Kōyasan to show us.

She believes that ancestors and the spirits of the dead are significant elements in everyday life and that illness is a request or moral reminder from the ancestors to the afflicted person. In particular she emphasises the importance of *mizuko* spirits—the spirits of those who die in the womb (*mizuko*) usually because of abortion. In Japan, after laws facilitating abortion were passed in 1948, some religious practitioners and Buddhist temples began to develop ritual memorial practices (*mizuko kuyō*) for the spirits they believed to be affected in this way. One such institution, a temple and associated society in Chichibu in the Tokyo region, founded by Hashimoto Tetsuma in the early 1950s, became especially prominent in this respect, establishing a series of rituals for the benefit of these spirits and performing pilgrimages to places such as Shikoku to pray for them.[10] Hashimoto's group, the Shiunkai (Purple Cloud Society), opposes abortion and considers that this caused unhappy

---

[9] The Ise shrines are considered by many to be the most significant of all Japan's Shinto shrines and are associated with the Imperial household and with Japan's national identity. They are also associated with mass pilgrimage activities. See, for example, Breen and Teeuwen 2017 and Nishigaki 1983.

[10] On the question of *mizuko* and its development in Japan, including the activities of Shiunzan and Hashimoto, see Brooks 1981; Hoshino and Takeda 1988; LaFleur 1992; and Hardacre 1997.

spirits to be released into the world and cause problems. The Shiunkai seeks to pacify the unhappy spirits of the dead while enjoining those who have had abortions to repent what the Shiunkai views as their pernicious actions. One of its activities is to do group pilgrimages to this end. Shiunkai members make regular circuits of the Saikoku, Chichibu, and Bandō Kannon pilgrimage routes, as well as Shikoku.[11] Because of her beliefs, and inspired by the now-head of the Shiunkai (Hashimoto *sensei* as she called him, a descendant of the founder Hashimoto Tetsuma), Terao joined the society and began to regularly visit Hashimoto's temple in Chichibu to pray for the spirits of aborted foetuses and for those who have had abortions and who, she believes, need to be spiritually healed as a result. She stated that every time she visits Hashimoto's temple she feels reborn and rejuvenated.

She also got involved in Shiunkai pilgrimages, notably to Shikoku, which she started doing with the group in 2011. Since then it has become her main pilgrimage focus. She has now done the whole pilgrimage seven times, roughly one complete circuit a year, done in two segments in spring and autumn and always as part of an organised Shiunkai tour by bus led by Hashimoto. She has also become a Shikoku *sendatsu*.

She views her pilgrimages as a way to help others by praying for them, caring for the ancestors, and pacifying unhappy *mizuko* spirits. The practice of pilgrimage runs deeply in her family; her six brothers and sisters and her four grown children and their families, she said, all have done various pilgrimages, notably Saikoku. She regards Kōbō Daishi as the reincarnation of the historical Buddha and has been on pilgrimage to Buddhist sites in other countries as well, including China, where she visited sites associated with Kūkai, Tibet, Bhutan, and India. At Bodh Gaya in India she chanted the *goeika* (pilgrimage songs) of the eighty-eight Shikoku temples, thereby in effect enacting the Shikoku pilgrimage in the birthplace of Buddhism, while in Bhutan she attended the International Buddhist Congress, dressed in full Shikoku pilgrimage regalia. She intends to keep doing pilgrimages, notably Shikoku, as long as she can, with the Shiunkai. She does various other religious practices as well, including chanting the Heart Sutra repeatedly, which she says she does in a similar way to the *hyakumanben* Nichiren

---

[11] On its website Hashimoto's temple Shiunzan Jizōji has a list of pilgrimages the society has done along with photographs and videos of its pilgrimages: see http://www.shiunzan-jizouji.com (accessed 23 January 2020).

Buddhist practice of chanting the *daimoku* mantra of the Lotus Sutra a million times.

Terao was in some respects strikingly different from virtually all the others we interviewed, in that she spoke so extensively and forcefully about spiritual issues—notably the presence of the spirits of the dead and what she saw as their influence in this world. Also she is the only person of those we encountered who had done multiple pilgrimages who has done Saikoku more times than Shikoku. At the same time she also indicated that her pilgrimage centre of gravity, as it were, had shifted to Shikoku and to her regular and recurrent visits to Kōyasan, which suggests that before long the number of times she has done Shikoku will surpass her number of Saikoku circuits. She also barely referred to the social dimensions of doing pilgrimages, even as she emphasised that she always does Shikoku as part of a pilgrimage party. Despite these variations, many aspects of her engagement resonate with those already touched on in this chapter, of someone who performs pilgrimages inspired by a special teacher and as part of a formally organised group with a remit to do pilgrimages. To that extent her experiences and associations with recurrent pilgrimage are framed by social engagement and the role of a spiritual authority figure who has inspired her to do the Shikoku pilgrimage repeatedly.

A pilgrimage group at Saba Daishi: sociability and enjoyment

These issues—of the social dynamics of pilgrimage and the presence of authority figures—were evident in early November 2018 when a small group of pilgrims was in the courtyard of Saba Daishi, the *bangai* temple mentioned in Chapter 2. Saba Daishi is one of the twenty Shikoku temples in the Shikoku Bekkaku pilgrimage (see Chapter 4) and is the site of a popular Kōbō Daishi legend. It also has connections with numerous pilgrimage confraternities and associations. Its head priest is known for having walked the pilgrimage multiple times and for maintaining close links with pilgrims.[12] Situated almost halfway along the eighty-kilometre stretch between Temples Twenty-Three

---

[12] See Reader 2005: 17, 44 for more on this temple and its support for pilgrims.

and Twenty-Four it is a temple often visited by pilgrims as they make their way down the eastern coast of Shikoku.

On this occasion a group of eight—six women and two men—from Fukuoka were at the temple, praying and chanting before the main temple hall. One of the men was acting as a general factotum, carrying all their pilgrim books and scrolls and getting them stamped, while the other man (the leader) oversaw the prayer rituals. The women, besides praying, also chatted with people working at the temple. From the way they were greeted by the head priest and others at the temple, and from the cheery conversation and bursts of laughter between them, it was evident that they were well-known regular visitors there. The women—all of whom appeared to be in their fifties or above—were also happy to engage in conversation with us and to talk about their group and leader. They were all dressed in pilgrimage attire and informed us that on this occasion they were visiting the twenty Bekkaku temples; they all held *sendatsu* rankings on both the Shikoku and the Bekkaku pilgrimages. The six ladies said they had done multiple pilgrimages together, including many circuits of the Shikoku and the Bekkaku pilgrimages, as well as the Saikoku Kannon pilgrimage, several regional eighty-eight-stage pilgrimages, and various regional thirty-six-stage pilgrimages associated with the Buddhist figure Fudō as well. They did pilgrimages at least twice a year together. While they were motivated by a strong sense of faith both in Kobo Daishi and in the leader of their group, whom they referred to as 'sensei' (teacher), they made it clear that there was also an intensely social dimension to their travels. They were not, however, an official confraternity, they said, just a group of friends who bonded together through their pilgrimages and devotion to their teacher, and who enjoyed each other's company as they travelled together. They were all married, but when asked what their husbands thought of their absences on pilgrimage, they all laughed; when they wanted to go off on pilgrimage together they (as one of them demonstrated with a smile and gesture) just waved goodbye and went off, leaving their husbands to fend for themselves. While pilgrimage was about reverence for figures such as Daishi and their teacher, it was also about enjoyment, companionship, and fun.

They spoke fulsomely of their teacher, Yasunaga-san, who was, they said, an ordained priest (*obōsan*) without a temple, who had done lots of ascetic practices (*shugyō*), including the Shikoku pilgrimage 220 times and who had, they said, a wholly red (*maaka*) pilgrim's book—something that clearly inspired them and that was in their eyes a marker of significance. As they were saying this, Yasunaga came over to join in the conversation. Shaven-headed and in black priestly robes, he informed us that he had been doing *henro* for over forty years. He always went to Kōyasan to perform a thanksgiving visit (*oreimairi*) at the end of each pilgrimage. He had also been doing the Bekkaku pilgrimage for around twenty-five years. He led many groups on pilgrimages, including this current group, which did several pilgrimages a year with him. He talked at some length about his attitudes to the pilgrimage, emphasising the importance of faith in Kōbō Daishi as a holy figure providing wonderful benefits to those who venerated him. Doing the pilgrimage was not just a matter of faith but also a form of *shugyō* (asceticism, practice) that, in his view, took nine to ten days to do properly. While he knew of people who had done the pilgrimage more often (and often more quickly) than himself, he was sceptical because he (like Nakagawa whom we mentioned in Chapter 2) thought it was not a matter simply of doing the *henro* a large number of times but of doing it properly, which in his view meant doing appropriate prayers and rituals at each temple and not rushing. Doing the *henro* took a lot of time and doing it 220 times (as he had) meant one had to have started, as he had, around forty years back; one could only do it so many times per year, especially if taking nine or ten days on it and then going to Kōyasan, as he always did. In addition he also did other pilgrimages with his followers, which of course limited the time he could spend doing Shikoku. In this respect—and in leading parties of pilgrims—he clearly differed from the pilgrims we cited at the end of the last chapter who appear to have focused primarily or exclusively on Shikoku. Nonetheless he had an extensive relationship with and immersion in the Shikoku pilgrimage not just in the duration of his involvement (forty years) or the number of circuits (220) but in the amount of time spent each year on the pilgrimage route. He averaged five or six circuits every year and spent around fifty or so days a year on the *henro*, alongside his other pilgrimage activities.

This encounter reiterated the themes we saw in the Sanwakai, of a respected teacher and leader with a long history of pilgrimage and multiple circuits to his name, enthusing others to do repeated pilgrimages. At the same time, while faith and veneration were clearly important, a key dynamic for those involved was a sense of sociability, in which pilgrimage was a joyous and convivial affair done with friends, something that encouraged members of the Sanwakai and the informal group from Fukuoka to keep on doing pilgrimages and that aided their leaders to increase their own numbers of circuits.

Sociability, scenery, and fun

The joyful atmosphere generated by the Fukuoka women's group and the convivial atmosphere as the Sanwakai pilgrims encouraged each other made their pilgrimages something to be looked forward to and enjoyed; that, too, spurred the wish to do such things again. This is a point that should be emphasised because it has not always been focused on in studies of pilgrimage. While there have been plentiful discussions about the relationship between pilgrimage and tourism, there has been comparatively little focus on the extent to which pilgrimage is enjoyable and fun, something that the Fukuoka ladies stressed. This is an aspect that entices and encourages many people to become pilgrims. While pilgrimage can have ascetic dimensions—something that we have drawn attention to as a significant factor in the development of the Shikoku *henro*—one should not overlook the point that asceticism and hardship need not be integral to it, and that fun and pleasure may also play their part.

This point came out frequently in our interviews with those who do the *henro* again and again whether by car or (see Chapter 6) by foot, with many such pilgrims emphasising the scenery, the change of pace they feel in Shikoku, the sense of friendship and warmth from local people and fellow pilgrims, and so on, when they talk about why they are attracted to the pilgrimage. In November 2019, for example, we talked to a couple from Hiroshima in their seventies who said they did their first Shikoku pilgrimage by bus and liked it. Thereafter did they decided to come again and do it by car in stages. While they initially did it seeking benefits (*riyaku*) for their children, they also had a sense of affinity (*en*) with Daishi. However, what was a particular factor in their coming back to do the pilgrimage again, the wife commented, was that the more they did it the more they found it to be enjoyable (*tanoshii*). Interestingly, as she said this she covered her mouth and made a sheepish face, as if she felt one should not talk of pilgrimage in such terms. Yet she was really articulating views that occurred repeatedly in our discussions and interviews: that doing the pilgrimage in Shikoku could be enjoyable and that this was in itself a stimulus to doing further pilgrimages. Often pilgrims have talked to us about the attractive nature of the island and the sense of being in a place that is Japanese and yet feels different, quieter, and more associated with rural life and traditions than the urban areas many of them come from. Being able to eat well, enjoy Shikoku's local cuisine, and feel the warmth and kindness of local people are also important attractions of the pilgrimage that have surfaced regularly in our interviews, and they have been cited often in pilgrim accounts of the *henro* as well as in assessments of its popularity in modern times.[13] Even if sometimes pilgrims feel they should not talk about enjoyment, it is an important aspect in pilgrimage in general, one that merits perhaps more consideration than it often gets.

Couples and their cars

The social and convivial dimensions of pilgrimage came through also in numerous encounters with one of the most common types of recurrent pilgrim: husband and wife combinations. We have at several points in this book already alluded to this, for example, in citing the couple who did over 300 pilgrimages together and only ceased when the husband died and the couple at Temple Thirty-Four who did several pilgrimages a year in their vehicle and were closing in on their goal of 100 circuits. Here we draw attention to some of the many couples met in our fieldwork and who had done the pilgrimage together multiple times.

At the end of October 2019 we met a retired couple from Yokohama outside the Maeyama Henro Salon in Kagawa prefecture. They were in their mid-eighties and were travelling in a van decked out with a bed and cooking equipment. They told us that they had done the pilgrimage sixty times, on average twice a year, although sometimes more often; one year, for example, they had done it seven times. (When we commented on how many times they had done it, they quickly said that this was nothing; they had met others who had done it far more often, including someone who had done it 700 times.) They slept in the van and showed us its interior, which had a mattress where they slept, cooking equipment and other items to make their travels comfortable. They had not limited their pilgrimages or travels to Shikoku but had spent much of their retirement driving around Japan visiting shrines, temples, and pilgrimage sites. Their van was covered in badges and stickers from various temples and shrines throughout the country, ranging from the southern island of Kyushu to northern Japan. Interestingly, given that they

---

[13] See, for example, Mori 2005, which examines how such themes have infused the pilgrimage and contributed to its growth in the modern period, as do Hoshino and Asakawa 2011 and Asakawa 2012. Reader 2005 and 2014 also discusses the importance of entertainment, good food, and enjoyment in this and other pilgrimages, while such themes surface also in various pilgrim diaries (Shultz 2009).

drove everywhere—thousands of kilometres a year it seemed—the temple and shrine stickers on their van all appeared to be charms for traffic safety.

Their main focus was the Shikoku pilgrimage, which had spurred their engagement with pilgrimage in general. They first went on the pilgrimage in 1991 to commemorate his sixtieth birthday and, finding a sense of peace while so doing, decided to return again—and again. As such they had been coming to Shikoku regularly for the past twenty-eight years. Finding that they enjoyed their experiences there, they had also branched out to do other pilgrimages and visit other religious sites. They said that doing pilgrimages and visiting shrines and temples made them peaceful and soothed their relations—adding with a smile that at home they would fight, while on the road they were at peace. The wife emphasised that it was this sense of peace and not faith in Daishi or anything religious (shūkyōteki) that motivated them. They would carry on doing their pilgrimages as long as her husband was able to drive, although she noted that since he was now eighty-seven they might have to give up fairly soon. In fact, they said they were already coming under pressure from their offspring to give up. Their adult children (in a fascinating reversal of normal patterns) worried so much about their parents that they had to call home every night to reassure their offspring that they were safe and had found a good place to park overnight. It might be, they thought, that family pressures along with increasing age might stop their incessant pilgrimage activities before long.

In early November 2019 a van carrying a retired couple from Fukushima in northern Japan drew up in the parking lot at Temple Eight. In their early seventies, they were on their fourth pilgrimage around Shikoku. They had, as with their previous pilgrimages, driven all the way from Fukushima—a journey of one thousand kilometres—in two days. They were doing the pilgrimage shachūhaku in a van customised for the purpose with a bed and equipment for preparing meals. Asked why they did the pilgrimage like this they responded that it was cheap; moreover sometimes at the places such as michi no eki where they stayed overnight they encountered other pilgrims doing the same thing and were able to socialise with them—something they enjoyed and that gave them a sense of community.

Asked why they were doing the henro, they said this was not because of faith but because they liked scenery and travel, and Shikoku provided them with the opportunity to enjoy both. They were not rushed or focused on piling up numbers and usually took between ten and twenty days to do the whole pilgrimage, stopping wherever they wished along the way. They had no set schedule except always doing it in one go, something that, since retirement, they had done every year around the same time in autumn when the changing colours of the leaves enhanced the scenery. They planned to keep doing the pilgrimage in this way until the husband (who did all the driving) was no longer able to drive. Asked if they knew the term *Shikokubyō* the husband laughed and said yes, and then gesticulated to his wife and said that it was she who had it. That, he stated, was the reason why he had to drive every year to Shikoku; she smiled and nodded as he said this. At this they headed off to the temple and began a long series of prayers and chanting of sutras that made us wonder whether, despite their saying otherwise, faith might also be a motive for them.

Sometimes (although not often) pilgrimage couples were emphatic about faith as a key motivation rather than just hinting at it. This came out in an interview at Temple Sixty-Four in October 2018 with a retired couple who told us that they were both *sendatsu* on the Shikoku and Bekkaku pilgrimages, that they venerated Kōbō Daishi, and that this was key to their pilgrimages. They commonly (as on this occasion) did the Shikoku eighty-eight and the Bekkaku twenty temples together as one circuit, and they had done this seventeen times in the past seven years, averaging two to three times per year and taking about ten days to do so. They travelled in their van, in which they slept overnight. The woman said that whenever they completed the circuit, they would go home and then soon after would want to do it again; it was a never-ending process. And yes, she said, they had *Shikokubyō*, as well as a deep faith in Daishi; the two complemented each other. They also had done the Saikoku pilgrimage some ten times and, although this pilgrimage is focused on Kannon, they also viewed this pilgrimage as being closely related to Kōbō Daishi, which is why they did it repeatedly.[14]

Yet at times, too, interviewees appeared mainly focused on getting temple stamps and portraying what they did as a retirement hobby while steering clear of anything associated with faith. Perhaps the most overt expression of this came from a retired couple met at Temple Thirty-Four in early November 2019, whose experience of the pilgrimage extended back over seventeen years. In that period they had done six pilgrimages and were now on their seventh circuit. They did it in short sections when they had time, always going by and sleeping in their van; they took their pet dog with them

---

[14] Several temples on Saikoku do have links to Kūkai and Kōbō Daishi, such as Sefukuji (Temple Four on Saikoku) where Kūkai spent some time and took the Buddhist tonsure.

and, when first met, they were carrying it in a bag, although they later put it on the ground to let it walk a little. They were adamant that they did their pilgrimages around Shikoku because they enjoyed travel and collecting temple stamps, and were explicit that what they were doing was a 'stamp rally'[15] that had nothing to do with faith. Indeed, they appeared to pay as much attention to their dog as to their temple surroundings. While they might have been something of an extreme case in the few if any others who so firmly proclaimed their pilgrimages simply as 'stamp rallies', they were indicative of a tendency among pilgrims to emphasise the social and enjoyment dimensions of doing the pilgrimage and a reminder that multiple performance need not be grounded explicitly in faith.

Couples and multiple means of travel

Not all the couples we met who had done multiple pilgrimages slept in their cars; the multiplicity of options of how to do the pilgrimage meant that we often met people who talked about trying it in various ways. Another couple from Hiroshima that we met in March 2018 at Temple Forty-Eight had done sixty circuits in the past few years at a rate of five or six times a year. They avoided our questions about faith and simply replied that they viewed the pilgrimage as something to do—something they had tried several ways, by car initially, then on foot, and now more commonly by car, staying as they did in various lodgings around the island.

The same was true of a couple from Ehime prefecture in Shikoku in their late sixties we met at Temple Sixty-Eight in October 2018. They had actually only done the pilgrimage together twice but both had done parts of it individually as well, while he had also done it twenty times with friends; so saying, he opened his pilgrimage book to show that it had been stamped numerous times and was awash with red ink. He carried a *kongōtsue,* a red pilgrimage staff adorned with esoteric Buddhist items, and wore a *sendatsu* badge, but at the same time he appeared rather embarrassed by these markers of status, saying that the staff had been given to him by a friend and that he was not a genuine *sendatsu* in that he did not guide other pilgrims; it was merely a formal rank accrued from doing several pilgrimages rather than because he was really capable of leading others. He was still working and farming in

---

[15] See Chapter 4, note 6.

Ehime prefecture, and so could not get away for extended periods, and so he does the pilgrimage in short sections between work commitments. Asked for reasons why he (and they) did the pilgrimage, they first noted that she had recently had serious health problems that incapacitated her for six months; as a result they were now doing the pilgrimage to pray for her health. He also added another reason why he had done it so much: whenever he finishes a pilgrimage or comes home after doing a section of the *henro* within a short time he starts wanting to go out on the road again. Why? He laughed and said '*Shikokubyō*'.

Sometimes, as we noted in Chapter 2, the allure of coloured *fuda* plays a part as well. A couple from Oita prefecture in Kyushu at Temple Seventy-Six told us that he was seventy-two and she seventy-five. They had done the pilgrimage five times and were happy (*ureshii*) on this occasion because, by reaching five times, they could now carry green rather than plain white *fuda*. This appeared to be very important for them, a spur to their pilgrimages. They had done their first *henro* seven years previously after retiring. The first time they walked in short sections, taking a year over it, but since then, because they were getting older and their legs were not good (he had a pronounced limp), they had to go by car. In fact, because of the poor condition of his legs they had been concerned that they might not be able to manage another circuit; however, since it would be their fifth, thus qualifying them to carry and hand out green *fuda*, they were able to overcome such worries and were thus able to strive (*ganbaru*) onwards. The husband then stated firmly that he was anti-religious (*han shūkyō*) and made critical remarks about various religious movements and traditions, ranging from Japanese movements that he thought caused social unrest to traditions such as Islam that he associated with conflict. However, his attitude to Kōbō Daishi was different; he respected him as a human figure and activist who accomplished many things. It was this sense of respect and value that drew him and his wife to the pilgrimage and spurred them to keep going together.

Individual pilgrims sleeping in their cars

Although there is thus a highly social dimension to the pilgrimage—something also emphasised in the notion of *dōgyō ninin*, that pilgrims are always accompanied by and in a relationship with Kōbō Daishi—many of the pilgrims we met who made repeated pilgrimages by car travelled on their own. This was the case, as we noted in the previous chapter, with the pilgrims with the highest numbers of circuits (and the fastest ones as well). Many such individual pilgrims likewise slept in their cars or vans. The female pilgrim mentioned in Chapter 2, whom we met in March 2018 who first used the term *shachūhaku* (sleeping in one's car) and showed us how she had customised her car to this end, is a good example. Iwaguchi Tomoe is from Tochigi prefecture and had at the time of meeting done close to fifty Shikoku circuits (she was a little unclear, initially saying over forty and then amending this to almost fifty) as well as three circuits of the Bekkaku pilgrimage. Her Facebook page (she gave us a link) indicates she has increased that number since we met as well as visiting other pilgrimage sites around the country. Proudly showing us her *sendatsu* badge, stole (*wagesa*) and pilgrim's book with its numerous red ink stamps, she told us she was a Shikoku *chūsendatsu* (the third rank of *sendatsu*) who first did the *henro* when she was aged seventy after retiring from work. She loved Shikoku so thought she would like to do it again and since then had initially averaged around three pilgrimages a year, although by 2018 she had increased this to five circuits a year, every two months or so all year round save for the hot sticky period in summer. Now in her eighties she wanted to keep doing the pilgrimage as long as possible. While she downplayed the idea of faith (*shinkō*) as a theme of her pilgrimages, she indicated that she had warm feelings for Kōbō Daishi, but in a manner we became used to (and that was reflected also in some of the questionnaire responses discussed in Chapter 4), she referred to him as a friend and companion. Indeed, she emphasised the point by switching from Japanese to say simply, in English, 'Kōbō Daishi my friend'.

Another female pilgrim met on successive days in November 2018 at different temples gave us further insights into the dynamics of car pilgrimages and about how people can develop deep lasting involvement with the *henro*. In so doing she brought out a new dimension to lifelong and multiple performance: of initial involvement in the pilgrimage through employment that led to the development of faith and lifelong attachment. She also provided an insight into the speed with which some pilgrims carry out their activities at the temples. We first met her at Temple Twenty-Seven late one afternoon in November 2018 when she said she was happy to be interviewed but added that she had little time to spare. Consequently we managed a short interview at breakneck speed in the temple parking lot. The next morning one of the authors was walking across the car park at Temple Thirty-One when he noticed a hand waving at him from the open window of a small car that sped into the car park. It was the same woman; as she locked her car and rushed across to the temple she said she was happy to talk more and flesh out her story as long as the interview was conducted as she did her rituals and got her book stamped at the temple. She moved very fast, haring up the steep temple steps, conducting her prayers (reciting the Heart Sutra and other incantations at the halls of worship at each temple) at a rapid pace, in between answering questions and narrating her story as the author in question strove to keep up with her.

She was single with no immediate family and lived alone in Hiroshima prefecture. Aged sixty-eight, she had a fifty-year-long history of doing the pilgrimage, which she first did when aged eighteen because of her work. She had been born and raised in Matsuyama in Shikoku and after school had worked for a local bus company that, among other things, ran pilgrimage tours.[16] Aged eighteen she was assigned to help as a bus guide on such tours, something she did for three years until she changed occupations and moved from Shikoku to Hiroshima. She did not elaborate on why she had moved to Hiroshima save to indicate it was connected to her work. However the experience of visiting the Shikoku temples with parties of pilgrims had spurred a desire to do the pilgrimage herself, not for work but as a pilgrim. The devotion showed by the pilgrims on the buses when she was a guide had made a lasting impression and had engendered a sense of faith in her—something that has been noted about other bus guides in Shikoku.[17] Thus she started making pilgrimages on her own to Shikoku and as a result had become immersed in the practice. The fact that she was from Shikoku also was important for her; she was reaffirming her relationship with her local culture and identity each time she returned to do the pilgrimage. As a rule, she said, she does it at least twice a year, usually in spring and autumn, but she has done it also in the hot summer period and in some years does it four or five times. She always goes in clockwise numerical order from one to eighty-eight and then visits Kōyasan. It takes her around five days each time to do it as she moves around quickly—something that we can readily testify to.

She said she would really like to do the pilgrimage like Kōbō Daishi, which she clarified as not just walking but sleeping out as a mendicant. However, being female she felt this would be dangerous, so she has adapted her car

---

[16] Although she did not say so outright it appears that this was the Iyo Tetsu Company, a bus and train conglomerate based in Matsuyama that has been heavily involved in running bus pilgrimage tours of Shikoku (Reader 2005: 152–155, 163–167).

[17] Reader 2005: 163–164.

and sleeps in it each night usually at *michi no eki,* service areas where, she said, she feels safe and where there are often other pilgrims staying, including other long-term pilgrims whom she has got to know. She did not carry a *fuda* of any colour, while her pilgrim's book was new. This was because, she said, she had, prior to this pilgrimage, put her previous *nōkyōchō* in the casket of someone who had died recently; since she said she had no immediate family now, we think this might have been a parent or perhaps departed spouse, although she would not say anything further on the matter. She gave a list of reasons for repeatedly doing the pilgrimage. Being brought up in Shikoku in the Shingon sect was important as it created a special link between her, Kōbō Daishi and the pilgrimage, while her initial job as a bus guide helped develop a sense of faith in Kōbō Daishi. She also said that doing the pilgrimage was a form of religious practice and a way to find out about and improve herself; basically each time she does it, it teaches her anew. Moreover it provided a way to see Shikoku, enjoy its nature and its people, and be refreshed. Enjoyment and returning to the roots of her identity thus played a role in her repeated pilgrimages. By this point we had reached the office where she had handed her pilgrim's book in to be stamped. After a few pleasantries with the temple official her book was passed back freshly inscribed and stamped. It was final step in her visit to the temple. With that she said goodbye, gave a wave, and marched off briskly to the car park to make her way to the next temple.

We also met many men who slept in their cars; since we have already referred to several such people in earlier chapters we will only mention one further example here. We were walking back to the car park at Temple Fifty-Four on a late October morning in 2018 when a van drew up there and a man dressed in pilgrim's clothes alighted. We immediately asked if he had done multiple circuits and whether he slept in the van; the answer to both was yes. He was in his sixties and from Kagawa prefecture. As a native of Shikoku he had initially done the pilgrimage with members of his family but it was after his wife died at the age of fifty-eight that he had really been doing it in earnest. Since her death he has done it ten times, always as a memorial for her. He always sleeps in his van, usually at roadside service areas. He does not do full circuits, but breaks the pilgrimage up into stages. He still works as a farmer and has fields to look after. Although he had already said a reason for doing repeat pilgrimages was because of his dead wife, he then added also that he had *Shikokubyō*. He also said that while on pilgrimage wonderful things happened to him, and he felt as if he were being cared for and protected by some power or other. Like those men mentioned in the previous chapter, bereavement and the loss of his wife was a precipitating factor in his doing multiple and repeated pilgrimages.

Individuals by car, day trips, and other means

While *shachūhaku*, sleeping in one's car, is a common and seemingly growing phenomenon among Shikoku pilgrims at present, it is by no means the only way people do numerous pilgrimages. We also met many individuals with rich Shikoku pilgrimage histories who used a variety of means of going around the route and who stayed in lodges. At Temple Fifty-Four, for example, shortly after talking to the aforementioned man who slept in his van and said he did the pilgrimage as a memorial for his wife and because he had *Shikokubyō*, another single male pilgrim drove into the car park in a small vehicle whose back seat was covered in a mound of boxes and papers. It looked as if it would be impossible for anyone to sleep in it, something the driver, a resident of Shikoku in his late thirties, confirmed. He did not appear in good health; quickly out of breath and with his hair seemingly falling out in clumps, he also appeared to be in a hurry, although he stopped briefly to answer a few questions. It was, he said, his seventh circuit of the *henro*. In addition he had also done the Bekkaku pilgrimage and was a *sendatsu* on both routes. He worked and so fitted the pilgrimages into his everyday schedules, doing them in short bursts, usually staying overnight in temple lodges or small local inns. Asked why, he initially used the word *byōki* (illness) but when we sought to clarify this by enquiring if he meant by this the idea of *byōki naoshi* (healing—a common prayer request) he said no, he meant *Shikokubyō* and then apologised that he had little time to spare and headed off to the temple.

Another example was a male pilgrim from Takamatsu who was returning to his car after visiting Temple Thirty-Three in early November 2018. Aged eighty-three, he had done the pilgrimage thirteen times, twice on foot and the rest by car. The first time was, he said, when he was 'young' (*wakai toki*). When asked how long ago this was, he said it was fifteen years previously, when he was sixty-eight. Young, apparently, for an eighty-three year old man, included being in his late sixties. At that time he had been diagnosed with cancer and told by doctors that he might die as a result. He did not; through surgery his doctors managed to save him medically, after which he went on pilgrimage to pray for continued good health. On that and one other occasion he had walked but now, due to age, he goes by car, usually doing the pilgrimage twice a year, always on his own and always in stages of around one week at a time. The focus of his continuing pilgrimages is on praying for continued good health and giving thanks for this benefit; after he said this he ceased the interview in order to turn back towards the temple, bow deeply, and recite a prayer before climbing into his car to head to the next temple.

Not long after this encounter we talked at Temple Forty-Two to Yamamoto-san, whose *sendatsu* badge was clearly displayed on his white pilgrim's shirt. He had first done the *henro* when he was twenty-four years old. He was now seventy-three. He had done the pilgrimage many times since then, although he could not give an exact number. Pressed about an estimate, he thought it was at least forty times. When he first did it, he walked and recalled that the roads were poor and everything was *inaka* (country, rural)—a term that implies being backward and undeveloped. He did not want to say exactly why he had done it that first time almost fifty years back save that it had helped him immensely in his life thereafter and that by doing it the first time he got a feel for the pilgrimage. However it was not until he was around forty that he began to do it repeatedly, when he had time and could fit it in with his work schedules. While he did it normally by car he had also on two occasions gone by motorbike. He retired at the age of sixty-six, some seven years previously, and it was from that time on, he said, that he could properly focus on the pilgrimage. Now he does it at least once a year, by car. Asked why he made two comments: *goriyaku ga warui kara* (because I have lots of misfortunes / things aren't good in my life)[18] and that he had a high regard for Kōbō Daishi, whom he portrayed as a 'wonderful man' (*rippa na hito*) who had travelled widely and accomplished many things in Japan. He added that he also does the Shikoku Bekkaku pilgrimage regularly as well and that he likes doing both that pilgrimage and the eighty-eight-stage *henro*; enjoyment and travel thus played a role in his continued and extended performance over the years.

A lady encountered twice in successive days in Tokushima prefecture—first at Temple Ten and then the next morning at Temple One—in October 2018 also talked about how she fitted the pilgrimage into her regular life, and how it helped sustain her. In her late thirties she was on her fourth pilgrimage by car and was from Nagoya, where she worked full-time; she added that she was self-employed, which meant that she could occasionally take time out

---

[18] This literally translates as 'because my worldly benefits are bad' but in essence means that he has misfortunes or lacks good luck in his life (and is therefore praying for betterment).

to come to Shikoku, doing the pilgrimage in stages and staying overnight in local lodges. Her family background was in the Shingon sect, as a result of which, she said, she has been brought up with faith in Kōbō Daishi. Her prime reason for doing the pilgrimage was to pray for worldly benefits related to her work and business. She wanted to do the *henro* as long as she could and planned to do it at minimum at least once every year; although a relative novice with just four circuits, she was mentally on the way to becoming a recurrent pilgrim. On this occasion she was doing the pilgrimage in reverse order and was planning to make her way back to Temple One, driving back to Nagoya that night. However, the next morning she drew up at Temple One and, seeing one of the authors in the courtyard, came up and said that she had not managed to get to this temple in time before the office had closed. As a result she had not been able to get her book stamped, and so had stayed overnight at a nearby lodge before returning the next morning, after which she was going to drive home to Nagoya. It was a reminder of how temple opening hours can be a problem for pilgrims, although in this case her flexible work structures meant that she was not unduly inconvenienced.

Another female pilgrim travelling on her own also indicated how the custom of pilgrimage could become embedded through family influences. Tsujimoto Reiko from Kobe was a *sendatsu* on her forty-fifth pilgrimage when we met on the steep steps up to Temple Forty-Five in early November 2019; now in her fifties she had been introduced to the *henro* by her grandmother, who took her (then aged just six years old) with her to walk the pilgrimage. Tsujimoto did it again on foot as an adult before getting married and raising children. She had then taken her children on the pilgrimage because she wanted to pass the tradition on to them just as her grandmother had done to her. Nowadays, however, she travels alone; her husband is too busy with work, and the children had grown, with other interests and demands on their time. She, however, continued to do it, now by car and in short stages; at the time we met she said she was going to visit half a dozen more temples in the next two days before returning home but that she had another visit to Shikoku planned for a few days hence when she was going to continue her pilgrimage.

Some pilgrims who go by car or van make even shorter visits to the route; especially for those who live in or close to Shikoku, it has become quite common to do the pilgrimage largely or wholly in day tips (*higaeri*). Thus a man in his seventies encountered at Temple Sixty-One in November 2019 lived on Awaji Island, which is close to Shikoku and linked to it by a bridge.

Handing us a gold *fuda* he told us he had done sixty pilgrimages over the past twenty-eight years, almost always in day trips. Citing faith in Daishi (*Daishi shinkō*) and *Shikokubyō* as his reasons, he rushed off as he had a schedule to keep; pilgrims on day trips whom we met appeared generally in a hurry. Another male pilgrim encountered near Temple Forty-Six (whom we mentioned briefly in Chapter 2 because of his collection of gold and brocade *fuda*) similarly did the pilgrimage regularly in day trips from his home in Ehime prefecture. Araki-san handed us a gold *fuda* indicating he had done fifty-five circuits thus far, beginning in 2009 when he retired. His interest and association with the pilgrimage involved both strong feelings towards Kōbō Daishi and a wish to help other pilgrims by giving them *settai*. For him Kōbō Daishi played a significant role in Japanese history. Japan, he said, had always been the country of the gods (*kami no kuni*), a term that has close associations with Shinto and Japanese nationalism (often of a narrow and insular kind) but then, he said, Kōbō Daishi (who brought esoteric Buddhism from China) came along to broaden the country's horizons.[19] Arita sees the pilgrimage as a means of continuing Daishi's work. His main purpose in doing the pilgrimage is to support other pilgrims, particularly those who walk and especially foreign pilgrims. In his retirement he has driven around the *henro* repeatedly (usually in day trips) in his van. Whenever he sees a walker or encounters a non-Japanese person on the pilgrimage he stops and offers them *settai* and encouragement. By supporting pilgrims from overseas with *settai* and kind words he felt he was helping make Japan a more engaging place and continuing what he saw as Kōbō Daishi's work. As well as giving out *settai* he carried a collection of notebooks and folders in which he asked pilgrims to write a message (he also took a photograph of each one and put that in his notebooks as well) and in which he collected the *fuda* of the pilgrims he met. In all he had records of over 1700 pilgrims (meticulously recorded by country for foreign pilgrims) he had met in this way. What was striking about him, also, was that unlike almost everyone else cited in this book, it was he who approached us first; normally when we have gathered information from pilgrims we have made the first approach and asked if they would speak to us. By contrast, Araki made the first approach on seeing one of the authors and assuming he was a pilgrim. When he found out that this was not the case and that our purpose was to do research on multiple performing pilgrims he was

[19] He was clearly speaking about the historical Kūkai at this point but, as is common among those we talked to, he in effect conflated the historical figure with the legendary one.

happy to tell us about his pilgrimage activities, show us his collection of note-books, and also the interior of his van, which was crammed with small gifts of *settai* such as bags of sweets and biscuits, along with boxes of notebooks and collections of *fuda*. Indeed, by talking about his activities with us he felt he was continuing to fulfil his mission of expanding Japan's horizons through the pilgrimage—a reason why he continued to keep visiting the temples and meeting other pilgrims.

A multiplicity of styles, a commonality of interests

In this chapter we have provided accounts of a number of the pilgrims and groups met during our fieldwork who have done the pilgrimage many times. The range of people we have introduced again demonstrates that there is a broad spectrum of modes, types, and means of multiple engagement, from those in groups to people travelling with a spouse to those who travel alone, to those who use their vehicles as a place to sleep and those for whom vehicles are just a means of transport. They also cover a broad spectrum in numerical terms. Some, for example, the lady met at Temple Ten and Temple One, have relatively short pilgrimage careers and have made only four or so pilgrimages; others have histories going back half a century; some have done over two hundred circuits and have established themselves as leaders of pilgrimage groups. Yet there is much that unites these people with apparently disparate levels of pilgrimage experience.

Those we have focused on in this chapter all make use of modern motorised means (usually their own car or van, but for some such as the Fukuoka group a microbus or similar vehicle) and indicate a continuing association with and wish to keep doing the pilgrimage as long as possible. In general there is a social dimension to their pilgrimages, most clearly evident in the groups for whom pilgrimage, while imbued with faith as well as deep respect for inspirational pilgrimage leaders, may be a highly social affair full of fun, enjoyment, and mutual encouragement. Those themes are evident, too, among husband and wife pilgrimage combinations. Individuals, too, often affirm a social dimension to their pilgrimages, whether in the man who spends much of his retirement doing the pilgrimage so as to engage with other (especially foreign) pilgrims or the people who sleep in their cars and talk about the sense of community that can emerge when staying overnight in a service area where they might have the chance to meet other pilgrims who are also parked there.[20] Not only have cars expanded the potential numbers of people who can do multiple pilgrimages but they have made it quicker, cheaper, and easier, especially when vehicles are adapted for overnight accommodation. The recent advent of *shachūhaku* pilgrimage has also increased the numbers of people who have done the pilgrimage many, even hundreds, of times while enabling people who previously might not have been able to do the pilgrimage at all, let alone many times, to develop extensive pilgrimage careers in Shikoku. This has particularly helped increase the number of female pilgrims who have done the *henro* multiple times, whether with their husbands or as with the examples cited earlier, of single women who are now doing many circuits in *shachūhaku* style.

We should also note that the very act of customising one's car in order to sleep in it represents a significant step in self-identification as a committed pilgrim, representing a significant amendment and expenditure in many cases. For pilgrims we met who had done this, especially those with small passenger cars, such as Iwaguchi and the female pilgrim met both at Temples Twenty-Seven and Thirty-One, customising was a major change in how they could use their cars. It required the removal of the front and rear passenger seats to accommodate the bed, which took up the left side of the vehicle, and thereby restricted their ability to have passengers and use it in social settings beyond the pilgrimage. To that extent customising one's car in this way is not just a means to facilitate pilgrimages but a statement of commitment to and unending association with the pilgrimage.

In this chapter we have focused on those whose prime mode of pilgrimage is motorised, in order to demonstrate how significant this mode of movement is in shaping and enhancing the scope of multiple and lifelong pilgrimage performance.

Some of those we have mentioned have done the pilgrimage by other means as well; as we have indicated, and as was evident in our survey introduced in Chapter 4, many pilgrims use and like to try a variety of means to experience the *henro*. Several of those mentioned in this chapter have also walked at some point. Walking, of course, has produced plentiful examples

---

[20] However, how much of a social and community feeling develops among those who sleep in their cars is unclear. On several occasions we went to service areas where we had been told such pilgrims often stopped, but we were unable to find any such people or see evidence of any such social engagements between them.

of lifelong pilgrims both in earlier times and in the present day as well. We have already introduced one type of walking pilgrim in the present day—the permanent itinerants discussed in Chapter 3—but there are also other pilgrims who, while not living on the route, walk the pilgrimage regularly in the present day. It is to such people that we turn in the following chapter.

6

Walkers on the way

Multiplicity, motivations, health, and retirement

Footsteps, origins, and multiplicity

The origins of the pilgrimage are in the footsteps of ascetics who, fired by the image and legend of Kōbō Daishi's incessant journey around the island, created a pattern of repetition and unending engagement that has resonated through the *henro*'s history. Until modern times all recurrent pilgrims went on foot, and there are still those who do this; besides the homeless pilgrims discussed in Chapter 3, there are various others in the present day who have extended histories of foot pilgrimages in Shikoku. Like those discussed in Chapter 5 who travel by car, such pilgrims manifest a variety of views, reasons, and motives for expending large amounts of their time both planning for and walking the long and arduous route multiple times.

What unites them is that they view their engagement with the pilgrimage not as a singular event but something more expansive—an engagement that can fill their lives. Some of them have only ever walked the *henro* while others have also done it other ways but primarily focus on walking. Some emphasise matters of faith, asceticism, and devotion. Others shy away from such things (or from talking about them) and instead emphasise interests such as keeping fit, hiking, and enjoying the scenery and landscape of Shikoku. Some always sleep out, and some try to live on very little, at times relying on soliciting alms; others say that they always stay in lodgings; some do the pilgrimage with almost seasonal regularity, often walking the whole route in one go at the same time each year (or in some cases, twice a year); others do it in sections whenever they have time. We will see all these themes and more emerging in this chapter, which looks at people who walked the pilgrimage a number of times and who have indicated in interviews that they intend to keep doing so as long as they are able (see Figure 6.1).

Pilgrims Until We Die. Ian Reader and John Shultz, Oxford University Press. © Oxford University Press 2021.
DOI: 10.1093/oso/9780197573587.003.0007

Figure 6.1 Pilgrim who pulls his belongings on a cart and who does multiple circuits

Asceticism, faith, and practice

We first made contact with Akiyama-san when one of the authors, walking part of the pilgrimage with a friend in May 2019, saw him outside one of the temples soliciting alms. At the time of the meeting, the author in question was carrying equipment to sleep outdoors, and this became a springboard for a conversation with Akiyama about pilgrimage and asceticism. We followed up that encounter in two ways, by sending him a questionnaire (he is one of the respondents cited in Chapter 4) and later arranging to meet him in November 2019, when we conducted a long follow-up interview in a restaurant by the gates of Temple Fifty-One. In that first encounter Akiyama indicated that he walked the pilgrimage frequently, always in an ascetic manner, relying on alms solicitation and sleeping out. However, when we met him in November 2019 he said that after many years of walking and asceticism he had 'graduated' (*sotsugyō shimashita*) from walking and now was going by car. In this he was a rarity, of someone who changed from walking to car pilgrimages and not out of physical necessity. His focus, he said, was on helping others, and this was a reason why he travelled by car, something he had been doing regularly since 2014.[1] He claimed that his earlier focus on walking was a form of ascetic training aimed at spiritual self-purification and self-development, after which he had become able to serve as a spiritual aide for others. It had helped him achieve a form of awakening, although he described it not as something universal, like the Buddha's enlightenment (*satori*), but as a local and small awakening.

He was sixty years old and from Kurashiki in Okayama prefecture—an area readily accessible to with close contacts with Shikoku and from which many pilgrims have come.[2] Since his teenage years he had had close links with a temple associated with the Shugendō mountain religious tradition, but initially he led what he called an 'ordinary' (*futsū*) life, working in a Japanese company, getting married when he was twenty-three and bringing up two children. However, he began to feel uncomfortable in this type of life and developed an interest in the spiritual world of the gods and buddhas (*shinbutsu*). He did various practices including waterfall austerities, mountain ascents, and meditation, experiencing a life transformation and spiritual rebirth (*umarekaware*) that led him to separate from his wife and offspring, though he retains contacts with the latter. His ascetic interests led him to walk the Shikoku pilgrimage in 2004. He was then aged forty-five. In 2007 he took a Buddhist ordination at the temple in Kurashiki where he first studied mountain asceticism. By 2019 he had done the *henro* on foot more than thirty times, twice every year, in spring and autumn, and 'around sixteen times' (*jūrokukai gurai*) by car. We should note that this latter number seemed problematic since he also said at one point that he started doing the pilgrimage by car in 2014 and that he did on average one whole circuit a year.[3]

Through his ascetic practices and pilgrimages he discovered an ability to help others by soothing bodily pains through using his hands, which he said were infused with healing powers.[4] He also studied various forms of spiritual healing, massage, and acupuncture to this end, and nowadays during his

[1] It is clear here that there were some contradictions in his statements, since in May 2019 he was soliciting alms and was walking, yet in November 2019 said he had been going by car since 2014.

[2] Especially since the road and rail bridge was built across from Okayama prefecture to Shikoku in the late 1980s, access has been quick and easy. Many multiple performers we met (including Nakano, discussed in Chapter 4) are from the Kurashiki area.

[3] We have noted before that sometimes interviewees were imprecise with recollections of when they started doing the pilgrimage and so on. This interviewee at times seemed to contradict himself (see also note 1), although his devotion to and engagement in the pilgrimage was certainly recurrent.

[4] Healing through the use of hands is not an uncommon aspect of Japanese folk medicine and practices and is evident also in some new religions in Japan.

pilgrimages he provides on-the-spot massages for those who give him alms. At one point during the interview he offered to massage one of the authors to demonstrate his abilities. He emphasised that he was an ordained priest but was not a *sendatsu*, regarding this ranking as merely superficial. Anyone, he said, could get *sendatsu* status simply by doing the pilgrimage four times. The implication was that he had achieved a special status as a priest through ascetic practice, unlike *sendatsu*; it was another instance in which a pilgrim portrayed and validated their particular standing while contrasting it favourably with that of others.

Akiyama commented that one views the pilgrimage in different ways when going by foot or car. He also noted a difference in economic terms. When he walked, he did not need money; he believed that doing it on foot was an ascetic exercise and that therefore one should live on next to nothing. He always slept out and relied on *takuhatsu*; indeed he believed that when walking the *henro* one should only spend what was received through alms solicitation. Although *takuhatsu* has a negative image in public consciousness associated with begging (*kojiki*) and 'getting things' (*monomorai*), he regards it as a religious practice (*shugyō*), as a means of learning about others, and as something embedded in the rules of the pilgrimage. However, he said, if one views *takuhatsu* simply as a way to get money, rather than as a religious practice, one cannot get satori (*satori wa hirakenai*). He added that if he did not receive anything while begging, he would not eat.

By contrast, doing the pilgrimage by car requires money, which he has to bring with him, to pay for fuel. His personal economic circumstances are difficult, and he is not well-off enough to own a vehicle himself, but he can occasionally borrow one from a friend for his Shikoku pilgrimages. He always sleeps in it, usually at service areas. He does not usually do *takuhatsu* when going by car because he could only borrow the vehicle for limited periods—on this occasion just seven days—and needed that time to concentrate on doing the pilgrimage. He did not have time to stop and solicit alms. However, he then somewhat contradicted himself by saying that he was going to take time out in the coming days to solicit alms. What he wanted to emphasise was that when travelling by car he did expend some of his own money; on foot he sought to exist solely on what he was given.

Whether walking or by car his philosophy was the same: not to plan in advance (*yotei nashi*), to go at one's own pace, and to go with the flow (*kawa no nagare*). He also added that while religious practice, *shugyō*, is a critical element in the pilgrimage, enjoyment is also central to it. Without enjoyment one cannot learn. Hence, one needs to find an enjoyable (*tanoshii*) way of doing things. For him this involved engaging in austerities and seeking to offer healing services to others. This was the current focus of his practice. Rather than visiting all the temples on the circuit, he now went from place to place offering his healing services to those he met on the route. When asked how long he would carry on doing the *henro*, he replied in terms we had heard many times before: *itsu made? shinu made* (until when? until I die).

Despite his occasionally contradictory comments and his use both of walking and car pilgrimages, Akiyama was not unique among those we met, especially in emphasising themes of asceticism and religious practice. There were many other frequent walkers who slept out, viewed what they were doing as a form of austerity, and saw faith as integral to their practice. A man dressed in pilgrim's clothes and with a backpack with a sleeping mat strapped on its top, for example, was walking briskly along the road in the late afternoon in early November 2019 some distance beyond Temple Forty-Four when one of the authors stopped to offer him a lift as *settai*. The man declined because he wanted to walk all the while, knew exactly where he was going—a place five kilometres down the road where he would sleep—and had plenty of time to get there. He was friendly and happy to stop and talk for a while, however, stating that he was seventy years old, from Fukuoka, retired, and on his fourteenth pilgrimage, always on foot. He walked every year around this time and always slept out (or, he qualified, around 90% of the time). He also includes the twenty Bekkaku temples in his circuits, which all take him forty-five days.

When asked why he did it he responded by talking about his deep faith in Kōbō Daishi. He, his family, and their ancestors were all in the Sōtō Zen Buddhist sect but he saw Daishi as transcending sectarian boundaries as a great and powerful Buddhist figure whom he venerated. He talked about Buddhism and its concept of *rinne* (the Buddhist cycle of birth and birth, the notion that all sentient entities are in a constant cycle of birth, death, and rebirth while seeking total liberation). He considered that doing the pilgrimage and following the path of Daishi was a way to liberation and breaking the cycle of death and rebirth. While he was not doing the pilgrimage specifically to escape the cycle of transmigration, he stated that in doing it he was engaged in a practice of self-learning and self-development, something that would aid subsequent transmigration. When asked whether the term *Shikokubyō* was relevant to what he was doing he laughed and said what he was doing was not an 'illness' (*byōki*) but something with spiritual foundations that kept him fit. He repeated that it was a religious practice linked to Buddhism and the cycle of birth and death and that he would keep doing it as long as possible. If he were no longer able to walk he might do another way. He then finished by making a circular gesture with his hand as he said that the pilgrimage was 'unending/eternal' (*eien*) just like the cycle of birth and death (*rinne*). His gesture of course could be seen as mirroring the structure of the pilgrimage as a circuit without start or finish, but it also clearly articulated the point that for him it was something that reflected Buddhist concepts of transmigration, death, and rebirth, and was endless.

Walking, sleeping out, and recurrent practice

Not all those who do multiple pilgrimages and sleep out are as overt in talking about asceticism, Kōbō Daishi, or faith, even if these themes often appear to be present in their practices. At Temple Thirty-Nine in March 2018 a man came into the temple courtyard carrying a pack and with a pilgrim's staff, although not wearing a pilgrim's white shirt (*hakui*). After putting his backpack down by a bench he walked across to the halls of worship but, rather than climbing up the steps so as to stand before the hall of worship as others were doing (and as is normal practice at Japanese Buddhist temples), he stood back a little at the foot of the steps and, rubbing his Buddhist rosary around his wrist, engaged in a series of recitations. After he had finished his prayers he did not go to the temple office (as he later told us, he did not carry a pilgrim's book because he could not afford the stamps) but returned to the bench, where we talked to him. He was fifty-eight, from Tokushima, and on his seventh pilgrimage. His first was when he was forty-two and was related to that being his unlucky (*yakudoshi*) year, which as we have mentioned before has traditionally been a reason for doing the pilgrimage. More recently he has gone round the pilgrimage once a year, always walking and sleeping out, although when the weather is bad he might shelter for a day or two. Usually the pilgrimage takes him around fifty days. Why does he keep doing it, we asked, and he replied that it was because he lacked good fortune (*goriyaku ga nai kara*) and had no work. He has little money and what he had was saved up from welfare payments. Because he smokes, he said, he needs around 1000 yen a day to support himself on the pilgrimage; otherwise he lives very cheaply on noodles and bread. He occasionally does *takuhatsu*, on average once a week, for economic reasons to supplement his small supply of money rather than because he viewed it as an ascetic practice that pilgrims should do. Nonetheless he saw the pilgrimage as a form of ascetic practice (*gyō*), although he was reluctant to say anything more than this or (despite having prayed extensively and talked about his lack of *goriyaku*) about his views on faith or Daishi.

We met another male pilgrim from Tokushima who slept out and did regular foot pilgrimages, on two occasions a year apart. Our first meeting occurred when one of the authors was driving, in October 2018, between Temples Eighty-Eight and One and spotted a man with a large and ungainly backpack out of which poked three umbrellas. He was extremely weather-beaten with long, unkempt hair and a straggly beard, and wore dark clothes, with a pilgrim's bamboo hat on his head. On closer view he appeared to be missing several teeth. He was marching along with his head down as if determined to get somewhere fast. Stopping the car, the interviewer explained what the research project was and asked if the man would be willing to talk about what he was doing. The man agreed but indicated that the conversation would have to be brief as he was intent on moving on. He said he was fifty-eight years old and from Tokushima where he had a house. He was on his way back there after calling in at Temple One to complete his current pilgrimage.

Currently unemployed, he lived alone, spending a lot of time walking the pilgrimage route. He said on this occasion that he did not have a fixed routine to his pilgrimages; he went when he felt like it and had been doing so for several years. He always slept out. Initially he carried a pilgrim's book but stopped doing so because of the cost of the stamps. He had no idea how many times he had done the pilgrimage. When asked why he was doing it he talked about being from Shikoku and how, as a *Shikoku-jin* (Shikoku person), the *henro* was part of his culture and customs; doing so was an expression of his own identity. At this point he said he needed to keep going and headed off; although he was not disconcerted by having a foreign researcher accost him by the roadside, he also was not very forthcoming and appeared keen not to disrupt his pilgrimage by spending any more time talking.

After checking our photographs from earlier visits to Shikoku it became clear that one of the authors had also briefly encountered him during an earlier visit to Shikoku, although at that time he had not been able to speak to him. A year after the meeting just described between Temples Eighty-Eight and One the same author was driving north of Cape Muroto when he saw this man again and, as before, stopped and spoke to him. The man in question was heading south towards Cape Muroto and Temple Twenty-Four, dressed

as before, although this time with only one umbrella sticking out of his backpack, which was as lopsided as the previous year. He immediately recalled
our previous conversation, stating precisely when and where we had met before, what our project was, and hence why he was once again being accosted
by the roadside by a Western male with similarly unkempt hair as his own.

He said he had now turned sixty and was receiving a pension on which
he lived. He repeated that he was a permanent resident of Tokushima where
he had a house and stressed that he was neither homeless nor itinerant. On
this occasion he was more precise in speaking about what he was doing; he
walked the pilgrimage twice a year without fail, each spring and autumn,
taking around forty days each time and spending eighty days per year on the
henro. He said he had done the whole pilgrimage around ten times now and
repeated what he had said on our first encounter: that on his first pilgrimage
he had carried a pilgrim's book and got it stamped but had not done so since.
He repeated that he always sleeps out; the reason for his large backpack was
because he carried a sleeping bag and other camping items. That evening he
would sleep at Muroto where there was a wayside empty house (*koya*) that
he always stops in. Since it was almost twenty kilometres away and it was already mid-afternoon, he would be walking for a while yet and had little time
to lose.

However he talked a little more, and this time did touch on matters of
faith, saying that he venerates all the *kami* (gods) and buddhas and that he
'likes' Daishi (*Daishi ga suki*). Nonetheless he was clear that faith was not
the reason for his pilgrimages; he does it because he likes walking, not because of faith in Daishi, *Daishi shinkō*. When asked directly on this point
he said three words vehemently, in English: 'no no no'. He used the same
three words when asked if he did *takuhatsu*; he does not need to solicit
alms as he has money from his pension. Since he slept out he did not need
much money anyway. With that he gestured that he needed to get on his
way, and the author agreed, especially since his car—stopped precipitously
when seeing the aforesaid pilgrim coming in the opposite direction—was
blocking traffic. What transpired from both these interviews was that the
pilgrimage provided a fixed point in his life, that he had got into a pattern of walking the pilgrimage regularly, almost as if a routine, and that it
played a part in his sense of identity as a resident of Shikoku. He had a fixed
style, always sleeping out and knowing where to stay each night, while he
spent a significant part of each year—around eighty days—sleeping out as
he walked the pilgrimage.

Schedules, faith, and other meanings

Not all those who walk repeatedly sleep out. The man met at Temple Thirty-Nine said he had met only seven such pilgrims during his current circuit and that this fitted a pattern he had noticed over the years, of declining numbers of pilgrims who slept out.[5] Sometimes pilgrims have to give up the practice even as they continue to walk repeatedly, as was the case with the man met at Temple Eighty-Five in October 2019 whom we referred to in Chapter 4 and who had walked four times before then doing the pilgrimage forty-six times by car in order to qualify for a gold *fuda*. Aged sixty-two and retired, he had gone back to walking after reaching his target of fifty pilgrimages and had done eight more circuits when we met him. He now did it on foot regularly twice a year. He had gone back to walking because he felt that going by car did not give him the same sense of meaning he experienced when on foot. He extrapolated further by talking about how he had a major spiritual experience on his second foot pilgrimage. Unlike driving, walking was a challenge that led to spiritual advancement; he talked about how runners who take part in marathons speak of 'hitting the wall', of the breakthrough that occurs by getting through this barrier, relating it also to his walking experiences on the pilgrimage. There came times when one just had to get through barriers of pain, and this led to mystical (*shinpiteki*) feelings. Walking the pilgrimage opened up such possibilities and enabled him to engage in a process of self-discovery in ways that going by car did not.

He related this to Kōbō Daishi, of whom he was a 'fan' (using this foreign loanword) and spoke of how Daishi had prayed for the safety of country and done numerous ascetic feats that had produced spiritual breakthroughs.[6] His walking style was clearly framed around speed and challenge, for he said he usually did it in thirty-four days—a rapid pace for a walker—although he then added that he was now slowing down a little. Moreover, although he had always previously carried a tent and camped out, his doctor had warned him against doing this in future due to his age and concerns about his health, so he now had to stay in lodges instead. He certainly kept to a firm schedule, stating that he had a plane ticket back home from nearby Takamatsu airport

---

[5] We have not found any statistics on this issue but note that a number of recent initiatives in Shikoku to provide cheap or free places to stay (including a number of wayside huts) might have had an effect here.

[6] He was yet another pilgrim who conflated the legendary Kōbō Daishi with the historical Kūkai, at one point referring to practices done by Kūkai as things done by Daishi.

to Saitama (near Tokyo) for the following night. He had bought it before he set out and had scheduled his pilgrimage around Shikoku to make sure he would get that plane; he estimated he would reach Temple Eighty-Eight by sometime in the middle of the next day, with ample time to get from there to Takamatsu airport for his flight.

We have already, with the example of Sasaki cited in Chapter 2, seen how some walkers have carefully organised schedules and routines around which their pilgrimages are framed, and this came out again clearly when Matsumoto-san, a man aged seventy-seven, agreed to meet us for an extended interview in October 2019. He lives in Osaka prefecture but is originally from Kagawa in Shikoku. His father died when he was ten and his mother when he was eighteen, after which he moved from Shikoku to Osaka where he had relatives. Since his parents' graves were in Shikoku he returned regularly there to perform regular customary grave visits (*haka mairi*), but he lived his working life in the Osaka region, employed by a major electrics company, continuing to live there since his retirement at the age of sixty. Since then he has lived on his pension and savings.

Matsumoto came to the interview bearing a large collection of materials about his pilgrimages in Shikoku, including detailed records of all his overnight stays, of the distances and amounts of time he walked each day, and how long it took him to do each section of the route. He first walked the *henro* aged fifty-seven after becoming very ill, requiring surgery and being told by doctors that he was overworking and needed to do more exercise. Because he was from Shikoku he thought of the pilgrimage and read a book written by one pilgrim about her experiences of walking Shikoku. He used this book to help plan his own pilgrimage, which he did in stages on foot, with the simple aim and purpose of getting better.[7] As a result he became attracted to the pilgrimage and since then had done it regularly, usually clockwise but on three occasions in reverse order. Through his efforts he had become a registered *sendatsu* (and had reached the rank of *daisendatsu*) as well as becoming a *sendatsu* on the Bekkaku pilgrimage, which he had done three times, each time in conjunction with walking the eighty-eight stage pilgrimage circuit.

He came to realise also that he had spent too long working and that he had no time for himself, so when he reached his company's retirement age of sixty he felt he had a chance to properly think about life. This fuelled his interest

---

[7] He is by no means the only person whose initial engagement was of this sort; see Reader (2005: 259–260) for how Miyazaki Tateki (see Chapter 2) initially became involved in the pilgrimage for similar reasons.

in walking the pilgrimage regularly, something he did from the age of sixty until 2015, when he was seventy-three. At this point he had taken a break from doing the pilgrimage because, having attained the rank of *daisendatsu*, he thought he would be unable to rise higher in the ranks or achieve really high numbers of pilgrimage (since he always went on foot). On this point he appeared quite critical of those who did the pilgrimage repeatedly by car and racked up very high numbers of circuits; however he also noted that since he himself did not have a car he really had little choice but to walk. It was also a reminder to us that status and ranks can be important driving forces for pilgrims.

However his association with the pilgrimage had not ended; he told us that he was thinking of walking again and that he definitely had *Shikokubyō*. Moreover during his hiatus from actual physical engagement with the pilgrimage he had devoted himself to all manner of activities centred on it. This was evident in the collection of materials he brought with him to the interview, such as numerous folders and files containing his meticulous records of every pilgrimage he has made to Shikoku. Prior to going off on pilgrimage he always spends twenty days preparing for the journey, drawing up charts of how long he intends to walk each day and arranging every night of accommodation. Such planning is part of the pilgrimage in his view, as it was in the case of Sasaki, cited in Chapter 2. He always, on pilgrimage, makes notes of everything that occurs, from the distances walked and time spent on walking each day, to places he ate and stayed, their costs, and so on. He then types everything up on his return home, and also uploads it to a personal website. (His website, we should add, is not just about his pilgrimages but includes materials about hobbies such as bird watching, hiking up mountains, and carving wooden Buddhist statues.) He also makes his own DVDs related to the pilgrimage, based on his travels in Shikoku and the photographs he has taken there. Indeed, he told us, even though he had not at that point been to Shikoku for over four years, his home life was largely taken up with activities related to the pilgrimage as he spends most of his time writing up his experiences and making files and DVDs of his photographs. He also has assembled a large collection of materials and articles related to the pilgrimage that he has cut out of newspapers and magazines and filed in plastic folders, along with printouts of talks by pilgrimage temple priests and many other items related to pilgrimage and Buddhism that he has similarly collected and filed. As such the pilgrimage was thus ever-present in his life.

When he first did the pilgrimage, Matsumoto indicated, it was for practical reasons, to walk and regain his health and was not in any way connected to faith. However, through the pilgrimage he has become a believer; he now has a statue of Daishi on his desk at home that he venerates, and he feels his constant pilgrimages are because Daishi keeps beckoning (*maneki*) him to Shikoku. Faith, in other words, has flowed from doing the pilgrimage, and it was this aligned to *Shikokubyō* (which he referred to as a 'spiritual illness' *seishinbyō*) that drew him back and kept him forever engrossed in the pilgrimage. He viewed Shikoku as a special holy island and a 'different world' (*betsu no sekai*); such views, along with his own identity as someone from Shikoku, meant that he had not done any pilgrimages apart from the *henro* and the Shikoku Bekkaku pilgrimage.

Matsumoto is clear that the pilgrimage is not for him a strict ascetic exercise; rather than sleeping out he stays in hotels, and local lodges, and drinks beer at night. He also admitted that he occasionally skips some of the ritual chants normally done by pilgrims at the temples and spends only a short time at each temple. At the same time he regards the pilgrimage as a 'religion' (*shūkyō*) to which he was devoted, even comparing it to 'other religions' (*hoka no shūkyō*) such as Pure Land Buddhism.

At this point Matsumoto talked about the importance of walking and the states of mind it induced. Life normally was so busy and complex that people had little time to think or reflect what life is about. The *henro* fills that gap and Daishi has given us this pilgrimage to help teach us these things. To walk is to think (*aruku wa kangaeru*) and reflect on life, while a key theme of the pilgrimage is that through walking one engages in the 'asceticism of thanks' (*kansha no gyō*) to Daishi. He added that for him the best part of the pilgrimage is the long section through Kōchi prefecture, where there are less temples and the distances between them are the longest, with the result that one just walks, often close to the sea, loses any sense of place and enters a state of selfless clarity (*mushin*, no mind). As he talked he exuded enthusiasm for and devotion to the pilgrimage. His wish to walk it again was evident. Indeed virtually his last comment in the interview was that he had learnt all about life from the pilgrimage. What was also striking was that he only once mentioned the fact that he was married. When we asked about his family circumstances and how it impacted on his pilgrimage activities, he replied that he had a wife but she did not seem to mind when he went off on the pilgrimage. She appeared to be less present in his thoughts than Daishi.

We encountered numerous other pilgrims with similar mixtures of faith and an interest in walking, such as a man from Nagoya who was walking between Temples Eighteen and Nineteen in early November 2019. Dressed head to toe in pilgrim's white (including white *tabi*- Japanese style footwear) and with an ancient gnarled pilgrimage staff, he said he was in his seventies and had walked the pilgrimage nineteen times every year at around the same time each year since his first circuit in 2001. Normally he took between thirty-three and thirty-five days each time, always in one go and clockwise. He generally stays in lodges, although if there is no option he does occasionally sleep out, although he tries to avoid this. He had also done one other pilgrimage: the Chita Hantō eighty-eight-stage route. He had done this because it was in his local area, and so he thought he ought to do it once. Otherwise his focus was simply on Shikoku. Why? It was a half-and-half mixture (*hanbun hanbun*) of faith (*shinkō*) in Daishi, who was an amazing person, and enjoyment (*asobi*). He had no intention of stopping and added, on being asked why he kept doing it, that he had not yet attained enlightenment (*satori wa mada haitte inai*), at which he laughed and set off again.

Hybrid styles, faith, and walking

In Chapter 2 we noted having multiple choices of how to do the pilgrimage can influence people to do it many times, while in Chapter 5 we showed that some pilgrims who usually go by car may sometimes walk for a change. Some walkers are also similarly hybrid in their modes of pilgrimage. This was the case with a man now living in Hiroshima (originally from Osaka) interviewed outside Temple Fifteen. He was in his late sixties, had done the *henro* eight times and was now on his ninth circuit: four were solely on foot, though occasionally he would accept lifts if offered as *settai*; three circuits were mainly by bus and train, while walking some parts of the route; and once was by bicycle. On this occasion he was again using a mixture of walking, buses, and trains; since there are several temples close together around Temple Fifteen he was walking that particular section. He never drove, he informed us, because he was very short-sighted. He had first done the pilgrimage five years earlier after getting into poor condition and becoming ill, at which point he was advised that he needed to get fit and that walking would be a good means to this end. This led him to come to Shikoku; he was another person who initially became involved in (and ultimately addicted to) the pilgrimage for reasons of health. Like Matsumoto he found the pilgrimage route offered a viable and accessible framework with a clear route and goals along the way (the temples) that allowed him to walk and get exercise. He found he liked walking and that the pilgrimage was 'easy to walk' (*arukiyasui*) as there were lots of signs indicating where the route went, plenty of places (hotels, lodges, cafes, and restaurants) where one could stay or eat, and lots of kind people who would help people such as him. Walking made him feel better, and on completion he decided he wanted to do it again; the *henro* has been a core theme in his life ever since. Shortly after his first pilgrimage he reached re-tirement age, and for the eighteen months after that he had more time to concentrate on doing pilgrimages. However, more recently, he has started some part-time work and also enrolled in the *Hōsō Daigaku* (the Japanese University of the Air). His time is more limited, so now does the pilgrimage in stages. He had also, he said, done the Saikoku pilgrimage but had not liked it anywhere near as much as Shikoku; it was not a walking pilgrimage and nor did he feel the people he met along the way were as friendly as those in Shikoku. As such, Shikoku was his pilgrimage.

On being asked about faith and Kōbō Daishi he initially responded that this was not a core motivation, but then amended this to say that he grew up in a Shingon Buddhist household and was introduced to Daishi veneration when young. As such it was part of his background, so he recognised that faith did play a part in his pilgrimages. Nonetheless he initially walked because of health issues; because it made him better and because he liked walking and wanted to continue looking after his health, he felt that in overall terms faith was not really a core factor in his repeated pilgrimages. He added that when he got better after being ill it was not a case of *byōki naoshi* (healing) in any sense related to the ways it is often seen in religious contexts (such as praying to a deity or Buddha and being cured), but was due to exercise. At the same time, he also recognised that his continuing engagement with the pilgrimage was strengthening his feelings towards Kōbō Daishi. As such faith in some form was also an element in his returning repeatedly to Shikoku.

Walking, nature, scenery

Not every pilgrim relates their repeated circuits on foot to faith—or even mentions it. Virtually every foot pilgrim we met who had done the pilgrimage more than once gave as one reason for this that they liked walking and loved

Shikoku's scenery and natural surroundings.[8] Some indicated that these attractions were so central to their pilgrimages that they rejected the idea of faith as a factor in their repeated pilgrimages. A good example was a retired man from Shizuoka in his early seventies who was carrying a rucksack and walking very briskly along the road near Cape Muroto. Suntanned and trim, he was on his eleventh pilgrimage, four of which (including this circuit) were in reverse order. When asked if his pilgrimages related to faith he responded by shaking his head vigorously and asserting that faith had nothing at all to do with it. Rather, he talked about *Shikoku no miryoku* (Shikoku's charms)— a term heard frequently when talking to pilgrims—as key to what he was doing. He expanded on this by saying that he lived alone and that this could be bad for one mentally; he pointed at his head at this point and indicated he would go stir crazy if he just stayed at home alone. Going on the *henro* was not just a way to enjoy Shikoku's charms, but to have something to do that involved being outdoors, walking, eating good food and meeting people. He used Miyazaki Tateki's guidebook as his compass on pilgrimage and always stayed in local lodges where other pilgrims stayed, so he had a chance to meet other people. The *henro* thus had an important social dimension that he lacked at home. It also helped him keep fit and healthy, and encouraged brisk walking; indeed, he said apologetically, he had a schedule to keep, so he could not tarry longer to talk but needed to press on to the place he planned to stay that night.

Another example was a man at Temple Eighty-Seven met on a late November afternoon in 2019. He had arrived there with two other men; they were walking individually but their paths had converged earlier. They had formed a temporary bond, arranging to stay in the same lodge nearby that evening and maybe share a beer or so. It was the sort of typical transient encounter and friendship that commonly occurs among pilgrims. Two were on their first pilgrimage; the third, from Tokyo, was on his twenty-fourth, all on foot. Puffing on a cigarette as he talked, he informed us that he was sixty-eight years old and had walked the pilgrimage twice a year, around the same time each spring and autumn, for the past fourteen years since he retired aged fifty-five. He always did it all in one go and took between thirty-eight and forty days each time. He also said he had walked the Shōdoshima

---

[8] This is not to imply these were not reasons for first-timers as well; indeed it was a common refrain from pilgrims that Shikoku's scenery and ambience played a major part in their initial wish to do the pilgrimage and in their subsequent enjoyment of it.

pilgrimage eleven times—something he recommended also to the other two men, saying that it was a good walk with excellent scenery, a smaller scale version of Shikoku that took under a week and where there were virtually no walkers or other pilgrims.

He was wearing a white pilgrim's shirt and a bamboo hat (*sugakasa*) but did not carry a stamp book; nor was he interested, he said, in becoming a *sendatsu*. In fact he quite adamantly rejected the idea. Nor does he ever sleep out; he always stays in lodges. When asked why he was doing the pilgrimage (and why so often) he was clear it was not related to faith but to his love of walking. Why then do the *henro* rather than (for example) a long-distance footpath or hiking course? He responded that his interest was in meeting people from all over Japan, which he could do by walking the pilgrimage, gesturing to his two companions as an example. By contrast, doing long-distance hiking routes was not to his liking; hikers were a different type of person, into smart hiking gear and marching along at a rapid pace rather than being friendly, engaging with others or, indeed, hanging out over a beer in the evening. He preferred the more casual and informal style of the *henro*. He then added a further factor behind his regular repeated pilgrimages: he had *Shikokubyō*, something that was, he added with a laugh, a 'serious illness' (*jūtoku na byōki*). For him the pilgrimage was a retirement activity in which he could engage with his love of walking, meet people, socialise, and enjoy Shikoku. When asked how long would he carry on doing this he replied as long as he could still walk. Would he at that stage go by car? No, he replied. Walking was his thing and the *henro* offered an excellent framework (with its route markers and plentiful lodges and places to eat) for him to engage in this pleasure. He also added that, although he did not carry a stamp book, he was on his fifth bamboo pilgrim's hat. Others had worn out and he had on such occasions stored them at one of the temples. Pilgrims sometimes do this so as to leave something of themselves permanently on the route.[9] The man in question was not just constantly engaged in repeated pilgrimages but had symbolically embedded himself there permanently through his pilgrim's hat.

At the bus stop by Temple Forty-Two a man with a pilgrim's staff, white pilgrim's shirt, and a backpack was waiting for a bus in November 2018 when one of the authors asked if he was on his first pilgrimage. No, he replied, it was his third time; this time he was doing it in reverse order for a change. He was from Nagoya and was seventy-three years old; he always did it in

---

[9] See Reader 2005: 68 on this and for a photograph of such items at one temple.

sections because he still worked much of the time and could only spare short periods for the pilgrimage, usually at weekends. He occasionally used buses but mostly walked, and although he was at the bus stop he was considering striking out again on foot as he was unsure if the bus would show up. He had first started the pilgrimage six years ago and it took him two years to complete, as did his second one. He was now halfway through his third but had done it slightly more quickly. He had in effect been engaged almost continually in doing the pilgrimage since his first steps along the route six years previously. When asked about his motivations he replied that the main one was that he wanted to live in nature (*jibun ni shizen ni sei shitai*); in saying this he talked about Shikoku's charms and waxed lyrical about walking in nature, seeing flowers, being in the mountains, passing through rice fields, and visiting old temples. He also talked about the joys of feeling the wind on his face and how he had learnt to appreciate nature through the *henro*. He also said that he would continue coming to Shikoku as long as his legs were good enough to carry him—if possible, until he died.

Similar themes emerged from a meeting with a retired man, also aged seventy-three, from Sapporo in the northern island of Hokkaidō in November 2018. Wearing a bamboo pilgrim's hat and a white pilgrim's shirt he was at the foot of the steps at Temple Seventy-One and had thus far taken fifty days to walk there from Temple One. Since retiring he had walked the pilgrimage every three years and was now on his fourth circuit. He had carried a book to be stamped on his first pilgrimage but not since then. He explained that it was nothing to do with faith; he did it because he liked hiking. Hokkaidō at this time of year was cold but Shikoku warm, so it was a way of escaping from the harsh beginnings of winter while getting exercise and keeping fit. His family was happy for him to go—something that seemed not uncommon for older men, perhaps indicating that going off on pilgrimage was a socially acceptable way for them to get away from the everyday world and have some 'me' time while allowing spouses who stayed at home time to themselves as well. Again it was a response and a reason that appeared with some regularity among the Japanese male walkers we met.

This was the case also with a man from Osaka in his sixties met at Temple Two at the end of October 2018 who said he was married and that his wife stayed at home while he came to Shikoku to walk sections of the pilgrimage. He had come by bus and was just going to walk a short section to Temple Six before catching a bus home again. He was in the construction business and only had limited time free for pilgrimages, fitted in between his work commitments, but in all had managed seven circuits in in the past five years, always on foot. His reason was that he likes walking; when asked why not instead do a hiking trail such as the Tōkaidō (one of Japan's historical long-distance hiking trails) he said it was because he had first come to Shikoku and had liked the atmosphere and ambience, and thus had come back again—and again. It was not connected to faith (*shinkō*); he just liked walking and added that in doing it he found out about himself—something that, as Hoshino Eiki has shown, has been a prominent factor in motivating pilgrims over the ages,[10] and that was at times mentioned by our respondents. He had no idea how many more times he might do the pilgrimage; he just would continue while he felt like it.

For him as for many other walkers we met, a major attraction of the pilgrimage was that it offered a viable framework and structure—from well-marked paths to plentiful places to eat and sleep—aligned with interesting places to visit (the temples), good scenery, nature, and surroundings with a supportive network and local culture for people who wanted to walk. For older Japanese in particular this seemed to be an aspect that attracted them, a point that emerged also in conversation with a male pilgrim met one evening by the gate of Temple Thirty-Seven. He was seventy, from Shizuoka, and had done four circuits on foot, twice clockwise and twice counter-clockwise. He had done it regularly in two sections, half in spring and half in autumn, each year since retiring. It kept him fit and mentally alert; his pilgrimages, he said, were not about faith, but about keeping going and staying alive, healthy, and mentally on the ball. He liked walking and found the *henro* provided a good structure within which to engage in his hobby of walking.

Such views resonated with those of a female pilgrim who walked into the courtyard of Temple Eighty-Seven in November 2019 shortly after the meeting outlined earlier with the man who had walked the *henro* twenty-four times. It was a striking encounter in that, while we had met a number of Japanese women walking the pilgrimage, they were all doing it for the first time. This woman was the first female Japanese pilgrim we met who had done repeated foot pilgrimages. She was seventy-eight years old and had done nine pilgrimage circuits—always in one go from the time she retired at the age of sixty. She walks much of the way but also uses buses and trains where appropriate, such as when there are very long stretches between temples and where there may be little respite from walking along busy highways. She said that

---

[10] Hoshino 2001: 353–378.

when younger she liked hiking and climbing or hiking up mountains, and had visited and ascended all the *Nihon hyaku meizan* (100 famous mountains of Japan). Doing the pilgrimage was in essence an extension of such activities. She started doing it as a retirement hobby; she wanted to travel and see Japan, and the pilgrimage appealed because overnight accommodation and food tended to be cheap in Shikoku. However, she complained, it had got dearer over the years. Nonetheless she continued to come to Shikoku and walk (with occasional buses and trains) around the pilgrimage route, enjoying nature and hiking. Although she insisted faith was not a factor, she also wanted to terminate the interview in order to do a series of prayers and rituals in front of the temple before going to find the place she was lodging that evening.

The last time?

We regularly asked pilgrims who had walked the route several times how long they thought they would continue making pilgrimages in Shikoku. As we have indicated in this chapter the most common response was along the lines either of 'until I die' or 'until I am no longer able to do so'. Sometimes those who gave the latter response said they might then do it another way (e.g. by bus or car) while others were clear that they would stop altogether once they could no longer walk the route. Concerns about age, declining health, and, poignantly, the realisation that their physical limitations clashed with their mental wishes to keep going, were present among many we met—perhaps unsurprisingly, given that many of them were in their seventies or above. (Indeed, we did not meet anyone who was walking who had done more than one pilgrimage and who was below their late fifties.) There were several times when, somewhat plaintively, pilgrims told us that they thought, or feared, that this would be their last time. Thus the man cited in Chapter 4, aged eighty-two, who had initially walked the pilgrimage aged seventy-three as a memorial for his dead wife and who, when we met him in March 2018, was on his fourth circuit on foot, wanted to carry on doing it as long as possible, but was aware that he was getting slower and might not manage it again. Another walker, aged seventy and from Kōchi, met near Temple Thirty-Eight in March 2018 was on his eighth foot pilgrimage; twice he had done it in one go but then had switched to doing it in sections to make it more manageable. However he felt this would be his final circuit on foot, after which he planned to go by car.

The feeling that the current circuit would definitely be a last pilgrimage came through most strikingly when talking to a couple who were on their fifth walking pilgrimage in November 2018. They had stayed overnight at Temple Thirty-Seven and had called into a nearby convenience store to get some breakfast because the temple lodge was not at that time providing food for overnight visitors. One of the authors was in a similar position and was greeted by the couple, who said they had seen him at the temple earlier that morning. On explaining the research project the couple—the Tanakas—were happy to take part in a long interview and outline their pilgrimage history and related matters. He was a former tax consultant who had initially retired aged fifty-seven and then worked privately—initially from an office and later from home—until he gave up entirely when aged eighty-four, while she ran their household.

He was ninety years old and she was eighty-three. Dressed wholly in white with bamboo pilgrimage hats, they had pieces of cloth draped across their small backpacks with signs in Japanese printed on them saying *kyūjū henro. fufu henro* (ninety-year-old pilgrim, husband and wife pilgrimage). They explained that they were walking it in one go, from Temple One on-wards, and were on their fifth circuit together. He had also done one pil-grimage with a group of twenty walkers led by the now deceased Miyazaki Tateki (see Chapter 2). Their first pilgrimage together was twenty-four years previously when he was sixty-six and she fifty-nine in the hot humid period of summer. This was after she had been diagnosed with breast cancer, was successfully operated on, and made a full recovery. To give thanks for this they did a 'thanksgiving pilgrimage' (*orei mairi*) on foot around Shikoku. It took them forty days and they stayed (as they always do) in local lodges or in temples that offered accommodation. They do not sleep out. Although they used the term *orei mairi*, 'thanksgiving pilgrimage', they both, throughout the interview, insisted that they were not driven by faith or religious motives and instead emphasised their love of walking, something that was a recur-rent theme in their discussions. At the same time they also had other reasons for each of their pilgrimages that had associations with faith and ritual commemoration.

They next did the pilgrimage was eleven years later, this time in spring, when he was seventy-seven and she seventy, doing what they called a *tomorai henro*—a memorial pilgrimage for the spirit of his mother who had died the year before, aged 100. This time it took them forty-three days. The third, again in spring, was in 2012 when he was eighty-four and she seventy-seven, in the aftermath of the Tōhoku tsunami and earthquake disaster of 11 March 2001, which they did it to pray for the spirits of those who died. On that occasion they wore a sign on the back of their rucksacks outlining the reason for their pilgrimage; it was the first time they had worn a sign. As a result of the sign they received lots of money as *settai*, and they saved it all—around 60 000 yen—and donated it to the *Asahi Shinbun* (newspaper) disaster relief fund. The *Asahi Shinbun* in turn published an article about them, their pilgrimage, and the donation, which led to a minor degree of fame for them.

Their fourth pilgrimage was four years later in 2016 to commemorate his eighty-eighth birthday (they called this their *beijū iwai*—celebration of the eighty-eighth birthday); there was of course also a correlation between his age and the number of temples. It took them fifty-seven days this time; as they commented, every pilgrimage took longer and required more preparation to arrange overnight accommodation as they got older. Initially they were going to stop at this point, but journalists at the *Asahi Shinbun* wrote again about them and then suggested that it would be a good idea for them to do it again when he reached ninety—a challenge they took up, but with the recognition that this would be their last circuit. They called it their *sotsujū kinen* (celebration of the ninetieth birthday) and thought it would take them sixty days in all. These latter two pilgrimages were done from October to November to coincide with his birthday.

Although each pilgrimage had a stated theme that could be considered as a specific motive, there was also a sense of continuity to their pilgrimages and a feeling of recurrent engagement with the *henro*. They had also done other pilgrimages on foot; he had walked the Chita Hantō pilgrimage with an organised group, and they had done the Shōdoshima eighty-eight-stage pilgrimage together. Moreover, when he was eighty-five and she seventy-nine they had walked around 800 kilometres along the Santiago de Compostela pilgrimage route from France across Spain to Santiago. On that occasion they were much helped, they said, by people met on the way, notably other Japanese. In addition to these pilgrimages they had visited and hiked up around half of the *Nihon hyaku meizan*, including Tsurugi in Shikoku, a mountain with close associations with religious mountain ascents. However, they no longer did such mountain hikes as it had become too difficult for them.

Throughout they emphasised their love of walking; he added that at home he did a five-kilometre walk every morning. Yet walking alone did not explain their involvement; while they were clear that they did not have any special or specific faith (*shinkō wa tokubetsu ni wa nai*) they also said that they had been helped by Kōbō Daishi. They had solicited *settai* on one pilgrimage (in order to donate it to a fund for those who died in Tōhoku) and were well aware of the meanings of the practice, saying that although they wanted to walk, they would, if offered a lift as *settai*, feeling obliged to accept it at least for a short way. The orientations of their pilgrimages (e.g. thanks for recovery from illness, prayers for the spirits of the Tōhoku disaster dead) also indicated that the faith dimensions of the pilgrimage were also present to some degree. They were also aware of pilgrimage history and especially of those who had walked the *henro* in the past and whose footsteps they were conscious of following. During the conversation they referred both to Miyazaki Tateki and to Nakatsukasa Mōhei, whom they cited as the person who had walked it most often. They also said they had met others who had walked it a number of times, the most being around twenty times.

They were the oldest couple, and he was the single oldest foot pilgrim, we met during our research. Their extended pilgrimage history stretched over twenty-four years and five foot-pilgrimages, plus other pilgrimage walks in Japan and Europe. Their expressed motivations were not dissimilar to many we met in that they liked walking but also touched on issues related to Kōbō Daishi, prayers for the dead and giving thanks for returning to health. It was clear, too, that, like many others we met, doing the pilgrimage had given them a sense of purpose and meaning in their retirement years as well as some public attention and recognition. The signs they wore drew attention to their pilgrimages, as did their willingness to talk to a major newspaper and even be persuaded to do another pilgrimage. At the same time they were coming to the end of their pilgrimage lives, realising that this would be their last time. It was a sentiment we heard from time to time from others, as we have already noted, and it reflected the sense that even the most avid pilgrims sometimes have to face the reality that their physical engagement with and performance of the pilgrimage will at some point have to end.

Foreign pilgrims

There is one final category of pilgrims we wish to introduce, and it constitutes a new and growing one in the context of long-term and unending pilgrimage engagement. This is of non-Japanese (and at present, predominantly Western) people who have long associations with and/or who have walked the pilgrimage a number of times. Reader cites the case of the American author Oliver Statler, who walked the pilgrimage, wrote a book about it, spent much of his later life making the *henro* better known to audiences beyond Japan, as well as leading parties of American students on sections of the route. He explained his immersion in it by simply saying that 'it's addictive'.[11] Pilgrims from overseas (most commonly but not exclusively from Western countries) are the main growth area of the pilgrimage currently,[12] and this has produced a small number who have come back again to walk the pilgrimage, sometimes more than once. We touched on this point in Chapter 2 with the example of the Canadian woman who works in Japan and regularly goes to Shikoku to walk sections of the *henro*. Others we met in this research include a middle-aged man from New York met at Temple Forty-Four in November 2019 who was on his second pilgrimage and, in November 2018, a Swedish female pilgrim encountered near Temple Seventy-One. She said she first came to Shikoku as a student in Matsuyama in the early 1970s. She then did a degree in Japanese in the United States and later returned to Matsuyama to teach for some years before marrying and raising a family in Sweden. Now that her children had grown and left home she returns to Japan from time to time, and when she does she walks along the pilgrimage path. She has walked it fully twice in such ways and was on her third circuit, this time doing it in two trips (due to getting a bit older and finding it less tiring to split it into two). She thought she would continue doing it as long as she could. She had a good knowledge of Japan and its religious traditions, and said that, given the time she had spent in Shikoku studying and working, the pilgrimage was part of her cultural background in Japan.

There are other Westerners who have also walked the pilgrimage several times; on two occasions officials at temple offices said to us that recently they had seen foreign pilgrims who had done more than one circuit. One was on his third and the other, the official thought, his eighth. We are also aware of a number of Western residents of Japan who regularly walk parts of the pilgrimage and who have close engagements with it, as well as some who have moved to Shikoku to deepen their association with the pilgrimage, in one case retiring there for this reason.[13] Moreover there are some who have

---

[11] Reader (2005: 255), where Reader also indicates that the same might be true for him; the fact that fourteen years later he is still studying the pilgrimage might appear to confirm this.

[12] The survey conducted by the Shikoku Araiansu Chiiki Keizai Kenkyū Bunkakai shows a small but growing cohort of overseas foot pilgrims in Shikoku; in 2007 there were, according to this study, just forty-four foreign pilgrims who walked the pilgrimage. By 2017 the number had exceeded 400 (Shikoku Araiansu Chiiki Keizai Kenkyū Bunkakai 2019: 8–9).

[13] Shultz 2020: 58.

become *sendatsu* through their repeated pilgrimages, including one Dutch man and a Korean female pilgrim. This, and the wider topic of contemporary non-Japanese engagement with the pilgrimage, is an area as yet little studied and that requires further research. At present we mention it here as a potential area of growth for the wider theme of unending pilgrimage we focus on in this book.

Recurrent walkers, prevalent patterns

Above we have outlined the stories and examples of a number of the people we met in our research who have walked the pilgrimage frequently and for whom their engagement appeared to be open-ended, with the caveat that many recognise that at some point, either through death, age, or infirmity, even the *henro* might have a finite temporal end. The cases we have outlined represent a broad spectrum of types, from those who talk overtly about faith, to those who see their pilgrimages through a lens of asceticism, to those who are more ready to present it in terms of health and a love of walking and nature. For some, issues of self-discovery and of challenging themselves were present. Many of course see these as intertwining themes. Some tend towards being solitary while others are happy to meet up and socialise with others on the way—and some even see the pilgrimage in part as a means of getting away for a period from their isolated lives at home to meet others. Extensive planning is often a feature of such pilgrims, while the pilgrimage appears rarely to be left behind, as it were, in Shikoku, but is taken home to become part of their home lives as well—something clearly evident in people such as Matsumoto, who recognises that the pilgrimage suffuses his home life as he spends much of his time working on his pilgrimage DVDs, folders, and website.

Every pilgrim we talked to had their own views and interpretations of what they were doing, and why. The walkers we have described here, who as they walk have extended periods on their own to reflect on their thoughts and intentions, have often developed specific philosophies and thoughts about the pilgrimage, as was evident, for instance, in Akiyama's views about *takuhatsu* and the rules he imposes on himself during the pilgrimage. While all pilgrimages are highly individual, the walkers we examined were particularly striking in emphasising the personal nature of their pilgrimages. They might at times socialise, often finding the friendship of the road to be part of the attraction of Shikoku, but they were also oriented towards being on their own. Apart from one couple cited earlier, the foot pilgrims we met in our fieldwork who had done several pilgrimages were all doing so on their own. Some did walk at times with fellow pilgrims, but few if any appeared to be intent on forming bonds with others throughout their travels; walking relationships were transient, to be enjoyed as and when they occurred but not intrinsic.

Compared to those who did multiple pilgrimages by car we noted that walkers tended to be less overt in talking about faith or related issues. Some viewed the pilgrimage through an ascetic lens, and several we have cited referred to their feelings for Kōbō Daishi or talked about matters of spiritual development and even enlightenment as important to them or as significant in their pilgrimages. Yet there were also many who shied away from such talk, outlining their motives through the prism of self-development and challenge or their enjoyment of walking and the benefits such activity brought them in terms of health and the like. For many people, in other words, Shikoku provides a structure for testing themselves, walking, and keeping healthy and active, that appeals to some people—especially older males—and offers a framework through which they can engage in such activities. The *henro* offers scope for long walks punctuated by the temples where they can, if they wish, pray and make requests for spiritual and worldly benefits, or just rest awhile and admire the temple architecture and ambience, and maybe meet and talk to other pilgrims. As several walkers indicated, their families appeared happy for them to go off regularly on the pilgrimage; it provided an acceptable reason for travel and for taking time out from family and home lives. It enabled them to enjoy nature in a managed way, with plentiful available facilities (besides the lodgings and places to eat, there are numerous convenience stores, public toilets, and other support structures all along the route) and in a context that is socially and culturally acceptable and meaningful. It also, in an age where people have increasingly shied away from overtly expressing belonging to religious institutions and from identifying themselves as having religious orientations,[14] enables them to take part in something traditionally

---

[14] This tendency in Japan since the 1990s has been widely noted especially in terms of declining support structures for institutional Buddhism but also new religions (e.g. Reader 2011, 2012; Ukai 2015; Kolata 2019). Interestingly, too, although sociological studies of religion in Japan (e.g. Ishii 2007) indicate that those in the older generations still tend to have higher levels of engagement in customary rituals and matters of faith, rituals and practices at temples, shrines, and other such places, that same segment of the population—the older generations—often appears ready to play down or even repudiate issues of faith when discussing why they walk the pilgrimage multiple times.

associated with such things while distancing themselves from any sense of affiliation and religious engagement.

We also noted that some walkers were conscious of the historical roots and patterns of the pilgrimage, and of those who had gone before them. Akiyama, for example, spoke of begging as an embedded ascetic practice of the pilgrimage and was conscious of the ascetic roots of the *henro*, while the Tanakas referred to past pilgrims such as Nakatsukasa. Others, too, indicated that by walking they were engaging with a long enduring historical strand within the pilgrimage. Indeed, that remains an element in the pilgrimage's appeal; various studies have shown that one element in the Shikoku pilgrimage's appeal, especially to older Japanese, is that of a place and practice in which traditions have endured and aspects of a Japan of earlier times can be still encountered.[15] This was a sentiment that many pilgrims (not just those on foot) have mentioned to us over many years of visiting Shikoku and interacting with pilgrims, and it remains an element in the pilgrimage's contemporary dynamic and attractiveness.

One final observation is that almost all our examples in this chapter (apart from some of the foreign pilgrims we referred to) are of people who are either retired or, if still working, nonetheless close to or above official retirement age. Almost all were over sixty, and many were in their seventies or above. This suggests that long-term engagement and multiple pilgrimage performance on foot is primarily if not almost exclusively an activity of the older generation. This is not because we have only selected people of this age group to focus on but because the pilgrims we met who had walked several times around the *henro* circuit were all of such an age. When we met younger pilgrims who walked they invariably indicated that they were on their first pilgrimage. As we noted also in Chapter 4, respondents to our questionnaire were commonly aged sixty or above, and only one was under forty.

This again suggests that multiple or incessant pilgrimage engagement is something primarily associated with age and ageing. This is hardly surprising. One needs an extended period of time to build up a history of multiple performance, whether by car or on foot. That requires time and, normally also, money—things more likely (especially time) to be available to older people. Retirement was an element in the stories of many of the walkers we have cited here; it was after retiring that pilgrims such as Matsumoto and the walker at Temple Eighty-Seven on his twenty-fourth pilgrimage, started doing the

---

[15] See, for example, Hoshino 1981; Reader 2005: 24–25; and Hoshino and Asakawa 2011: 159–175.

henro repeatedly. That does not mean that younger pilgrims walking the pilgrimage for the first time now will not do it multiple times; historical patterns along with evidence provided in this book show that many people—perhaps the majority—who do the pilgrimage will then repeat it. As such some of those whom we met while doing their first pilgrimages in 2018 or 2019 might well do it again and, as they get older, retire, and have more free time, become like the older pilgrims discussed in this chapter. As it stands, however, people of retirement age and above are always likely to be the most dominant group within the wider rubric of multiple and unending performance that we have identified as a significant characteristic of the Shikoku pilgrimage.

Concluding comments and new challenges

Multiple performance and infinite pilgrimage

At Temple Eighty-Five at the end of October 2019, we talked to two youngish men wearing white pilgrim shirts and with backpacks. They were both were walking the pilgrimage, although not together. They had just arrived at the temple around the same time. Both had started from Temple One, had been walking for several weeks, and were now only a day or so away from completing the pilgrimage, each for the first time. Would they do it again? we asked. Both replied similarly: no, once was enough.

This incident stood out because we could not recall any other case of people during our research being so adamant about this being a one and only time. Usually when people expressed the view that this might be their only pilgrimage it was due to age or circumstances; more frequently they appeared inclined to do it again, sometimes trying it another way. As we have shown in this book, there are many who have done this, using a variety of means of doing the pilgrimage, often completing it multiple times and spending much of their lives immersed in it. Moreover, many of those who had only done it once or twice appeared already to be embarked on a path of continuing pilgrimage, as was the case with a woman met at Temple Eighteen in November 2019 who was on her second pilgrimage. She said the following year was a leap year so she would do the pilgrimage again, albeit *gyaku uchi* (in reverse order), following a popular practice of doing it this way in leap years. The year after, she said, she aimed to do it again, for her fourth time. Asked whether she planned to do the pilgrimage every year thereafter, she said she was not sure whether she could do it *every* year, but she certainly aimed to do it again and again.

It was the sort of encounter we had repeatedly—people had only just started out as pilgrims in Shikoku, but who were already thinking ahead to future performances. To them pilgrimage was, as we commented in the Introduction, temporally unbounded[1] and not limited by the period spent

---

[1] Shultz 2020.

Pilgrims Until We Die. Ian Reader and John Shultz, Oxford University Press. © Oxford University Press 2021.
DOI: 10.1093/oso/9780197573587.003.0008

on the route; it was a continuing activity and engagement, not just practiced physically but also mentally evoked when away from the pilgrimage route and projected into the future. Illustrative of this were people we met who had done the pilgrimage sometime in the past—even many decades ago—but for whom the experience and thought of pilgrimage had remained alive, at times also manifest in a wish to do it again before they died. This was something we heard from a man dressed in pilgrimage clothes who climbed out of an ancient van that chugged up to Temple Sixty-One in November 2019. He was eighty-eight years old and on his third circuit. His previous two had both been over a quarter of a century ago, once in 1991 and then again in 1994. Since then he had not had the time to do the pilgrimage but had always wished to; the thought never went away. Since he was now eighty-eight and feeling his age, it was now or never. He added that he had done his earlier pilgrimages in the same van he was still driving. Since both he and the van (over thirty years old) were on the way out, he said with a laugh, he wanted to do the pilgrimage once more in it before one or both of them expired.

Such encounters encapsulated the themes that we found throughout our study. There may be those for whom doing the *henro* is a single experience, but there are many who repeat their journeys multiple times and for whom the pilgrimage never goes away. In the early 2000s Satō Hisamitsu's sociological studies and surveys indicated that 42% of Shikoku pilgrims were on at least their second pilgrimage and that over 5% had done it ten times or more.[2] In that era, too, the single largest provider of bus pilgrimage tours, Iyo Tetsu of Matsuyama, reported that around half those who went on their pilgrimage tours were doing it at least for a second time.[3] While patterns of pilgrimage have changed and bus pilgrimage numbers have declined significantly in very recent years (most strikingly since 2010), the dynamic of repetition has continued through the increasing focus on car pilgrimages. These have now become the most common means of Shikoku pilgrimage travel, while car pilgrims, as we have indicated in earlier chapters, often do multiple pilgrimages.[4] Many walkers, as we showed in Chapter 6, do not limit

---

[2] Satō 2004: 224–226.

[3] Reader 2005: 90.

[4] Shikoku Araiansu Chiiki Keizai Kenkyū Bunkakai 2019 indicates clearly this shift from bus tour to more individual car pilgrimages. We state this both through observation (in that we barely saw any buses of pilgrims during our three visits to Shikoku in major pilgrimage periods in 2018 and 2019) and based on information given to us by numerous priests, temple officials, and experienced pilgrims during our fieldwork. We plan to discuss this issue elsewhere in a projected study of transformations and changes in contemporary pilgrimage.

themselves to one circuit but return time and again, while the approximately 9000 living *sendatsu*, people who have at minimum done the pilgrimage four times, also serve to show how widespread the practice of repetition. It is, in other words, not something limited to a marginal group or tiny minority in Shikoku but a dominant pattern in the pilgrimage. Those who repeat the *henro* constitute a significant part of the Shikoku pilgrimage world and are highly prominent within it.

In Chapter 2 we talked of a spectrum of types of multiple performance, and throughout this book we have introduced examples of people across this spectrum: pilgrims who live wholly as itinerants sleeping out and living on the pilgrimage route (usually reliant on alms); people who perform dozens of circuits a year and who live for long periods in their cars, perhaps spending 300 or more days a year on pilgrimage; people who walk the pilgrimage regularly and spend many weeks a year on the *henro*; and so on. There are also those who may have done it relatively few times but who are nonetheless conscious of an all-embracing absorption in the pilgrimage and those who feel, even when they are home, that they are somehow 'on pilgrimage' and are preparing for their next journey around Shikoku. There are many, too, who are influenced by pilgrims who have done it hundreds of times, and who envisage themselves becoming similar to such figures.

Across this broad spectrum there is a commonality that unites such diverse practitioners and modes of pilgrimage; whatever means they use, all are taking part in the same pilgrimage even as they express participation in a multitude of different and often highly personalised ways. This notion of commonality is expressed in the phrase *dōgyō ninin* that is written on pilgrim shirts, a phrase that states each pilgrim travels together with Kōbō Daishi, the holy figure who in pilgrimage lore is forever travelling around Shikoku as an eternal pilgrim. As such all pilgrims, no matter how they do it, are involved in the same pilgrimage, one that is, like the Daishi's travels, unending.

This image of the pilgrimage as unending was strikingly brought home to us when we called in at a shop selling pilgrimage goods next to Temple One. One of the items on sale was a white T-shirt with a pilgrimage motif. The shirt was inscribed with the words 'Shikoku Henro 88' underneath two sideways figure eights. The two figure eights together, of course, indicated the number eighty-eight. Written sideways, each eight also depicted the symbol for infinity, thereby presenting a clear association between the pilgrimage, the number eighty-eight, and infinite practice. Each infinity symbol thus also depicted an endless circuit, while on the upper infinity figure circuit there was a small temple image along with a line of pilgrims. The pilgrim figures were, as such, going around the figure eight on an infinite journey with no discernible end or, indeed, beginning; as such the T-shirt appeared to sum up an image that is evident in the very structure of the *henro* and in the travels of those who do it: a pilgrimage that is unending and infinite in nature (see Figure C.1).

There are, as we have indicated in Chapters 1 and 2, many reasons why this is so. Some are historically embedded, from the Japanese traditions of repetition and asceticism, to the influence and images of repeated and unending circumambulation in the *henro*'s legendary foundation stories and the footsteps of actual early ascetics. Some are grounded in the physical structure in which pilgrims, by doing the customary thanksgiving visit to the first temple, complete a circle and thus return to their starting point again. Repetition is certainly aided by structural and contingent contexts, including modern economic and transport developments that enable people to have the funds and means, via their pensions, savings, customised cars, and free time, to do the pilgrimage as and when they wish. There is a culture of encouragement in the pilgrimage that is emphasised through the practice of almsgiving that helps pilgrims, the words of support people receive at temples and from other

SHIKOKU HENRO 88

Figure C.1 Pilgrimage T-shirt with infinity sign and the number eighty-eight pilgrims, the *sendatsu* system with its array of ranks and offers of status for performing the *henro* multiple times, and the allure of brocade *fuda*. Kōbō Daishi, not just as a figure of veneration but, as many viewed him, a friend, is part of this culture of encouragement too, as are prominent pilgrimage activists and leaders of confraternities, who derive authority from their multiple pilgrimages and serve as inspirations for others to follow their paths. The very framework of the pilgrimage offers immense scope for different ways of performance, enabling pilgrims to set their own agendas, be highly autonomous, and become figures of authority. For many pilgrims, as we noted in Chapter 2, the first pilgrimage was an initial learning experience that made them realise they needed to discover more both about the pilgrimage and themselves, thus leading them to subsequent pilgrimages. A culturally accepted and happily embraced notion of 'addiction' and 'illness' specifically associated with Shikoku, and that is not seen as needing a 'cure' since taking part in the 'illness' is in effect the cure, further reinforces the pilgrimage's repetitive dynamic. Moreover, doing the *henro* can be enjoyable, offering pilgrims the chance to experience fine scenery and temples, immerse themselves in cultural history, and sample the local cuisine and atmosphere of the island, thus developing a desire to do it again.

As we indicated in earlier chapters, many (but by no means all) of the pilgrims we have referred to in this book have done other pilgrimages besides Shikoku. To that extent the focus (and addiction) may not be purely related to Shikoku but to the wider idea of pilgrimage, with it being an activity that extends beyond one place to become a life path. Nonetheless, almost invariably the Shikoku pilgrimage is central to such endeavours; participants might do other pilgrimages from time to time but, like Nakatsukasa, whose almost endless circumambulations of Shikoku were interrupted twice by his pilgrimages to other Japanese sacred places, their absorption in the practice of pilgrimage is primarily if not wholly a Shikoku-centric one.

A reflection of wider pilgrimage patterns—or a special case?

Pilgrims and priests alike claimed repeatedly that the *henro* is unique, with a special and singular nature that brooks no equal. Of course any pilgrimage will have its special characteristics and may similarly be promoted by its devotees advocates as unique and unequalled. Such an emphasis on uniqueness does, however, raise significant questions about the themes of unending engagement and repetitive pilgrimages that we have been discussing. Are these themes unique to Shikoku because of its special nature? Do they apply to Japanese pilgrimage culture more broadly? Do these themes have wider meanings and implications for studies of pilgrimage more generally?

In our view it would be seriously mistaken to view the Shikoku pilgrimage as a singular entity. This is not just because many pilgrims in Shikoku do other pilgrimages and hence view pilgrimage in general as a lifelong practice or that such immersive engagement in pilgrimage is a particularly Japanese phenomenon. As we indicated in the Introduction, some of the themes that we have identified in Shikoku, and some of the terms that we have used to describe those phenomena and themes, have been mentioned or discerned in studies of pilgrimage elsewhere. When scholars talk of 'serial pilgrims', of pilgrimage sites as second homes, or when they refer to the idea of 'permanent pilgrims', they are talking in various terms about issues that are also manifest in Shikoku. Likewise, scholars discussing Muslim pilgrimage experiences indicate that pilgrims they interviewed who had done the *hajj* pilgrimage to Mecca commonly view it as the central event and key organising principle in their lives, which they would do it again if they had the wherewithal[5]—views that are clearly evident among the Shikoku pilgrims we talked to.

We argue that Shikoku should be seen not as a unique outlier but as a manifestation of a potentially recurrent phenomenon, but one that has been rather overlooked in pilgrimage studies—namely repetition, long-term, temporally unbound, and unending pilgrimage engagement. As we noted in the Introduction there has as yet been no sustained examination of such issues that can stand as a corollary to our study. This is a lacuna that extends also to the wider practice of pilgrimage in different cultural and religious contexts. We have drawn attention to the point that many pilgrims in Shikoku also do plentiful other pilgrimages, even if their core focus is on Shikoku. In other words, pilgrimage as a general practice may be multiple and pervasive in their lives, not simply limited to the practice of one special pilgrimage.

We suggest that this is an issue that requires more research in other pilgrimage contexts; for example, while there are 'serial pilgrims' at the Catholic pilgrimage site of Lourdes, as Agnew states,[6] are such pilgrims just devotees of Lourdes or do they also make other pilgrimages, for example, to other

---

[5] Tagliacozzo 2013: 271–283.
[6] Agnew 2015.

Catholic sites such as Medjugorje, Fatima, and so on? Do those who have made Walsingham a 'second home' also make pilgrimages elsewhere? Do the pilgrims for whom the *hajj* is a central life experience and who would do it again if they had the means (or, in the case of those who do have the means, do it regularly) do other pilgrimages as well? We recognise that studies of pilgrimage have provided plentiful examples in a number of different religious and cultural contexts of pilgrims going to a number of sites, for example, by taking part in tours that visit a number of pilgrimage locations in a single journey. However, thus far such studies have tended just to mention that pilgrims going, for example, to Santiago de Compostela or on tours to Lourdes, might call in at other sites along the way, or that Hindu pilgrims in India might visit a variety of sites.[7] There has not, however, been any systematic study of the extent to which such practices indicate a wider and continuing relationship with pilgrimage in general, of the sort we have drawn attention to here, and this is a matter we think that needs to be considered by those researching pilgrimage sites and practices around the world.

We would just add a brief observation in this context about the recent rise in numbers of non-Japanese walkers on the Shikoku *henro* that we mentioned in Chapter 6. One of the factors boosting such numbers has been the popularity of the Camino, the pilgrim's way, to Santiago de Compostela, which has seen an exponential rise in walkers in recent times.[8] We heard from various sources that this has had an impact in Shikoku, in that some of these Camino walkers, on completing that pilgrimage, had become interested in doing other long-distance routes and hence had turned their attention to the *henro*. We had confirmation of this at a Shikoku pilgrimage lodge in November 2019, where we met two Frenchmen. They told us that they had previously walked the Camino and through that had become keen to walk other long-distance pilgrimage paths. It was for that reason that they were now walking the Shikoku *henro*. This again appears to reinforce our suggestion that doing a pilgrimage is an act that can readily lead to taking part in more pilgrimages.

---

[7] For example, Frey (1998) mentions at various points that pilgrims going to Santiago de Compostela may visit other shrines along the Camino. Dahlberg (1991) is one of many discussions of a single pilgrimage site that mentions tours that also call in at other sites, while Fedele (2018) indicates that people she terms 'energy pilgrims' also visit a variety of sites in their search for spiritual energy. In Indian terms, Feldhaus (2003) draws attention to how Hindu sites form networks of connected places that may be visited. However none of these delves further into the issue or provides any analysis of the idea of multiple practices and long-term engagement.

[8] See, for example, Frey 1998; Roseman 2004; and Sanchez y Sanchez and Hesp 2016.

This is a question that needs to be asked more often when studying any particular pilgrimage, whether to Hindu, Catholic, Buddhist, or any other sites. One of the authors elsewhere discussed the example of a Japanese couple who had done multiple pilgrimages in Japan and then started to visit numerous other pilgrimage sites around the world, first Buddhist and Hindu sites in India and Nepal, then Catholic sites in Europe, and who saw their primary self-identification (in terms of faith) as 'pilgrims'.[9] While much of the academic literature on pilgrimage operates from within the parameters of specific religious frameworks or focuses on specific sites, more attention should be paid to the idea of people viewing or identifying themselves not as members of a particular faith or devotional path who then go on pilgrimage to places associated with that tradition but primarily as pilgrims who, through that identity, do not feel bound to one specific tradition but may make visits to various places that are seen as pilgrimage sites from a variety of faiths and cultural contexts.

Life is a pilgrimage

In Chapter 2 we cited the commemorative stone erected by a high ranking *sendatsu* at Temple Fourteen engraved with the phrase *jinsei wa henro nari*—'life is a pilgrimage'. This is a theme that emerged in various conversations with pilgrims, and it is also the title of a booklet about the *henro* by Hatada Shūhō the head priest of Anrakuji (Temple Six), in which he discusses the pilgrimage as a ground for Buddhist practice and path to enlightenment.[10] While Hatada's main intention is to present the pilgrimage through a Buddhist lens, relating it to the structures of esoteric Buddhism while emphasising the notion, manifest in its symbolic structure, of the *henro* as a four-stage journey to enlightenment, he also relates it to a journey in and through life, from childhood onwards through various stages of life. There are resonances here with the thematic origins of pilgrimage within the Buddhist tradition, based initially on the idea of the Buddha's life as a pilgrimage with four major stages: his birth, enlightenment, expounding his teachings, and his entry into nirvana. These four stages were articulated in pilgrimage terms in early Buddhist history via monastic visits to the four

[9] Reader 2001: 127–132.
[10] Hatada 1996.

sites, Lumbini, Bodh Gaya, Sarnath, and Kushinagar, associated with them. Early Buddhist monastics, too, were on a life pilgrimage in which they had no set abode and lived a life of mendicancy; theirs were, in effect, lives of pilgrimage. These structures were prominent in Shikoku, too, both in terms of the mendicants whose travels, following the imagined itinerant path of Kōbō Daishi, were important in the development of the Shikoku pilgrimage, and in its fourfold structure and envisioned path of practice. Pilgrimage for such figures was a life journey and commitment, one that was unending and served as an articulation of the path of life.

While few pilgrims we talked to related their understandings of the pilgrimage to the philosophical themes of Buddhist text and practice articulated by Hatada, they often recognised the underlying meanings of pilgrimage as a metaphor for life and talked of their pilgrimages in ways that similarly placed it at the centre of their lives and gave meaning to all they did. They envisaged life as a pilgrimage and pilgrimage as a life journey, both in the physical sense of actual performance and in the sense of thinking about it even when they were not actually on the road.

The notion of life as pilgrimage is not confined, of course, to Buddhism or to the thoughts of priests and pilgrims in Shikoku. Scholars have similarly indicated how such concepts have been significant in the development of Christian pilgrimages. Dee Dyas indicates that in early Christianity 'life pilgrimage' refers to the view that life itself is a pilgrimage—a journey towards a heavenly home, to God, and an afterlife. She argues that 'place pilgrimage' (pilgrimage as a physical journey to sacred places, and as a place-centred activity) developed initially in Christianity as a metaphor for journey of the soul to God and became included in Christian practice as a localised version of that spiritual journey.[11] Life pilgrimage was thus the real journey. While place pilgrimage (the physical aspect of journeying to a sacred location such as Rome or Jerusalem) might be the most overt manifestation of pilgrimage in early Christianity, it was in effect a physical expression of a deeper notion—of the person/soul and life itself as being embedded in a permanent path of pilgrimage. Donald Howard similarly argues that the writings of medieval Christian pilgrims portray the pilgrimage to Jerusalem not just as a physical journey but as one that enacted symbolically 'the passage from birth to salvation'; it was, as such, 'a symbol of human life, and the corollary, that life is a pilgrimage'.[12]

---

[11] Dyas 2001: 246; cited also in Albera 2018: 177–179, which discusses these notions further.
[12] Howard 1980: 11.

234 PILGRIMS UNTIL WE DIE

The roots of pilgrimage in such terms (and likewise in Buddhism and in the foundation stories and symbolic images of the Shikoku pilgrimage) are in the idea of pilgrimage as a life journey and of life as a pilgrimage. The pilgrimage inscription cited in Chapter 2 and at the beginning of this section reiterates that point about Shikoku, and it reflects themes that emerged repeatedly in our interviews. The root images of the pilgrimage relate to Kobo Daishi the wandering pilgrim and holy figure forever on pilgrimage. His physical journey (according to legend) in Shikoku and his constant presence there, always potentially available to pilgrims who travel with him, manifest a life pilgrimage that is grounded in place, as were the pilgrimages of figures from Shikoku history such as Shinnen, Tada, and Nakatsukasa, who made the *henro* their life's journey.

The pilgrims in contemporary Shikoku whom we have discussed manifest similar themes, whether they live permanently on the route, endlessly circle the route in their adapted vehicles, or simply keep travelling along the *henro* whenever they can do so. The businessman discussed in Chapter 2 who goes each Friday night to Shikoku, by Monday morning is no longer on the pilgrimage in a physical sense, while walkers we discussed in Chapter 6 may on an annual basis complete their walks around the route and return home. Yet they are constantly living their association with the pilgrimage and thinking about the next time. In such contexts the Shikoku pilgrimage conflates the notions of place and life pilgrimage into one; place and route are a metaphor for life and the situation in which it is enacted.

Specificity, theory, and the relevance of Shikoku

In the Introduction we drew attention to the problems of specificity in the study of pilgrimage: while studies of pilgrimage often view or understand pilgrimage as something quite universal and extending across religious traditions and cultural spheres, they are frequently focused on specific case studies that might produce phenomena and characteristics that appear potentially highly particular. That naturally leads to the question, as we recognised, of how far one can develop a theory from one pilgrimage and context that might be applicable to pilgrimage more generally. That question is intensified in this current case in that the pilgrimage being studied and used as an example appears to especially lend itself, for various structural, historical, and contemporary reasons, to repeated and unending practice in ways that have not thus far been identified in other pilgrimage contexts.

While we recognise these issues, we also wish to point out that, as we said earlier, the types of issues we have focused on and the questions we have raised in this book have rarely been examined elsewhere. Moreover we have drawn attention to examples where some similarities (of serial pilgrimage and notions of permanent pilgrims, for example) to the Shikoku case have been identified or alluded to, while noting that such issues have rarely been given fuller attention in the field. As it stands we offer the example of the Shikoku pilgrimage as an avenue through which to ask further questions about the nature of pilgrimage in general. It raises the question of permanence as a dynamic in pilgrimage and suggests that pilgrimage, rather than being related to issues such as goals, ends, and contrasts with stasis, may be unending. Those who do (or aspire to do) multiple pilgrimages in Shikoku are in effect saying that through these place pilgrimages they are undertaking a life pilgrimage, one whose only boundary and limitation is the acceptance that physical inability or death will eventually occur. Even these are not necessarily endpoints. Being physically unable to travel any more may not stop mental involvement, while the custom of being buried in a pilgrim's shroud, often with a pilgrim's book, and illustrated by such examples as the confraternity members met in Chapter 5 who carry white pilgrims shirts to be stamped in preparation for their final journey, indicates that the pilgrimage is not terminated by the end of life in this world. The Shikoku *henro* tells us that pilgrimage is not a transient activity set apart from home or routines, but an unending journey and concept that permeates the lives of participants and resides at the very core of their being.

References

Abe, Ryūichi 1999 *The Weaving of Mantra: Kūkai and the Construction of Esoteric Buddhist Discourse.* New York: Columbia University Press.

Agnew, Michael 2014 *Where Heaven Touched Earth: Encountering Place and Person at Lourdes.* Unpublished PhD diss., McMaster University.

Agnew, Michael 2015 "Spiritually I Am Always in Lourdes": Perceptions of Home and Away among Serial Pilgrims. *Studies in Religion/Sciences Religieuses* Vol. 44/4: 516–535.

Albera, Dionigi 2018 Afterword: Going Beyond the Elusive Nature of Pilgrimage. In Simon Coleman and John Eade (eds.) *Pilgrimage and Political Economy: Translating the Sacred.* New York: Berghahn Books, pp. 173–190.

Araki Michio 1990 Junrei no genshō. *Bukkyō* No. 12 (July 1990): 65–75.

Asai Shōzen 2004 *Henro kudokuki to junpai shūzoku.* Osaka: Toki Shobō.

Asakawa Yasuhiro 2008 *Junrei no bunkajinruigakuteki kenkyū: Shikoku henro no settaibunka.* Tokyo: Kokon Shoin.

Asakawa Yasuhiro 2012 Michi o burikorāju suru: Shikoku henro no junreiro saisei undō. In Yamanaka Horishi (ed.) *Shūkyō to tsūrizumu: Seinaru mono no henyō to jizoku.* Kyoto: Sekai Shisōsha, pp. 149–169.

Bawa Yamba, C. 1995 *Permanent Pilgrims: Role of Pilgrimage in the Lives of West African Pilgrims.* Edinburgh: Edinburgh University Press.

Bouchy, Anne Marie 1987 The Cult of Mt. Atago and the Atago Confraternities. *Journal of Asian Studies* Vol. 46: 255–277.

Bowman, Glenn 1991 Christian Ideology and the Image of a Holy Land: The Place of Jerusalem Pilgrimage in the Various Christianities. In John Eade and Michael Sallnow (eds.) *Contesting the Sacred: The Anthropology of Christian Pilgrimage.* London: Routledge, pp. 98–121.

Brooks, Anne Page 1981 *Mizuko kuyō* and Japanese Buddhism. *Japanese Journal of Religious Studies* Vol. 8/3: 119–147.

Chavez, Amy 2013 *Running the Shikoku Pilgrimage: 900 Miles to Enlightenment.* Volcano, California: Volcano Press.

Coleman, Simon 2000 Meanings of Movement, Place and Home at Walsingham. *Culture and Religion* Vol. 1/2: 153–170.

Coleman, Simon, and John Eade 2004 Introduction: Reframing Pilgrimage. In Simon Coleman and John Eade (eds.) *Reframing Pilgrimage: Cultures in Motion.* London: Routledge, pp. 1–26.

Dahlberg, Andrea 1991 The Body as a Principle of Holism: Three Pilgrimages to Lourdes. In John Eade and Michael Sallnow (eds.) *Contesting the Sacred: The Anthropology of Christian Pilgrimage.* London: Routledge, pp. 30–50.

Dyas, Dee 2001 *Pilgrimage in Medieval English Literature: 700–1500.* Cambridge: Boydell and Brewer.

Eade, John 2000 Introduction to the Illinois Paperback. In John Eade and Michael Sallnow (eds.) *Contesting the Sacred: The Anthropology of Christian Pilgrimage,* new ed. Champaign: University of Illinois Press, pp. ix–xxvii.

Eade, John, and Michael J. Sallnow 1991 Introduction. In John Eade and Michael Sallnow (eds.) *Contesting the Sacred: The Anthropology of Christian Pilgrimage.* London: Routledge, pp. 1–29.

Eck, Diane 1983 *Banares: City of Light.* London: Routledge and Kegan Paul.

Ehime ken Shōgaigakushū Sentā 2001 (ed.) *Shikoku henro no ayumi.* Matsuyama: Ehime ken Shōgaigakushū Sentā.

Fedele, Anna 2018 Translating Catholic Pilgrimage Sites into Energy Grammar: Contested Spiritual Practices in Chartres and Vézelay. In Simon Coleman and John Eade (eds.) *Pilgrimage and Political Economy: Translating the Sacred.* New York: Berghahn Books, pp. 112–135.

Feldhaus, Ann 2003 *Connected Places: Region, Pilgrimage and Geographical Imagination in India.* New York and Basingstoke: Palgrave.

Frey, Nancy Louise 1998 *Pilgrim Stories: On and Off the Road to Santiago.* Berkeley: University of California Press.

Goodwin, Janet 1994 *Alms and Vagabonds: Buddhist Temples and Popular Patronage in Medieval Japan.* Honolulu: University of Hawaii Press.

Gorai Shigeru 1975 *Kōya hijiri.* Tokyo: Kadokawa Sensho.

Gorai Shigeru1989 *Yugyō to junrei.* Tokyo: Kadokawa Sensho.

Hakeda, Y. S. 1972 *Kūkai: Major Works.* New York: Columbia University Press.

Hamaya, Mariko 2009 'Kojikihenro' no seikatsushi. *Tokushima-chiiki-bunka-kenkyū* Vol. 7: 103–117.

Hardacre, Helen 1997 *Marketing the Menacing Fetus in Japan.* Berkeley: University of California Press.

Hatada Shūhō 1996 *Jinsei ha henro nari: Shikoku hachijūhakkasho to taizōkai mandara.* Itano, Tokushima: Anrakuji.

Havnevik, Hanna 1998 On Pilgrimage for Forty Years in the Himalayas: The Female Lama Jetsun Lochen Rinpoche's (1865–1951) Quest for Sacred Sites. In Alex McKay (ed.) *Pilgrimage in Tibet.* Richmond, UK: Curzon, pp. 85–107.

Hayami Tasuku 1983 *Kannon shinkō.* Tokyo: Hanawa Shobō.

Hinonishi Shinjō (ed.) 1988 *Kōbō Daishi shinkō.* Tokyo: Yūzankaku.

Hoinacki, Lee 1996 *El Camino: Walking to Santiago de Compostela.* University Park: Pennsylvania State University Press.

Hoshino Eiki 1979 Shikoku henro to sangaku shinkō. In Miyake Hitoshi (ed.) *Daisen: Ishizuchi to Shikoku Shugendō.* Tokyo: Meicho Shuppan, pp. 310–328.

Hoshino Eiki 1981 *Junrei: Sei to zoku no genshōgaku.* Tokyo: Kōdansha Gendaishinsho.

Hoshino Eiki 2001 *Shikoku henro no shūkyōgakuteki kenkyū.* Kyoto: Hōzōkan.

Hoshino Eiki, and Asakawa Yasuhiro 2011 *Shikoku henro: Samazamana inori no sekai.* Tokyo: Furukawa Kōbunkan.

Hoshino, Eiki, and Dōshū Takeda 1988 Indebtedness and Comfort: The Undercurrents of *mizuko kuyō* in Contemporary Japan. *Japanese Journal of Religious Studies* Vol.14/4: 305–320.

Howard, Donald R. 1980 *Writers and Pilgrims: Medieval Pilgrimage Narratives and Their Posterity.* Berkeley and Los Angeles: University of California Press.

Ieda Shōko 2009 (2014) *Shikoku hachijūhakkasho tsunagi henro.* Tokyo: KK Besuto sera-zu.

Imai Misako 1981 *Oyako henro tabi nikki*. Tokyo: Tōhō Shuppan.

Ishii Kenji 2007 *Dētabukku: Gendai nihon no shūkyō*. Tokyo: Shinyōsha.

Kaell Hillary 2016 Notes on Pilgrimage and Pilgrimage Studies. *Practical Matters* Emory University, Spring 2016, No. 9: 1–10.

Kiyoyoshi Eitoku 1984 *Michi shirube—tsuke Nakatsuka Mōhei nikki*. Shin Niihama: Kaiōsha.

Kiyoyoshi Eitoku 1999 *Henro hito retsuden: Gyōgi bosatsu kara Nakatsukasa Mōhei made*. Shin Niihama: Kaiōsha.

Kobayashi Shinji 2003 *Kusahenro Kōgetsu*. Kobayashi: Kawanoue, Ehime.

Kōgetsu 2003 *Kazefutokoro ni kachi zanmai*. Fuchu, Hiroshima: Shinmedia.

Kojima Hiromi 1989 Junrei: 'meguri' to 'monomorai'. In Setouchi Jakuchō, Fujii Masao, and Miyata Noboru (eds.) *Bukkyō gyōji saijiki*. Tokyo: Daiichi Hōkan, pp. 168–178.

Kolata, Paulina K. 2019 *Doing Belonging in Jōdo Shinshū Temple Communities: An Ethnography of Buddhism in Japan's Depopulating Regions*. Unpublished PhD diss., University of Manchester.

Kondō Yoshihiro 1982 *Shikoku henro kenkyū*. Tokyo: Miyai Shoten.

Kouamé, Nathalie 1998 *Le pèlerinage de Shikoku Pendant l'Epoque Edo: Pèlerins at sociétés locales*. Unpublished PhD diss., Institut National Des Langues et Civilisations Orientales, Paris.

Kouamé, Nathalie 2001 *Pèlerinage et société dans le Japon des Tokugawa: Le pèlerinage de Shikoku entre 1598 et 1868*. Paris: École Française d'Extrême-Orient.

LaFleur, William R. 1992 *Liquid Life: Abortion and Buddhism in Japan*. Princeton, NJ: Princeton University Press.

Maeda Takashi 1971 *Junrei no shakaigaku*. Kyoto: Mineruba Shobō.

Matsuzaka Yoshimitsu 2003 Maegaki. In Kōgetsu *Kazefutokoro ni kachi zanmai*. Fuchu, Hiroshima: Shinmedia, p. 1.

McKevitt, Christopher 1991 San Giovanni Rotondo and the Shrine of Padre Pio. In John Eade and Michael Sallnow (eds.) *Contesting the Sacred: The Anthropology of Christian Pilgrimage*. London: Routledge, pp. 77–97.

Mori Masato 2005 *Shikoku henro no kindaika: Modan henro kara iyashi no tabi made*. Osaka: Sōgensha.

Mori Masato 2014 *Shikoku henro: Hachijū hakkasho junrei no rekishi to bunka*. Tokyo: Chūkō Shinsho.

Mori Masayasu 1986 Shikoku henro no hijiri: Nakatsuka Mōhei. In Hagiwara Tatsuo and Shinno Toshikazu (eds.) *Bukkyō minzokugaku*. Tokyo: Meicho Shuppan, Vol. 2, pp. 99–116.

Morinis, Alan 1981 Pilgrimage: The Human Quest. *Numen* Vol. 28/2: 280–285.

Morinis, Alan 1992 Introduction: The Territory of the Anthropology of Pilgrimage. In Alan Morinis (ed.) *Sacred Journeys: The Anthropology of Pilgrimage*. Westport, CT: Greenwood Press, pp. 1–28.

Nicoloff, Philip L. 2008 *Sacred Kōyasan: A Pilgrimage to the Mountain Temple of Saint Kōbō Daishi and the Great Sun Buddha*. Albany: State University of New York Press.

Nishigaki Seiji 1983 *O-Ise mairi*. Tokyo: Iwanami Shinsho.

Obigane Mitsutoshi 2002 *Sairai Yamamoto Genpōden*. Tokyo: Daihôrinkaku.

Osada Seiichi, Sakata Masaaki, and Seki Mitsuo 2003 *Gendai no Shikoku henro: Michi no shakaigaku no shiten kara*. Tokyo: Gakubunsha.

Ozaki Makoto (pseudonym) 2018 *Hajimete no arukihenro: Shikoku hachijūhakkashohenro*. Osaka, private publication.

Rambelli, Fabio 2002 Secret Buddhas (Hibutsu): The Limits of Buddhist Representation. *Monumenta Nipponica* Vol. 57/3: 271–307.

Reader, Ian 1988 Miniaturisation and Proliferation: A Study of Small-scale Pilgrimages in Japan. *Studies in Central and East Asian Religions* Vol.1/ 1: 50–66.

Reader, Ian 1993a Dead to the World: Pilgrims in Shikoku. In Ian Reader and Tony Walter (eds.) *Pilgrimage in Popular Culture*. Basingstoke: Macmillans, pp. 107–136.

Reader, Ian 1993b *Sendatsu and the Development of Contemporary Japanese Pilgrimage*. Nissan Occasional Papers on Japan No. 17, Nissan Institute for Japanese Studies, Oxford.

Reader, Ian 1999 Legends, Miracles, and Faith in Kobo Daishi and the Shikoku Pilgrimage: A Commentary and Selected Translations from Shinnen's *Shikoku Henro Kudokuki* of 1690. In George J. Tanabe (ed.) *Religions of Japanese in Practice*. Princeton, NJ: Princeton University Press, pp. 360–369.

Reader, Ian 2001 Reflected Meanings: Underlying Themes in the Experiences of Two Japanese Pilgrims to Europe. In Adriana Boscaro and Maurizio Bozzi (eds.) *Firenze, Il Giappone e L'Asia Orientale*. Florence: Leo S. Olschi, pp.121–139.

Reader, Ian 2005 *Making Pilgrimages: Meaning and Practice in Shikoku*. Honolulu: University of Hawaii Press.

Reader, Ian 2011 Buddhism in Crisis? Institutional Decline in Modern Japan. *Buddhist Studies Review* Vol. 28/2: 233–263.

Reader, Ian 2012 Secularisation R.I.P? Nonsense! The 'Rush Hour Away from the Gods' and the Decline of Religion in Contemporary Japan. *The Journal of Religion in Japan* Vol. 1/1: 7–36.

Reader, Ian 2014 *Pilgrimage in the Marketplace*. New York and London: Routledge.

Reader, Ian 2015 Japanese Studies of Pilgrimage. In Dionigi Albera and John Eade (eds.) *International Perspectives on Pilgrimage: Itineraries, Gaps and Obstacles*. New York and London: Routledge, pp. 23–46.

Reader, Ian, and Paul L. Swanson 1997 Editors' Introduction: Pilgrimage in the Japanese religious tradition. *Japanese Journal of Religious Studies* Vol. 24/3–4: 225–270.

Reader, Ian, and George J. Tanabe 1998 *Practically Religious: Worldly Benefits and the Common Religion of Japan*. Honolulu: University of Hawaii Press.

Rhodes, Robert F. 1987 The Kaihōgyō Practice of Mt. Hiei. *Japanese Journal of Religious Studies* Vol. 14/2–3: 185–202.

Roseman, Sharon R. 2004 Santiago de Compostela in the Year 2000: From Religious Center to European City of Culture. In Ellen Badone and Sharon R. Roseman (eds.) *Intersecting Journeys: The Anthropology of Pilgrimage and Tourism*. Urbana and Chicago: University of Illinois Press, pp. 68–88.

Saitō Akitoshi 1984 Kōbō Daishi shinkō ni kansuru jittai chōsa. *Bukkyō bunka ronshū* No. 4: 400–479.

Saitō, Akitoshi 1988 Kōbō Daishi densetsu. In Hinonishi Shinjō (ed.) *Kōbō Daishi shinkō*. Tokyo: Yūzankaku, pp. 49–61.

Sallnow, Michael J. 1981 Communitas Revisited: The Sociology of Andean Pilgrimage. *Man* Vol. 16: 163–182.

Sallnow, Michael J. 1987 *Pilgrims of the Andes: Regional Cults in Cusco*. Washington, DC: Smithsonian Institution Press.

Sanchez y Sanchez, Samuel, and Annie Hesp (eds.) 2016 *The Camino de Santiago in the 21st Century: Interdisciplinary Perspectives and Global Views*. New York and Abingdon, UK: Routledge.

Satō Hisamitsu 1990 Osamefuda ni miru Shikoku henro. In Nakao Shunpaku Sensei Koki Kinenkai (ed.) *Bukkyō to shakai: Nakao Shunpaku sensei koki kinen*. Kyoto: Nagata Bunshōdō, pp. 437–459.

Satō Hisamitsu 2004 *Henro to junrei no shakaigaku*. Kyoto: Jimbo Shoin.

Satō Hisamitsu 2014 *Junpaiki ni miru Shikoku henro*. Osaka: Toki Shobō.

Shikoku Hachijūhakkasho Reijōkai 1965 *Shikoku hachijūhakkasho reijōkai kōnin sendatsu bangikai kisoku*. Shikoku: Shikoku Hachijūhakkasho Reijōkai Jimusho.

Shikoku Hachijūhakkasho Reijōkai (ed.) 1984 *Shikoku hachijūhakkasho reigenki*. Sakaide: Shikoku Hachijūhakkasho Reijōkai Honbu Jimusho.

Shikoku Araiansu Chiiki Keizai Kenkyū Bunkakai 2019 *Shinjidai ni okeru henro ukeiri taisei no arikata: Henro shukuhakusetsubi no genjō.kadaitō chōsa*. Takamatsu, Kagawa: Shikoku Keizai Rengōkai.

Shingyōkai Honbu (ed.) 1981 *Henro*. Nagahama: Shingyōkai Honbu.

Shinjō Tsunezō 1982 *Shaji sankei no shakai keizaishiteki kenkyū*. Tokyo: Hanawa Shobō.

Shinnen 1981 (1687) *Shikoku henro michishirube*. In Iyoshi Dankai (ed.) *Shikoku henro kishū*. Matsuyama: Ehime ken Kyōka Tosho, pp. 69–116.

Shinno Toshikazu 1976 Henro no takuhatsu. In Wakamori Tarō (ed.) *Nihon shūkyō no nazo*. Tokyo: Kōsei Shuppan, pp. 221–230.

Shinno Toshikazu 1978 Shikoku henro no hijiri to sono shūkyō katsudō. In Sakurai Tokutarō (ed.) *Nihon shūkyō no fukugōteki kōzō*. Tokyo: Kōbundō, pp. 83–108.

Shinno Toshikazu 1980 *Tabi no naka no shūkyō: junrei no minzokushi*. Tokyo: NHK Bukkusu.

Shinno Toshikazu 1986 Junrei no gyōja: sono shūkyōteki na tassei. In Hagiwara Tatsuo and Shinno Toshikazu (eds.) *Bukkyō minzoku taikei Vol 2: Hijiri to minshū*. Tokyo: Meichō Shuppan, pp. 173–196.

Shinno Toshikazu 1991 *Nihon yugyō shūkyōron*. Tokyo: Yoshikawa Kōbunkan.

Shiragi Toshiyuki 1994 *Junrei.sanpaiyōgo jiten*. Osaka: Toki Shobō.

Shirai Kazushi 1982 Shikoku henro jittai. *Tokushima Kenkyū* Vol. 7: 218–219.

Shultz, John A. 2009 *Characters on a Page, Characters on a Pilgrimage: Contemporary Memoirs of the Shikoku Henro*. Unpublished PhD diss., University of Manchester.

Shultz, John A. 2011 Pilgrim Leadership Rendered in HTML: Bloggers and the Shikoku Henro. In Erica Baffelli, Ian Reader, and Birgit Staemmler (eds.) *Japanese Religions on the Internet: Innovation, Representation, and Authority*. New York: Routledge, pp. 101–117.

Shultz, John A. 2013 Shock Treatment on an Inpatient Island: Finding Anxious Cures in Shikoku. *The Journal of Intercultural Studies* Vol. 38: 27–41.

Shultz, John A. 2016 The Way to Gyō: Priestly Asceticism on the Shikoku Henro. *Japanese Journal of Religious Studies* Vol.43/2: 275–305.

Shultz, John A. 2018 The Gaijin Henro: Outliers, Discrimination, and Time Variability with Pilgrimage in Shikoku. *Kenkyū Ronshū* Vol. 107: 1–12.

Shultz, John A. 2020 Pilgrimaging Through Time: The Theoretical Implications of Continuing Journeys on the Shikoku Henro. *International Journal of Religious Tourism and Pilgrimage* Vol. 8/1: 51–59.

Speidel, Manfred 1977 Anthropological Notes on Architecture: Japanese Places of Pilgrimage *A + U Plaza*.

Stevens, John 1988 *The Marathon Monks of Mount Hiei*. London: Rider.

Tagliacozzo, Eric 2013 *The Longest Journey: Southeast Asians and the Pilgrimage to Mecca*. Oxford and New York: Oxford University Press.

Tanaka Yoshitaka 1979 Awa no reizan to Shugendō. In Miyake Hitoshi (ed.) *Daisen Ishizuchi to Shikoku Shugendō*. Tokyo: Meicho Shuppan, pp. 344–367.

Taylor, Philip 2004 *Goddess on the Rise: Pilgrimage and Popular Religion in Vietnam*. Honolulu: University of Hawaii Press.

Teeuwen, Mark, and John Breen 2017 *A Social History of the Ise Shrines*. London and New York: Bloomsbury.

Tezuka Myōken 1988 *Ohenro de meguri atta hitobito*. Tokyo: Ryonsha.

Tsurumura Shōichi 1978 *Shikoku henro: 282 kai Nakatsuka Mōhei gikyō*. Matsuyama: Matsuyama Furusatoshi Bungaku Kenkyūkai.

Turner, Victor 1973 The Center's Out There: Pilgrim's Goal. *History of Religions* Vol. 12/ 3: 191–230.

Turner, Victor, and Edith Turner 1978 *Image and Pilgrimage in Christian Culture*. Oxford: Blackwell.

Ukai Hidenori 2015 *Jiin shōmetsu*. Tokyo: Nikkei BP sha.

Webb, Diane 2000 *Pilgrimage in Medieval England*. London: Hambledon Continuum.

Yamamoto Wakako 1995 *Shikoku henro no minshūshi*. Tokyo: Shinjinbutsu Ōraisha.

Yoritomi Motohiro, and Shiragi Toshiyuki 2001 *Shikoku henro no kenkyū*. Nichibunken Sōsho No. 23. Kyoto: Kokusai Nihon Bunka Kenkyū Sentā.

Television documentary

NHK 2003 *Ningen dokyumento: Ikite yuku kara aruku hito da: Kōgetsu san*. Documentary about Kōgetsu, broadcast June 27, 2003.

Newsletters, magazines, and newspapers

Henro monthly newsletter for *sendatsu* published by the Association of Shikoku Pilgrimage Temples.

Josei Sebun 2003 July 31, *Taiho made no hachijūhachi fudasho meguri 80sai ohenrosan*. Tokushima Shinbun, pp. 52–53.

Shūkan Shinchō 2003 *Taihosareta manuke otoko no 'ohenrobidan' wa daiuso*. No 28, July 24, pp. 50–51.

Internet sources

https://autoc-one.jp/suzuki/every/special-5007515/photo/0046.html?fbcli d=IwAR3tUPShGoGIRxyF8XLB7b8XCuUAS-tLlocPQ5Uqh66awUHG6FaJQW0JM1k (accessed 5 June 2020).

http://blog.goo.ne.jp/fukujukai/e/be4dfcb8d3528ae6612968ef352795d5 (accessed June 2018; no longer available).

http://blog.goo.ne.jp/goo623695/e/a5dd5f4b6dda2dabf73491b6ec2daf00 (accessed 9 Dec. 2019).

http://blog.livedoor.jp/sanmeigaku/tag/%E3%81%8A%E9%81%8D%E8%B7%AF (accessed 9 Dec. 2019).

http://junitarou.blog95.fc2.com/blog-entry-188.html (accessed 24 Oct. 2019).

http://taiyohanasaku.waterblue.ws/chieko/wordpress/tag/%E9%81%8D%E8%B7%AF%E5%B9%B8%E6%9C%88/ (accessed 11 Dec. 2019).

http://www.gokutsuma.com/henro2/index.htm (accessed 3 Jan. 2020).

http://www.kushima.com/henro/news/030517.htm (accessed 11 Dec. 2019).

http://www.maenaem.com/henro/sp.htm (accessed 24 Oct. 2019).

http://www.shiunzan-jizouji.com (accessed 23 Jan. 2020).

http://www7b.biglobe.ne.jp/~karasumoridounin/sikokue3.html (accessed 24 Oct. 2019).

https://ameblo.jp/garagarahebi/entry-10013834408.html (accessed 24 Oct. 2019).

https://doroashi.com/henro3-sadhu (no longer available; accessed Nov. 2018).

https://getnews.jp/archives/2084645 (accessed 11 Dec. 2019).

https://henroseika.exblog.jp/i8/5/ (accessed 24 Oct. 2019).

https://www.chugainippoh.co.jp/article/news/20190802-001.html (accessed 10 Dec. 2019).

https://www.ohenro-portal.jp/doucyu/193/201404/2209.html (accessed 14 Jan. 2020).

Index

For the benefit of digital users, indexed terms that span two pages (e.g., 52–53) may, on occasion, appear on only one of those pages.

Figures are indicated by *f* following the page number